Praise For
Around the Table

Diana Reyers' book, "Around the Table: Escaping the Cycle of Insanity" is a tribute to the determination and self-awareness that was required of her in order to navigate, heal, and eventually, overcome deeply complex familial rituals and relationships. It is a must read, particularly for daughters with the desire to understand difficult relationships they have with their parents and grandparents, as well as the cultural and religious upbringings that they may be questioning in order to step fully into who they are, and not who others want them to be.

Tana L. Heminsley, Author
Awaken Your Authentic Leadership—and adaptations
& *Ease Amidst Challenging Times*

Growing up a child of the early '70s, the poignant way that Diana writes her memoir insights familiar passages of hierarchy, protocols, and generational dynamics. I was transported through her words to a place where I was a benefactor of her experience—a voyeur of life with her family. It's hard to explain, which is why I believe you need to read this offering, the feelings that arose, leaning into a young Diana's thought processes. What starts with a literal lesson over 'spilt milk', soon sets the stage for a figurative measuring stick as to her place then, and now, in the world. The renderings of her soul unfold as she invites you to reconcile with her, her belief systems, her dynamic translations, and her softened approach to relationships that developed through her childhood and on into her own family dynamics. Diana is the fresh take on 'Chicken Soup for the Soul', perhaps readily accepted as a new version like 'Bone Broth for the Brain' in as much as it is no longer enough to wish and feel good, but rather, do the shadow work and heal. She takes you to a depth and back again that personifies 'doing the work'. Thank you, Diana, for once again highlighting authenticity and prescribing it for us all.

Candace Chisholm, Bestselling Co-Author,
She Changed Me: One Ordeal; Two Perspectives
CEO and Co-Founder of He Changed It and She Changed It,
mobile apps for health and wellness prevention.

I

Around the Table

Escaping the Cycle of Insanity

Diana Reyers

 Daring to Share Global

Published by Daring to Share Global™
April 2022 ISBN: 9781777548223

Copyright © 2022 by Diana Reyers

All rights reserved. No part of this publication may be reproduced, stored in, or introduced into a retrieval system, or transmitted , in any form, or by any means—electronic, mechanical, photocopying, recording or otherwise—without the prior written permission of the publisher. This book is sold subject to the condition that it shall not, by way of trade or otherwise, be lent, resold, hired out, or otherwise circulated without the publisher's prior consent in any form of binding or cover other than that in which it is published and without a similar condition including this condition being imposed on the subsequent purchaser.

Editor: Diana Reyers
Typesetter: Greg Salisbury
Book Cover: Olli Vidal
Interior Illustrator: Olli Vidal

DISCLAIMER: Readers of this publication agree that Diana Reyers or Daring to Share™ Global will not be held responsible or liable for damages that may be alleged as resulting directly or indirectly from the use of this publication. Neither the lead publisher nor the self-publishing author can be held accountable for the information provided by, or actions, resulting from, accessing these resources.

More Praise For
Around the Table

There is something very profound and beautiful about reading someone's story and having the permission to be immersed in their world. Not only do we learn about the writer's feelings and perspective on life and events, but it gives us an opportunity to be curious and to reflect on our own perspectives, relationships, quests, battles, wins, behaviors, and triggers. Diana's Reyers' memoir definitely enables us to do that. Many readers will relate to the desire for love from a parent as a child and the sentiment of inadequacy when the latter's perception is the failure to achieve the quest. Mrs. Reyers not only shares with us the different sufferings from her childhood traumas with authenticity and vulnerability but genuinely paints the relatable addiction for belonging in a palpable way: living day-to-day in search of the hit.

Julie Gauthier, Bestselling Author
Hungry To Be Me: A Quest to be my Own Hero

This beautifully written story opened my eyes to Diana's reality of an understandable struggle with acceptance and unworthiness many cannot comprehend. Her descriptions of necessary distraction to avoid inevitable trauma brought me along on this journey with an injected humour, relating to what she was going through in moments of chaos which others referred to as normality. It was like she was describing a story from centuries past based on family tradition and ideology, which understandably took its toll regarding self-identity and self-worth. With descriptive focus, she brought me with her, bringing out multiple emotions in the process through a strict yet skewed upbringing, which in my view, is not relative to the modern era. After reading "Around the Table," I will never look at a glass of milk the same. Ironically, I have a hard time "Forgetting about it," and I can guarantee you will too.

Corey Laine Hilton, Bestselling Author
Take it Off: Revelations of a Male Exotic Dancer
Authenticity Coach & Introspective Influencer

Diana's story takes you on a journey through the lens of her sensitive, young, and loving soul. You will truly feel the difficulties that she endured while navigating through her childhood as she was indeed loved but from a distance. Sadly, a love that came in a maze of conditions. I found myself cheering her on as she attempted to understand the meaning of unconditional love at such a young age—affection and adoration, which she would find in the heart of her grandmother, her Oma.
This story tells of such a deep longing for loyalty, trust, true friendship, and the meaning of this beautiful but wild ride called family.

Maureen Rooney, Bestselling Author
A Child's Nightcap: My Soul's Survival Story
Trauma and Paediatric RN

Reading "Around the Table" has opened my eyes to the hierarchy of parental control and the unique perception and interpretation of each child's experience and how this shapes their beliefs into adulthood. A greater understanding of families and generational trauma and control that often changes within the place you land within your family dynamic often determines the degree of dysfunction. I am impressed with and honoured to know Diana as a friend yet did not know her story. She has evolved into a woman who is seen and heard in the world for her authenticity and ability to support others to share their vulnerability when telling their stories. I am not surprised that Around the Table is a story that resonated with me, having been born of the same generation, and proving that everyone has a story to tell, and humanity would thrive better if more people like Diana dared to share their truth as she has.

Donna Fitzgerald, Bestselling Author
Creative Healing Through Transformation:
Conversations with my Soul
donnafitzgerald.ca

I have known Diana Reyers for over a decade and have always thought of her as a courageous, vulnerable, inspiring leader. And now I know more of the backstory of how she became the remarkable woman that she is. Hers is an exquisitely heartbreaking, brave, enlightening exploration of her roots, the origins of her inner critic, her familial behaviour patterning and the courageous self-reflection and personal growth to become the authentic woman she is today. I saw parts of myself in her story, and I imagine you will too. A spellbinding read and an inspiration for your own personal self-discovery and journey of growth.

Laura Mack, MBA, Co-Author
WOW Woman of Worth:
16 Women Who Are Thriving Through Turbulent Times
CEO at Authentic Leadership Global, Inc.

Diana has this wondrous way of transforming fear of vulnerability into heartfelt connection between author and writer, speaker and audience, and even strangers who bravely say hello after turning the pages in one of her books. Despite the personal hardships, and emotional trauma Diana has faced, she continues to rise above all adversity by shining light on darkness and exposing truth with courageous love. These are just some of the gifts Diana brings along with her each time she dares to share, while inspiring countless others to do the same. Grateful to know her and love her; Diana has become a cherished confidante and lifelong friend.

~Michelle Elleana Nadeau, Bestselling Co-Author
Daring to Share Deception to Truth

The endorsement of Diana's memoir is both among the easiest and most difficult writing tasks I have had come across my desk in quite some time. It's easy to write many heartfelt words about who Diana is and the emotional content of her story. My difficulty comes in the attempt to keep it brief as our dynamic is one that has many layers.

I first met Diana on the set of a community television program I was spending time volunteering at. She was a guest promoting one of her other books, and I connected with her right away. I knew she was an authenticity coach and spent time helping women with addictions. She was so polished, self-assured, and confident as she talked about her then current project and what it meant to her. We became fast friends. My wife and I got to know Diana even better over the years during various ways our lives crossed paths from time to time. When it came time to write our book, Diana was an integral part to my wife and me. She was our guide, editor, coach, strategist, and cheerleader.

Diana has many gifts. She can be stone cold logical and hold reams of emotional empathy for people, seemingly at the same time. She is brilliant, insightful and has the ability to both inspire and motivate. Her communication skills are superlative. So too is her fierce desire to help people. I would not be a published author were it not for her. How did someone become so impressive? Was she always like this? Was she just wired this way?

In getting to know Diana, like any relationship that finds its way moving below the surface, answers to that question started to pop up like pieces of the puzzle: a comment about her childhood here; a sharing of something going on with one of her parents there; and every once and a while, the retelling of a major life event or two. All revealing that this amazingly put-together woman, who seemingly was just naturally impressive, was indeed the result of a lot of fucking work with a lot of fucking history—some of it extremely traumatic.

The tapestry of trauma in all our lives makes us who we are in an intertwinement of events and emotional effects of those events. Couple that with our own perceptions, dreams, skills, insights, and self-awareness, and you see the actions and results of those actions that become our lives. Diana has authentically taken all of these things into account in this powerful, heartfelt, sometimes difficult sharing of the ingredients that life gave her and what was made, and still is being made with those ingredients. She pulls no punches and talks about the things many of us never talk about, while giving us, the reader, both the ability to see what has made her who she is and relate to similar things that occur in our own lives.

She shows us an insightful nature in which her journey of experience and culture combine and continue to constantly develop and help her grow to this very day. And we get the good fortune to be a part of her journey thanks to her allowing us to bear witness by reading the words in this volume.

Diana was a little girl who grew into a woman that just wanted to do something right, and perhaps she is such a high achiever and helps others achieve great things because of that nearly impossible, unquenchable mandate. And while nobody does everything right every time, she sure tried. I am grateful she dared to share all of the stories contained in this volume. I look forward to you holding the same regard for her that I do.

Mike Chisholm, Co-Author
She Changed Me; One Ordeal, Two Perspectives
Host of *He Cast*, the official podcast of HeChangedIt.com

~ Author's Note ~

All accounts described in this book are true to my recollection.
They are shared from my perception based on the level
of self-awareness I had as a child, teenager, and adult
when they were experienced and interpreted.

Emotional trauma must be processed and not shamefully hidden
so, I wrote this story, including my uncomfortable bits,
to inspire you to acknowledge yours.

This book is dedicated to anyone who thought
they could not escape the cycle of insanity for even one moment.

Your story's validity exists
simply because you do.

Stay sane & find your willow tree.

I

∼ Escaping the Cycle of Fear ∼

There I sit, tucked in tight at the retro sixties, Formica kitchen table with silver aluminum legs and matching yellow vinyl seats. When I move my thighs, they stick to the plastic because I reluctantly agreed to wear a dress. My mother sits at one end close to the stove, counter, and sink. My father is opposite her at the other end of the table with the kitchen door a few feet behind him. One of my siblings sits beside me, and the other is across from me; both appear calm and obedient on the outside, doing what I know I should be doing. Viewing this through my adult lens, I assume a correlation of seat placement to familial status, ranked first by the patriarch, then the matriarch, and then the age-appointed designation of the children from oldest to youngest. From my five-year-old perception, I believe I have been slighted, having been assigned the least important place around the table—a shared side with one of my sisters, who sits closest to my mother. The oldest sister has the luxury of space with an entire side at her disposal, and my parents have each assumed their roles as heads of the table. I am sure there was no discussion determining my mother's seating assignment due to her need to have quick access to food preparation and service. Knowing that age would not have been a factor, I wonder if any thought would have been needed if one of us were a boy.

I see my clumsy self knocking over my glass of milk. Spilled milk is such a simple thing, a fast-flowing quick-spreading mess that I managed to fit into most meals. At the time, I didn't know why; it seemed to just happen. I now know that I was a spontaneous child with a lot of suppressed energy. I would have been better off in my eldest sister's spot with more room and less risk of hitting things in my way. Although that would have set me up for success and been more reasonable, it would have disturbed the solidly-planted generational hierarchy that never seemed possible to alter.

The spilled milk shifts my mother's intended harmony for our daily gathering around the table to one of discordance, and I immediately tap into the uncomfortable shift. I absorb everyone's thoughts—*she did it again*—as everyone, but my father jumps up at the same time in an attempt to avoid the white liquid landing on their laps. The chair legs scraping along the linoleum like chalk on a blackboard make me shiver, and I nervously look at my mother for reassurance. Seeing she has everything under control, I glance up to my father to assess his reaction before checking in with the other presence in the room who sits high above him on the

Around The Table

crucifix over the door. I was told he is the son of God and diligently watches over our family to keep us safe, but he never stops me from spilling my milk. We begin every meal with the same prayer, thanking Him for our food...

Bless us, oh Lord,
and these thy gifts which
we are about to receive from thy bounty,
through Christ, Our Lord.
Amen

    I have recited it hundreds of times precisely as taught and rehearsed. As I repeat each word with my eyes closed, they seem heartfelt, but when I'm done and look up, His eyes piercingly look down at my spot at the table as if He is disappointed in me. For a moment, I become distracted, thinking about how He must have suffered hanging like that from the nails in the cross—what if the blood dripping from His hands was real? I picture a stream of blood slowly progressing down the wall through my father on its way to the table with droplets landing in my spilled milk. I become overwhelmed with guilt because I have imagined my father and Jesus as one. I believe what I am thinking is a sin because I intuitively know I must keep it a secret. I have sinned before. I quickly erase the image out of my mind and glance back at my father to assess his mood.

    He doesn't have to move because my mother is quick, having done this cleanup many times before. In three rote moves, she stands up, grabs the cloth from the sink behind her, and strategically swipes it across the table in front of my father before it reaches the top of his plate. His three daughters, including the infamous milk-spiller, stand with our plates swimming in the wet mess before them. My sisters look at me with the same look my father has. They are annoyed but unreactive. I am thankful they don't say anything; they know better than to elevate the tension at the dinner table.

    My mother takes the time to look over at me and smile while proceeding to wipe the rest of the mess, *It's okay; it's just milk.* I feel ashamed. Why do I always spill my milk?! I keep my head down but peek over to the right at my father to see his expression of discontent; it's ever so slight, so I'm not really sure which way he will go. He remains silent until my mother completes the cleanup. That could be a good thing—the ambivalence about my dinner table accident that day. I'm fine without the interrogation we've had in the past surrounding why I always seem to spill my milk because I don't have an answer. I'm also confused because not saying anything doesn't mean he's okay with what just transpired. It just means he's probably working the day shift and had a good sleep the night before—he's more tolerant as a result.

    Like many men who work in factories back then, he's significantly affected by inconsistent sleep due to the gruelling four-days-on, three-days-off schedule, but I'm a kid and don't understand that. I'm aware that there are times he's grumpier than others, and I'm best to evaluate his mood and then choose my response accordingly. Spilling my milk never supports the night-shift state of mind and is better tolerated during the day-shift scenario. My mother often explains, *Not getting enough sleep can make people grumpy.* She encourages me to be more understanding, *Of course, he doesn't mean it. He's just tired.*

She finishes sopping up the remaining bit of milk that also flows through the crevice where the extra slat sits to make the table bigger for a family of five, of which I am the youngest. I watch her skillfully wipe above, below, and in between the crack that wouldn't be there if I was never born. My mother finally sits down and smiles while scanning everyone's face around the table, ending with my father. Then she looks back at me and asks me if I would like another glass of milk. I politely say, *No, thank you,* and my father looks over at me for a moment and tells me to *just forget about it* without skipping a bite. It becomes one of what seems like a million times he tells me this throughout my life.

As a child, I was filled with the push-pull of clarity and ambiguous turmoil while sitting around that table. Experiencing the dinner ritual provided the comfort of my nurturing mother through the satiation of my stomach by her incredible cooking. But the very feeling that my Dutch relatives refer to as *gezelligheid* or *connection* in English quickly dissipated via my interpretation of emotional discomfort that encompassed the process. From one moment to the next, the pleasure my stomach freely danced in became replaced by an insecure, disciplined two-step within its confusion-based pit.

I misunderstood and thus, repelled the patriarchal confidence my father exuded. At the same time, I longed to understand and be part of it; a sense of belonging became the driver I spent decades yearning for. Eventually, it also became an obsessive search for my definition of love. It wasn't until much, much later that I discovered that my perception could either determine or slant my truth. I also realized that sitting around the family table seemed more complicated for me than for those sitting alongside me. I viewed it as an additional place where I didn't belong while enduring the time between my milk being poured and subsequently spilled. I tried hard to manage my chaotic thoughts and be as tranquil as my sisters were. I desperately wanted to fit into what I believed I didn't because the repeated words *you're too sensitive* were too difficult to absorb and manage. I didn't know how to stop interpreting and expressing my emotions.

Not ironically, this uncontrollable natural response became my weakness over time and the culprit of my dinner table angst. My soulful inner passions easily guided me very early on but eventually became detrimental to my emotional survival. With each passing childhood year, I became scarred with deeply embedded stories that concluded I was not worthy of following my heart's messages; they became deemed unreliable, invalidated, and above all, indefensible. Swirls of thoughts dictated that my way of being was unacceptable no matter what I did. Many years of repeated failed attempts defending my truth became exhausting to an irreparable degree. Still to this day, I am fraught with the burden of waves of disapproval within how I interpret others' responses to me. Trauma is impossible to erase fully.

Sunday dinners were held in the dining room with the china cabinet looming behind me; it was filled with the good china and pinwheel crystal that my mother collected. We abided by the same seating plan as in the kitchen. As I grew older, I thought it was normal for families to constantly disagree while eating dinner, to come together to dispute each other's opinions. It didn't matter who began the argument, with my father introducing a topic to start the debate. He persistently egged us on in what felt like an attempt to prove the other wrong. It was similar to the tactics applied to our weekend board game routine, with the primary goal to win rather than create familial connection. So, sitting in the formal dining room for dinner instead of the kitchen made no difference as I was still torn between the welcoming matriarchal meal set lovingly on the table and the discouraging patriarchal competitiveness that began once served.

My mother cooked several go-to Sunday dinners, but my favourite was roast chicken, rice, and vegetables. Each component was generally always the same. However, my mother sometimes substituted the rice with mashed potatoes and created a little pond by pushing the bottom of the ladle into the middle of the mound, allowing the gravy to fill the moat. I have wondered why I often reflect on those Sunday dinners now that I'm an adult. It's usually when I'm overwhelmed with chaotic thoughts and crave a ready-made rotisserie chicken from the grocery store. There's no question there's a correlation to the obsessive-compulsive behaviour I defaulted to as a child, seeking comfort during Sunday dinner. The ritual became an automatic distraction to get through to dessert emotionally unscathed. It began with focusing on one bite of my mother's loving offerings to quiet the noise around me. I then moved on to the next item on my plate. One by one, I savoured the unique attribute each element offered me: the crunch of the chicken's crispy skin between my teeth, the velvety stream of curried gravy touching my lips, and the granular bits of Minute Rice gently bumping along my tongue. Next, I became mesmerized by the perfectly cut frozen carrots and peas that bathed in the curry; I hoped for equal numbers of green and orange as I counted and sorted them— *one pea, one carrot, two peas, two carrots...* It didn't take long for this to become a preoccupation, providing a haven from the chaos around me. Now and again, I glanced up at what seemed like my very tall glass of milk perfectly placed on my mother's Dutch impeccably-ironed white linen tablecloth. I never drank my milk at Sunday dinner; it was far too risky. This prompted its unique trail of comments, but I knew the trade-off of routine criticism was worth the alternative deep shame I could not seem to shake if my milk seeped through the tablecloth onto the good colonial table.

I had no idea that my brain had developed this meticulous method of diversion, allowing me to balance out surrounding levels of comfort and discomfort; it was like a reflex. I used it subconsciously and then carried that approach of rhythmically swaying from one end of the spectrum to the other to the kitchen table from Monday to Saturday as well. Over the years, various habitual behaviours were transferred to other areas of my life, using them to move through accumulated emotional trauma—small Ts as they are now labelled. They became automated responses, using various focal points of distraction to counter the unbearable physical and emotional sensations presented when uncomfortable voices and vibrations elevated around me. Ever so tightly, they allowed me to hang on to anything that resembled a bit of hope while blocking out anything that did not. Ultimately, this became the dysfunctional lifeline I used for decades to manage my frustration with my perception while determining whether it was true or not. It was so effective that most people thought I was the most functional person they knew.

Yet, my perception of reality has been my greatest struggle throughout my life. It created turmoil in my mind, in my life, and within my closest relationships. The ambiguity of not knowing if my thoughts were real or fake, right or wrong, accepted or rejected, took me to the closest feeling of what insanity must be like. Many times, I sat questioning every thought that entered my mind, and other times, I made confident deductions that ended up being complete fantasy. The latter were the ones that caused me the most grief and almost destroyed one of my most meaningful relationships with my mother. Over time, the interpretations my mother and I had of each other's intentions became remarkably skewed. And without having conversations around the confusion created, we sadly spiralled into acute disconnection, pushing each other beyond the line of being sane to functional insanity. What each of us did with that eventually determined the destruction of what could have been.

We went through waves of letting things go that should have been addressed to being passionately consumed about other things that didn't matter. More often than not, we simply didn't get each other, and yet, many times, we did. I realized that it was sometimes best just to walk away, but that wasn't always easily done. Living through this continued decades-long process is painful for both, to a lesser degree at times. And when that lull presents, I am very aware of the vortex of unbearable suffering that lies waiting to spiral out of control again. It happens within seconds and always depends on how we respond to one another. And I know that I find some sort of twisted solace within the judgement of her in a moment of weakness, reverting to my ever-lingering need to be right. My parents unknowingly birthed that need, a detrimental programmed reaction sitting dormant, waiting for the opportune defensive moment to wake up and surface—it's never appropriate, and it's always damaging.

Well into my 30s, my quest for independence from what I believed was my mother's control became my greatest need to move from there to here; *there* was a very foreign external existence motivated by other peoples' expectations, and *here* was a familiar inner way of being inspired by my unique characteristics that had laid dormant for so long. I diligently used the strength my mother subconsciously modelled to survive the patriarchal world I was born into. The same resilience that supported me to hide my natural self also allowed me to uncover it many decades later. I learned how to fully live guided by my essence by managing the need to defend it.

Yes, I am grateful that I finally reached this destination at the age of 60, but suffering was never something I welcomed into my life, even when I knew blissful relief would be achieved on the other side. I also didn't relish in the agony of inflicting pain on my mother but saw no way out as the fundamental core of my personality did not seem welcomed by her or my father. I concluded they were drawn to the abstract person they dreamed I should be but repelled the essence of the person I indeed was. The torment that came hand-in-hand with being manipulated by another—whether purposefully or not—was barely tolerable. As a result, I swore I would tirelessly fight my inherited self-centred side, vowing I would never inflict this turmoil on either of my children. And yet, there were times when I did. At one point or another, the conditioning was more potent than my level of self-awareness; I often regret not having been opened to attaining a higher degree of wisdom earlier in my life.

I now accept that I was meant to move through the elated deep connection with my mother, then the subsequent tumultuous breakdown of that initial bond, and finally, the partial recovery of it. I believe I was intended to evolve through the frustrating, painful parts, as well as the unexpected, pleasant ones. The eventual wisdom I discovered through this 55-year process has supported me to establish meaningful connections with my children. Miraculously but not seamlessly, I have fostered nurturing relationships with their beautifully insightful partners. As I stepped into the position of matriarch for my children, I desperately wanted to learn what not to do from the matriarchs who came before me. I was motivated to reflect deeply about how I wanted to show up for my family, intending to gracefully support them through their child's need for dependence to an adult's natural progression to independence. I knew how I interpreted and responded to their transition into adulthood could highly impact them…and me…with the power of either greater good or destructive evil. The choice was mine as a female influencer, and the struggle of duality came into play and continues to create a juggling act of where I stand within my role in my family—*to be or not to be*—do I lead as a domineering matriarch or an unobtrusive guide?

The latter became as obsessive as counting the peas and carrots on my plate, driven by my passionate fight against deeply embedded intergenerational patterns that continuously tugged at my apron strings—damn them!! To this day, I am cautiously aware of when they approach, and I allow them to tap at the door because they effectively provide me with clarity about how I do not want to be. Letting them in just a bit offers sufficient warning to quickly analyze, process, and discard them within seconds. It's a fine line between sanity and insanity, and sometimes

Escaping the Cycle of Fear

I falter because the centuries-old familial systems I dread somehow sneakily weave through the value of grit my mother instilled in me. I know I need to fight that programming by utilizing the patient army of confidence waiting to march with me. Suddenly called to war, I thank my mother for modelling that strength so I can, ironically, fight parts of the matriarchal prototype she instilled in me—the elements that do not represent my soul. I want to fight to overcome the generational stereotypes of those who came before me—to model an intuitive, kinder, more genuine way of being. But I cannot do that a moment before it is absolutely necessary because there is always the chance that fighting too soon could elevate the emotional upheaval my armour is not yet equipped to endure. I need to receive a clear realization before attacking the set-in-stone familial archetypes.

The yearning to belong has been my greatest weakness, and envisioning the choice to fight that urge, if only in the distance, provides the freedom from it—to not feed into the enemy that presents themself as an ally by becoming their prisoner. That feels right. But alternatively, the stigma of not belonging motivates me to want to surrender because isn't any form of connection better than none? No, it is not. That feels wrong. Clarity provides the confidence to turn and walk away. This becomes another fine line of where I sit on the spectrum of belonging or not belonging—being sane or insane—both have trade-offs, and it comes down to determining which fight is worth its perspective backlash. Either way, it seems like an ominous war. And it becomes essential that I understand which battle is worth engaging in; is it the autonomy of not caring if I belong or the conformity of choosing to belong at any cost? Do I forge ahead or listen to my father and *just forget about it*? In my mind, it once again boils down to what is right and what is wrong—but from whose perspective?

My existence began on September 3, 1960, with two people questioning this exact debate. My mother had a roast in the oven while methodically doing her house chores like any other day. She felt dizzy now and again and had to sit down. Her mother, who was visiting from Holland, watched my mother being interrupted by several of these dizzy spells while ironing my father's shirts. My grandmother pointed out that her daughter must be in labour, but my mother balked at the idea that being light-headed could be a sign of my entry into the world because she claimed she had no pain...at all. Finally, my wise grandmother insisted that the episodes be timed, and my mother reluctantly conceded that, yes, she was likely in labour as they presented regularly, with not much time apart.

My father was at work, so my aunt, who lived close by, was called, and off they sped in the direction of the Catholic hospital. My aunt focused on getting my mother to the hospital on time and went through a red light, which prompted a police officer to stop her. She explained the situation in her broken English, and the officer immediately led the way to the hospital with his lights and sirens blaring. The end of the story is that my father got there just on time, and I was

Around The Table

born ten minutes after the entourage arrived at the hospital. My mother insisted she didn't feel one contraction through the entire birth...not one.

My mother told this birth story at least a hundred times, and each time, it never felt like my story, but only hers. I entered this realm as a child who craved attention, just as I believe my mother did. I often think that attention-seeking must be a genetic component because both my mother and I have required a high degree of it at various times in our lives. When I was young and unaware, having someone respond to me in a positive light invoked an abnormally high surge of approval through my body like a bolt of lightning. It immediately created affirming connection with that person, and I became part of them. I craved that sensation like a drug that accompanied a welcomed sense of belonging rarely experienced around the dinner table. As a result, attention became approval and approval translated into a perception of being loved. I became a people-pleaser, particularly a mommy-pleaser, because she provided powerful positive attention from the matriarch in our family. This became the force behind belonging, approval, and what I defined as love. My mother became my addiction for love, providing me with my drug of choice—the more I did for her, the more she smiled, and her happiness fueled my addiction for my definition of love over and over again. The only glitch was that there were many spaces between when my highs came crashing down and my lows rose up again because her happiness was unsustainable.

The first five years of my life became my most significant, cementing a belief that shaped how I responded to any human being crossing my path for the next 40 years; *you are not loved unless you make others happy* became my subconscious mantra. As a wee five-year-old, I tiptoed into my parents' room at sunrise before my father got home from the night shift. I slipped into bed with my mother, who kept her eyes closed, and she reached over to me to hold my hand while I lay beside her. I was one with her, and I believe she felt the same. There was safety within her reach, and this tiny gesture of physical touch through the warmth of her hand provided another confirming hinge on my love connection. This made me smile.

From the moment I shot out of my mother like a cannonball, I idolized her 100 percent. Initially, I physically attached to her for her milk and touch. However, over time, her presence in my life became a necessity for nurturing my essence, a motivator for my creativity, and a driving force behind obtaining her approval as I sought to be loved. When I was very young, my mother encouraged me to openly express all the stories and characters that continuously popped into my head because, deep down, she knew that my imagination corroborated my authentic existence. I played endlessly in my bedroom with my dolls and stuffed animals. Watching me, one might have thought I was playing the matriarch to my children, but no, they were my audience as I shared conjured up tales with them. Along with my mother, they validated what I thought love was by feeding my need for attention with their permanent smiles of approval staring at me for hours on end.

I became a storyteller at a very young age because the feedback I received, whether real or imaginary, fed my endless search for belonging.

My bedroom was a safe place where I went to be by myself without worrying about the possibility of scrutiny. It was a sanctuary where the pre-planning of thought or behaviour wasn't necessary, and it presented a different reality from the one that sometimes unfolded beyond my protective bedroom door—in the kitchen or the dining room, around the table. It was calm versus chaos with a safety barrier in between. But the barricade was not bullet-proof because there was no lock, and the door could be opened by anyone at any time. So, when my mother interrupted my storytelling one day and announced I would be going to kindergarten soon, my heart sank. She told me how fun it would be, and I came up with every reason I should not go. She countered me, saying there would be lots of children and toys to play with, that my teacher was nice, and I would learn a lot. I persisted, telling her I didn't want to go to school, didn't care about playing with other kids, didn't want to play with other toys, and didn't need to learn anything else. These were all excuses because the reality was that I intuitively knew I would not fit into the exterior world. I would not survive beyond the four walls of my bedroom without my stuffed animals or my mother.

No matter how sensible my intuition seemed, the first day of school arrived, and my mother walked me to the kindergarten just blocks from our house. I'm sure she sensed my trepidation because she worked hard at making me feel comfortable, talking about the pretty flowers strategically placed in our neighbours' gardens and what a lovely day it was. She also used distraction as a weapon against the fear of expressing emotion—the weather was the go-to topic of discussion. But flowers blooming and the sun shining were not intriguing enough to distract me from a deep knowing that something greater was about to unravel. At the age of five, walking along the shoulder of the road beside the ditch, all I wanted was to go back to my bedroom, shut the door, and continue living my imaginary existence with my mother on the other side of that partially-safe space.

I made one final attempt at getting out of this predicament with a stern, *I don't want to go to kindergarten.* I had never raised my voice or talked back to my mother, and it resulted in her retaliating with a firm and adamant, *You're going, and you are going to have a good time!!* I quickly noted this was not a question. She was not asking my opinion, and her tone indicated no room for argument. This in itself was disturbing, with a new side of my mother that resembled my father, presenting as detached and cold. The matriarch had suddenly placed herself alongside equal billing with the patriarch, making a decision void of emotion, flexibility, or compromise. At that moment, I understood that she was in control instead of me, and I immediately retreated within myself as we headed silently down the street to meet my first teacher. This is also my first recollection of wanting to prove that I was right and believing my mother was not while experiencing the same intimidation when being told I was wrong as I did with my father.

Around The Table

It's true, I loved kindergarten, but I also worried about not being with my mother every day, questioning who would make her happy and who would make her smile. At this young age, my first bouts of anxiety emerged. I couldn't determine or articulate the discomfort that escalated inside me when my mother left my side. She was seemingly unscathed and even appeared happy, easily turning around with a wave while walking away from the kindergarten yard. None of this made any sense to me because I believed our happiness was conducive to being together…all the time. So, as she disappeared down the street with a skip in her step, I immediately grieved the absence of her presence. And even though she was the one who left me standing there, I blamed myself for abandoning her because there was no one else at home to keep her company.

I spent the next eight months going to the little basement kindergarten down the road. I made a few friends, but I knew I didn't fit in with the other kids; not only did I look different from them, but I really believed that I interpreted the world the exact opposite of how they did. My teacher looked like Mrs. Butterworth with her heavy-set stature, tiny round spectacles, and knotted bun on top of her head. She took on my mom's role by encouraging me to be creative. This fed my need for approval—love. She gave me a sense of being special, and she smiled a lot. With gratitude yet sadness, I remember my first year in school in 1965 as the best one out of 14.

My mother did the right thing transitioning me into the real world, and I was blessed to have an incredibly nurturing teacher. But, just before summer vacation began, my mother told me I would be going to the big school in September. She was wise to get that embedded in my brain early, and of course, I knew that was the next step. However, in response to my newly-developed anxiety, that was also the year I began consciously compartmentalizing and ignoring things that made me nervous. Change was uncomfortable, and I did not welcome it, so I learned how to masterfully block any discomfort that came my way—similar to the daily ritual of counting the food items on my plate at dinner.

Once again, my mother told me how wonderful grade one would be instead of encouraging me to chat about my doubt or what I could do to cope with it; most parents didn't do that back then. So, after a summer of ignoring my fate, I distracted myself by pretending to be optimistic like she was as I went off to my first day at the big school. True to her word, there were old and new friends there, but my optimism dissipated as soon as I stepped on the playground. She did her familiar schtick, smiling and turning around with her little wave while I noticed the hair on my neck rise. Suddenly an icky feeling of being different tugged at my stomach. This physical indicator was new, but it was similar to the discomfort I moved through on my first day of kindergarten. Over time, it became the red flag I counted on to manage bouts of anxiety brought on by extreme loneliness. Standing there beside the playground equipment, I was confused and frantically tried to make sense of wanting to run away from the pain of not belonging.

Quickly scanning the rest of the playground, I determined a pecking order of conformed, stereotypical children, who were distinctly categorized. First, there were the good-looking and confident males and females. I recognized them as future patriarchs and matriarchs who decided where everyone landed in the scheme of an established hierarchy; they controlled the fate of their peers from most important to least significant. Then, low on that scale were the stigmatized, awkward, less self-assured children who presented as loners scattered around the yard—I resonated more with them than their upper-level counterparts. Most of these panic-ridden souls stood by themselves, but some were fortunate to have found an equally floundering friend to cling to as a pillar of security.

In most cases, relationships were developed out of necessity, to be a part of something—anything really— to fit into an established societal role somewhere on the ladder of acceptance. There wasn't much choice unless one was willing to be banished entirely from this ancient-ranking prototype. Within moments, I assessed where I sat within the chain of command, which was nowhere near those superior to me. I wasn't quite at the bottom, but anything midway or below was equally rejected by those at the top.

For a moment, I remembered that other first day a year ago when I tried to convince my mother to take me home. In desperation, I looked behind me and saw her walk away and instantly knew it was a waste of time to start that battle again. So, I stood there, simultaneously, absorbing and fighting the discomfort of being an outsider. Momentary turmoil encompassed me, resembling familiar disapproval at home when I spilled my milk. But I took a deep breath, and an inkling of confidence washed over me when I realized this was no different than being at home around the table, and I resorted to counting my vegetables. It was all too familiar, actually, and I knew what was necessary to survive the wrath of being at the bottom of the totem pole; I needed to find some peas and carrots to count.

Being somewhat empowered within the norm of my discomfort, some strength bubbled up when I realized I could survive it. So, I took a step forward into familiar yet unwelcomed territory. This warrior memory would become the first of many. I became aware of my ability to use my soul's patient courage that waited for me to tap into and utilize its power. Later in my life, I decided to give myself full credit for my resilience rather than thank God for it. Instead, I became grateful for my willingness to endure suffering because I discovered that each sad episode was a beautiful gift of awakening, even though it was often painful beyond belief. I eventually valued the discomfort of restorative truth more than the comfort of destructive fantasy.

I am now certain that perception only becomes reality when I believe it. And as a little girl with squinty eyes, a long nose, a pixie haircut, and a scrawny body, I fed into the societal belief that my looks determined the measurement of my worth. And I was different from every girl within ten feet of anywhere I stood on that playground. I saw groups of kids gathered together, with not one asking

Around The Table

me to join them. Beautiful girl-next-door species with big brown or blue eyes, little curled up noses, and long glistening ponytails skipped in unison before me. Boys congregated and taunted the less favourable children who clung to pieces of playground equipment as if representing the security of one of their parents. Every ounce of my being indicated this would end with prevailed anguish. It was the beginning of a long journey hindered by a firm conviction that I was not good enough without conforming to the approval of others—mirrored acceptance equalled belonging, which translated into love. My only saving grace was knowing I could survive rejection. I knew this because my mother instilled that belief in me. She also taught me how to use strength as protection, but I never understood its merit as much as I did on that first day of grade one.

I don't think my mother was aware of my despair because I never told her. I didn't want to show her that I was weak, sad, or insecure; I just wanted to make her smile and show her that I was strong and as happy as she seemed to be. Something deep inside me knew that if I asked her for advice, she would give it. However, I also believed she would not offer without asking her for it because my mother wore one of those fake veils, protecting her from emotional pain and suffering. It was her peas and carrots. So, I followed her lead and chose not to push her by tugging at her veil. I took great care to keep it hanging safely between us because I believed I would cause her discomfort if I shared my fearful encounters, and I was confident she would not love me if I attempted to discard her protective barrier.

Any bravery I developed came from the thought that I needed to make my mother happy, and part of that was not to be bad. As a result, I found a method of distraction to be good by counting the minutes, hours, and days to the weekend. Every week I endured the trauma of five terrifying back-to-back days that included the marching steps and jingling of a hundred keys hanging off the principal's robe. She was a nun and a nasty person, so when the incessant noise of those keys stopped, I knew a child in one of the classrooms was about to receive the strap for whatever reason she deemed fitting. I erred on the side of caution, staying small, quiet, and inconspicuous. I was not a risk-taker, avoiding pain at all costs.

I put my hand up when I had to go to the bathroom after initially holding my pee for as long as I could, hoping I wouldn't have to walk down that hall with the possibility she would suddenly appear. But straining my bladder was not the answer because it always created the sudden need to go, accompanied by having to run down the hall to avoid a mess in my leotard. Running was not allowed, and the principal had a sixth sense when it came to being right there the moment a sprint began. The result was always the strap.

In second grade, I was summoned to the front of the class when the boy behind me whispered, *Trick or treat, smelly feet, give me something good to eat,* and I giggled aloud. The teacher never asked me what I was laughing about but instead sat in her chair in front of her desk and put me over her knee, lifted my skirt, and spanked my bum ten times. The entire class was my audience, and they laughed

Escaping the Cycle of Fear

until she told them to settle down. I was so ashamed but also angry because none of my classmates were reprimanded for laughing while I was humiliated for a little giggle. I learned early on that life isn't fair and even more so for those who don't stand up for themselves.

Sadly, my encounters with Catholic punishment were the least of my worries when I suddenly became a victim of elevated bullying. I saw it coming. After all, I already endured classmates running up to me every day, asking if I could see when I smiled because my eyes became narrower than they already were when I didn't. My last name was integrated into a chant, *Pitter-Patter, let's get atter*, that groups of girls and boys sang over and over again while dancing around me. But I did what I thought my mother would do: be strong, never cry or react, and focus on the happy children in the distance on the round-about circling around and around. With every turn, the chanting eventually subsided because I didn't give them the reaction they were waiting for, and they ran off. I was grateful they didn't resort to the physical abuse I witnessed other victims receiving, and yet, I had moments when I wished they would just get it over with by punching me in the face. Eventually, I determined that if I made myself disappear as soon as the recess bell rang by running out to the fence that backed onto the Protestant school, I was less of a target. Distance became my ally because it wasn't worth it for them to travel to get to me. Resourcefulness became one of my attributes of emotional survival.

One day, a bit of hope trickled in when I was befriended by a girl that I thought was part of the bully pack. But she was nice to me and used my naivety to trap me. We chatted and joked around for a while, and a glimmer of camaraderie that comes with not being made fun of for a brief moment came over me. We walked by where the bikes were parked, and she asked me if I knew how to swing by one leg around the steel bike holder. I told her I had never done that but had seen others do it, and it looked like fun. I was determined not to disappoint this newfound friend, so when she encouraged me to try, I walked over to the higher bar with the logic I would have more space to clear the pavement beneath it. She encouraged me to go to the shorter one because she thought it would be easier for me on the first try. I trusted her and went for it by lifting my right leg over the bar and wrapping it around my dangling left leg like I had seen other children do.

Sitting high on the bar, I was proud I had come this far until I saw a group gather around me, yelling their usual, *Pitter, Patter, let's get atter*. I looked over at the girl who had initiated our newfound friendship and saw her laughing hysterically alongside the others. Humiliation overtook me, and for a brief moment, I saw my mother smiling in front of me with her beautiful veil of courage. And just like that, I turned to strength, believing I had no choice but to go for it. I wanted to jump off that bar and run to the safety of the fence, but instead, I put on my veil, pretended all was fine, and delved into my fate of misery. To my detriment, I swung myself forward, and my brow scraped along the hot black pavement. The impact was a damaging reiteration that not only had this girl thrown me into the dark den of her taunting peers, but she had also been willing to risk my life to secure her sense of belonging within this pack of wolves.

The limited trust I had in anyone was obliterated when I was rushed to the nurse's room while waiting for my mother to come and take me either home or to the hospital. Sitting on a chair, I looked towards the open door and saw the trail of blood that had dripped from my head down the hallway when the parent on yard duty brought me in. Holding a bag of ice on my cut, I wondered if the principal would give me the strap for swinging on the bike rack. Of course, we weren't allowed to do that; it was sure to be another notch on my wall of sin.

As my mother turned into our driveway that day after picking me up, I glanced at our weeping willow tree in the backyard. Its long branches swayed back and forth in a rhythmic dance as the breeze picked up, and it seemed to be calling me. I immediately claimed it as my sanctuary, where the distance from the rest of the world became less motivation for others to disrupt my solitude. This tree became my security blanket like the fence and the round-about on the playground. I endured each school day with the distraction of knowing it waited for me at the end of the day. Laying beneath its umbrella of leaves became a daily ritual. This willow tree and all that transpired under it served me just as I believed I served my mother. It brought me happiness because no one hurt me under the willow tree, and it made me as close to safe as I thought possible.

Day after day, I stared at the clouds through the wisps of twine, and I discovered intricate stories floating above. It was as though the wind flipped through tattered pages as the clouds moved quickly past me. I was sure that the expansive blue and white backdrop was an ancient storybook provided by God, and I wondered how this mighty being chose which ever-changing tales He shared. At that time, it never occurred to me that God wasn't responsible for creating the stories I saw and heard while lying below the great weeping willow. I realized much later that the gift of my powerful imagination was responsible for them. But back then, I was told that God had the highest power and automatically assumed it was His magic at play before me. After all, He forgave all creatures, big and small, no matter how many glasses of milk they spilled, so he must have given me this precious gift of the tree against the sky as an act of acceptance. By doing so, He also made me smile, which was proof that He must be someone who loved me. Unfortunately, so did the little girl who manipulated me into smashing my head on the pavement, and it made me wonder if God would also betray me after being so kind by sharing His stories.

My admiration for God slowly began to wane alongside the deterioration of my self-esteem, impacted by the torment of daily bullying. My reliance on this higher power began diminishing at the same rate my worthiness did. I struggled with trusting His power because the kids at school also had power, as did my father, and something was off. Around the age of 16, I concluded that control evolved from hierarchy, with the highest positioning having the highest power. None of

Escaping the Cycle of Fear

it seemed fair as I learned that age, sex, and status did not equate to wisdom, intelligence, and virtue. And yet, I was still somewhat attracted to the concept that a male who was older than me deserved respect no matter what they did—I had a decade and a half of programming that told me so. This became a dangerous game of cat and mouse, good versus evil, and right versus wrong. I was reminded of this any time my awareness fell short, which happened more often than not because the wisdom I needed to be decisive about what I really believed had not yet fully percolated.

A lot of time passed until I found clarity about what God meant to me, but this backyard space remained my haven as a young girl. It was where I read books to my stuffed animals and dolls and expressed gratitude to Him for the stories in the clouds. This continued until around the age of eight, when I heard my parents talk about the problematic roots of the willow tree and how they were growing under the house's foundation. My angst around what that meant supported me to express my deep concern to my mother about losing this special place that ignited my imagination. I didn't share my emotions very often, but I knew she was my only chance at saving the tree that created the view to the sky where God so willingly narrated His inspiring stories and instilled a sense of belonging in me. I pleaded with her without telling her why I didn't want the tree cut down because I didn't know how to articulate that!! I simply cried and begged her not to take it away.

The tree was never cut down and remained my haven until our house was put up for sale later that year. I'm not sure if my mother ever expressed my worry about removing the tree with my father, but I know she transferred my desperation into her own and pleaded with him not to destroy it. She probably also cried as an effective tool, knowing he would not have understood the importance of my time and space with God in the clouds. And being uncomfortable, he would have wanted the emotional outburst to end as quickly as possible.

So, my first eight years on this earth ended with my mother winning the fight for a tree's life. She didn't realize that she also saved my soul's life by getting my father to agree to keep it. I entered the following year, ultimately grieving its loss when the house it stood behind was sold. Little did my mother know that she ripped the security of that tree from me by moving me far away from it. And I thought the almighty power of God was taken away from me when we moved away from the willow. The reality is that my mother initiated a landslide of awakenings when I eventually concluded He was not the source of my power at all. Instead, I realized that it was me who empowered myself. From that day on, I concentrated on avoiding fear by keeping my eyes level while sitting around the kitchen table. I vowed never to look at the cross above the door again.

II

˞ Escaping the Cycle of Authority ˞

I was nine years old in 1969 when my parents sold their first home, a duplex purchased with a 1000-dollar down payment borrowed from a friend, and bought a larger, elevated bungalow in a nicer part of town. As hard-working immigrants from Holland, this was a huge step up the ladder of life. In 1957, my father brought his family over on what was commonly referred to by immigrants of that era as *the boat*. Thousands of Dutch people crossed the ocean to start a better life with more opportunities than back home. Like so many immigrating to Canada, my parents were filled with hope, sailing for weeks with their first-born daughter and 50 dollars in their pocket.

Their daughter was only one when they rented a second-story apartment in the north end of a downtown area stigmatized as low-income and unsafe. The apartment was run down and infested with cockroaches, which my mother became accustomed to rhythmically stomping on to protect her baby. This place was all they could afford, and although the situation was dire, she and my father forged ahead with optimism, determined to create the life they dreamed of. My father began looking for a job, which became complicated because his career credentials as an accountant in Holland were not valid in Canada. Out of necessity, he pushed this setback aside and solved his financial burden by taking a job at a factory, or as we called it, the nylon plant. This ended up being a life-long gig in a factory, working on the line through gruelling 12-hour shifts. Sadly, for those who lived with him, his volatile and sometimes unpredictable temper was one significant indication of his ill-fate.

I don't know if his fluctuating moods were always part of his personality because I wasn't born until after he began working those long shifts. Still, they are what I remember more than the stories my mother told me about what a great father he was—most of which were expansions of the truth or what she would have liked me to experience. That incongruency in perception often confused me. But, she had her wifely and motherly roles to uphold, and God was her guide. *Honour thy husband* was the unmistakable message I got, and that sometimes meant leaving not-so-pleasant parts of the story out. She immersed herself in daily housewife duties as if they were part of her job description…because they were back in the 60s. My mother was the epitome of what a wife and mother were expected to be back then, striving to do everything that served her husband and children. She protected and defended my father, her God, and her children—in that order, as required, and with the passion of a pit bull. But, although she was devoted to God, her loyalty to Him was overridden by the power she gave my father. And she didn't have an allegiance to everyone's God, just the Catholic one.

One morning in that cockroach-infested apartment, my mother was bathing her baby in a portable plastic basin beside the kitchen window when the bell rang from the lower-level door to the building. With one hand on her child's tummy, she lifted herself on her tiptoes and saw a few women standing on the small porch directly under the window with pamphlets in their hands. Not knowing who they were, she lifted her baby out of the water and wrapped her in a towel. Next, she carried her down the stairs to the front entrance. Opening the door, she was welcomed by members of the Jehovah's Witnesses. They seemed friendly, and she was polite, patiently letting them finish their spiel while rocking her child. Then, with her Dutch accent, she politely told them that she was a devout Catholic and not interested in changing religions. They smiled, handed her the pamphlets, and then walked to the next house. My mother climbed the stairs back to the second level, added warm water to the basin of now cold water, and immersed her daughter back into the tub.

The next day, the entourage returned at the same time. Multi-generational matriarchs trained my mother to maintain a strict schedule of daily tasks, so her baby was back in the little tub having her morning bath when the doorbell rang for a second time. Peeking through the window again, my mother recognized the well-dressed ladies in their suits, hats, and heels, and she decided to wrap her daughter up one more time to reiterate her answer to their recruitment request the day before. This time, she didn't let them get too deep into their sermon and gently pushed their hands that held new pamphlets back towards them. She wasn't as polite and firmly told them, *No, thank you!* They smiled and waved goodbye while turning to walk away.

Although inconvenienced and frustrated, my mother was confident her message was received, and she would not hear from them again. She was wrong. They returned the same time the next day, interrupting her routine again. My mother did not head down the stairs to greet them this time but wrapped her daughter up and laid her in her bassinette. She then opened the window with no screen, lifted the basin of tub water, and threw it out on top of them. They shook their wet heads like dogs out in the rain and looked up towards my mother in shock. She repeated her response to them from the day before, yelling, *No, thank you* and slammed the window shut. They never came back.

When tapping into her essence, my mother has been described as kind and giving by many. However, her patience is not to be tested! When slighted, she has no barometer of control, quickly shifting to a place of retribution. She will do anything to make her point, including sacrificing a relationship should the other person involved not accept their responsibility in the altercation. I have been just as self-righteous because there was a time when I followed suit, believing that the act of forgiveness involved the admittance of fault by my adversary. Ironically, as much as my mother agrees with this integral piece of accountability, she often compromises her role within that equation by using her matriarchal status. Therein lies a dilemma because I cannot turn the other cheek simply because she leverages her familial hierarchy as a reason for her innocence.

On the other hand, she adheres to strict hierarchy rules, assuming she will be forgiven and proven not guilty simply because she is the matriarch. She used her privilege to alter details and their context in an attempt to establish her righteousness any time I challenged her when catching her in a lie. One unknown deception occurred in my 20s and developed into catastrophic revelations when I turned 60. A revealed 40-year-secret completely altered my perception of my mother and whether I could forgive her or not because she refused admittance. I struggled greatly because I could not accuse her without facts to back up my suspicions.

And yet, in general, she had no problem following the hierarchal protocol she had conformed to, automatically forgiving those above her, admonishing her husband and God of all transgressions. In the case of God, there was no reason other than He earned her grace due to His ranking. As an extension of the Catholic teachings from her parents and those before them, she must honour Him no matter what. In my father's case, he simply deserved compliance by virtue of being her husband, our father, and the head of the household—the male. He decided where her loyalty went first, second, and so on based on the ancient patriarchy guideposts—unconditional devotion to God, then man, and then women and children. Outside of an emergency, she freely served her children after God and man were taken care of first; that's just the way it was. However, she also used her matriarchal influence when she wanted something from those beneath her in the familial lineup. When it was to her advantage, I understood my place in the chain of command.

I remember having dinner with my parents one day after I got married. My husband was away, and it was just the three of us at the table. My mother shared a conversation she had with my mother-in-law the day before. Hoping for my approval and camaraderie, she told me how ridiculous it was that my husband's mother shared that her children were everything to her, and she would do anything to support them. My mother told me how hurtful that must be for my father-in-law, and it was wrong for his wife to put her children before her husband. My father sat beside her and agreed that my mother-in-law should find other things to fulfill her, like spending time with her husband. So, there I was, sitting around the table with my parents again, telling me what seemed normal to them, but not to me. Years of trauma loomed over me as I tried to absorb and process what they said as quickly as possible, so I could respond in a way that represented what I believed without triggering an argument. However, I had been at that same junction so many times before and knew it would be futile. Becoming caught in the vortex of indecisiveness, I leaned towards agreeing to establish the same camaraderie my mother enjoyed. But my desire to defend was what I believed was much more prevalent. At this point, I was in my 30s and had yet to learn how to manage the constant shame of being coerced into agreeing with them.

The expectation of having the same beliefs as my family was beyond complicated. I learned I could never uphold their standards because we rarely agreed on anything for as long as I can remember, which was always problematic and made me different from my sisters. They seemed to always agree with my parents, particularly my father. Early on, I also nodded in agreement in response to anything he said, even if I disagreed. However, as I got older, there were times when I stated my opinion, and the consequences were dire; perhaps my sisters were also afraid of him. But for me, a time came when my truth practically burst out of my chest without me having any control over it, and I began my quest to be credited with being right, knowing full well that would never likely happen. Something in me could not be contained because the longing to share myself grew equally as fast as the hair on my head.

The head of our household had difficulty respecting opinions based on emotion and no patience for hysterical viewpoints. Some time in my teens, I realized that not only did he want to be right, but he enjoyed proving me wrong. I also figured out that he didn't know how to respond to my vulnerable rants, and being pragmatic was far more comfortable for him; perhaps even the only way he knew how to be. He and I were exact opposites, yet we had a few similar characteristics. He could be quiet—introverted—and as a child, I was the same until I had to adapt to socially surviving. People who meet me for the first time now define me as an extrovert. But back in Catholic elementary school and through high school, I was an outsider without the self-confidence to make friends easily, even with those who felt mutually less-than. I wore the badge of an outcast and have since wondered if my father did as well. I don't think either of us intended to—we were just both surviving. No one chooses to suffer due to the unique disadvantage they are given when brought into the world.

I related to my father's discomfort in social situations, having jumped into the deep angst of my own. Still, I never resonated with his choice not to express empathy for others and blatantly share his lack thereof. And yet, I had trouble empathizing with him; I wanted to understand, but I didn't. Having always had an intuitive sense that compassion is the gateway, I struggled when he almost made a point of being the opposite. Watching his awkward interactions with family members, acquaintances, and my children, I had difficulty relating to his typically arrogant response to the world. I was never sympathetic to this because, ironically, he conditioned me not to be. The strength instilled in me by my mother, alongside the skill of squashing emotions modelled by my father, were highly valued family characteristics. As always, my father ended every disagreement with *just forget about it*, especially after I bravely expressed how I felt—he couldn't handle it. Over the years, this repeated statement invalidated most of what I shared. Not long ago, I was vulnerable about something I told my mother and father, and both became defensive. When the uncomfortable conversation ended, my father looked at me, and I mouthed those same words in unison with him, *just forget about it*.

Through my teens and into adulthood, I questioned myself many times, wondering if my judgment of him came from being terrified that I might become him or that I already had. I became very good at shelving my emotions and distancing myself from anything uncomfortable. Recently, a friend provided pause for reflection, suggesting that a piece of my pragmatic resilience might come from my father rather than my mother's rigorous strength-training program. It made some sense to me because he showed me how to detach from painful things, both physically and emotionally, just as seamlessly as he did. I sat in the dark that day, thinking about this possible gift from my father—did he give me the ability to push my soul to the sidelines to make room for that army of confidence I needed to soldier on? And was this a gift? Perhaps I should be more grateful.

My dad loved to read and was a seeker of knowledge. He was intelligent and always ready for a debate. So, while he was uncomfortably quiet more often than not, he relied on his ability to share his accumulated knowledge while simultaneously comparing it to someone else's lack thereof. I understand this methodology because I am also more secure in engaging in conversations about topics I am well-educated and familiar with. Somewhere along the line, I came to believe that subjects like math, science, geography, or politics were not within my realm of understanding—I'm a girl—but my father was knowledgeable in all of them. When I was younger, I diligently shared my limited knowledge during a brief crusade to connect with him by acquiring the ability to discuss anything that used the left side of my brain. This back-fired because I could not compete with his intellect and analytical thinking; I viewed them as weapons against my deep insights and intuitive thoughts that I was naturally drawn to. We differed in so many ways; I am creative, empathetic, and an advocate for the underdog, whereas he was logical, impassive, and critical of others who differed from him. We are both stubborn, so my desperate need to connect with him consistently evolved into disconnection with out-of-control arguments as I persisted in getting him to agree with me. Although I became much more conscious of this dysfunction over the years, if I let my guard down, I was still highly motivated to win the right or wrong game because I believed I might belong.

This argumentative undertone became more evident after we moved to the bungalow in the township when I was nine. I remember my father sitting at the head of the table, strategically controlling each conversation. Over time, I interpreted our back-and-forth engagement as an intention to prove me wrong, no matter the topic. He was an adult, the man of the house, the patriarch, and he was very good at seeming right, which of course, made me perceive I was not. Well into adulthood, we sat around the dinner table in our delegated seats or around the coffee table on the loveseats in the living room. Society's goal in creating such seating is to spark conversation, but my father's quest became the reality of any interaction we had. Due to my insecurities, I was usually defeated before we even began to speak. Over the years, this contributed to my ill-health because I continually emotionally sacrificed myself.

At the same time, I was unaware that any degree of resilience I had was working in the background, growing a coat of armour—slow and steady. It would eventually prove to protect me from the consequences of being considered weak and too sensitive. And, if I had an ounce of awareness of this fortitude back then, I would have asked my father why it was so horrible that I dared to care to be an advocate for myself and others. But I didn't because, by the time I reached an age when I could stand up for myself, I was far too absorbed in trying to win whatever fight we were fighting. Even with the small degree of confidence I sometimes managed to muster up, I used it for all the wrong reasons. To this day, I trust myself more while supporting others than myself.

Being moral and ethical became my focus. I learned to voice my opinion, but my father always successfully countered it. To this day, my husband shares memories of conversations around my parents' dinner table with my father stirring up shit with me. They ultimately resulted in me defending what I believed and my father rarely conceding. He typically had a condescending smirk on his face throughout the entire argument, and my interpretation was his delight in getting me riled up. Unfortunately, the story I created in my head was that I needed to be a good girl and agree in order to be loved, or, if there was any possibility, prove I was right with the consequence of being bad and unloved.

When I entered my late teens, the affliction of believing I was marginally insane began to surface. I was conscious of a little person running around in my brain yelling, *Just be wrong, and you will be loved or Do what they want, and they will accept you*. I was confused about which would provide the desired result because both seemed fake and calculated. This was my father's deal, refusing to agree with me just because he could. Finally, I realized that it didn't matter what route I took because he would never give me a morsel of compliance. So, following his lead, I decided to use his tactic, pointing out falsehoods in things he stated. I had become him, and I finally understood the pathological drive that inhabited his brain because it began motivating me as well.

On one occasion, when I was in my 50s, sitting beside my father on my sofa, I was intrigued when he pointed his finger in my face and called me a narcissist. He then asked me if I even knew what that meant. *Narcissism is an acute condition whereby someone is so self-involved that they lack the emotional and social intelligence to be aware of how their behaviour negatively impacts others,* I responded, and he floundered with nothing to say. I knew the answer because I had been working in the coaching industry for several years, supporting others to live authentically, which often included my clients having to manage the narcissists in their lives.

This was one of the few times I recall him struggling to win an argument with me, and it wasn't as satisfying as I thought it would be. As much as I thought I should celebrate this accomplishment, I empathized with his insecurity, having lived through it a hundred times myself. I was also devastated, recognizing it as an uncomplimentary part of me that I had developed from interacting with him. Regardless, I revelled in the fact that I dared to stand up for myself and won. The irony was that the initial argument started with me defending my husband about how my parents had disrespected him—the very thing my mother would be proud of me for and that my father would expect his wife to do if he were in my husband's shoes. And yet, neither supported my position due to ranking higher than my husband on the hierarchy scale. I had brought my father down a notch on his egoic ladder, and I'm sure he felt defeated, given the importance of his lineage standing.

I remember wondering what my grandmother would have thought seeing her son finally being put in his place. Knowing her, I think she would have been proud of my determination to save my soul. All those years were worth every moment I fought to be right for once. I know she would have understood because she also endured her own fight with a man much like my father. Like so many women in the early 1900s, my father's mother stayed home to run the household. Back then, way more so than now, people were defined within their roles of either a man or woman. My oma spent her days cooking, cleaning, and raising her four sons. Spending this much time with her children, she created a powerful emotional bond with them. Consequently, I questioned why my father struggled so much with expressing his emotions after being brought up by a mother who was so nurturing and showered him with heart-felt love; until I met my grandfather, and everything became crystal clear.

It was obvious that my opa was the polar opposite of my oma, and he scared me. I met them both for the first time when they came to visit us in Canada when I was around two or three, but I have no recollection of their stay or even if they came to visit more than once. I only have a few photos of them picnicking with us along the side of a road. These images are carefully pasted in the tattered childhood album my mother filled with memories and passed on to me when my parents moved from a house to an apartment—they didn't have room for them anymore. My grandparents look happy, sitting on a blanket, smiling, and eating. I seem to be untainted by soon-to-be-created stories in my head.

I was reunited with my grandparents at the age of 11 when my parents sold the bungalow in town and everything we owned to move back to Holland. Unlike the one with the willow tree on, I had no particular attachment to the one with the red floor. However, I do remember it having a partially finished basement with a bright red painted floor, and I wondered why anyone would paint a floor red. I also have fond memories of a blizzard in March 1971. It was so massive that it became known as the storm of the decade. We had a driveway that sloped down into the garage, and my parents parked their car just outside the garage door at the lowest end. So much snow fell that it completely covered the car overnight. Our family sat around the table that morning listening to the news on the kitchen radio and cheered when we heard that schools and businesses were closed for the day. It was one of my father's scheduled days off, so we all went outside to shovel ourselves out. This became a collaborative family effort, with everyone doing their part to complete the task at hand.

We enjoyed spontaneous moments that day, making snow angels, having snowball fights, and building snowmen and forts, which my oldest sister was a master at. She always invited me into her most recent build. We experienced a sense of togetherness that day, and it continues to reside deep within my soul. Long ago memories like these inspire the overflowing love I intentionally offer my husband, our children, and their extended families. I struggled to identify with that evolved love from a very early age because it conflicted with elements that contradicted it. However, I know it was developed from an accumulation of other hand-picked childhood feel-goods that I desperately tapped into in an effort to belong. They are memories that keep me from tipping over the borderline of my egoic fight between love and hate and encourage me to return to those I am hurt by the most. I am astounded that such a simple thing as a bowl of my mother's homemade chicken soup on a Saturday afternoon after cleaning the house together has stuck on my brain like gum to a shoe. Or that savouring Long Johns from the local donut shop after coming home from church continues to be worthy of clinging on to. There was nothing better than the 25-cent Dairy Queen cone during the car ride home after a day of sun at the beach; of course, I had to be different, asking for the added chocolate dip. Playing board games with my parents and sisters was passed down as one of the most significant things my kids enjoy doing together even now. These childhood moments significantly shaped another part of me—the undamaged part that was unconditionally gifted before our big move across the ocean.

Moving to Europe was a significant, life-changing event, ranging from incredible to horrible within the seven-month span we lived there. I dove into the excitement of flying on a plane during this transition to an entirely different culture and meeting my paternal grandparents for what seemed like the first time. I embraced visiting my maternal grandmother, aunts, uncles, and cousins; my mother had 13 brothers and sisters, with around half living in Canada. We relocated to Holland because my mother missed the other half and her mother, who still lived there. Her father had passed many years before at the age of 65. However, my father's parents still lived, and he had one surviving brother and sister-in-law and their two sons.

I don't know how my mother convinced my father to sell everything and return to Holland, but she did. Like so many overcrowded countries, there are long waitlists for house sales and rentals, so we moved in with my father's parents, who made room for us in the house he lived in as a child. The plan was that we stay with them until a place became available. They lived in an old row house along a cobblestone road. This was where my father grew up, and the house was narrow and deep, with the highest ceilings I ever saw. The living room was at the front, the dining room in the middle, and the kitchen at the back with a bedroom on either side. There was a long hallway that ran through the middle from the front door to the kitchen at the back, and a *kachel*—coal heater—sat between the dining room and living room and heated the entire house. This was where my oma sat every afternoon with a glass of Dutch *jenever*—gin. She instantaneously fell into a light slumber after swallowing the shot of gin and automatically woke up after 15 minutes; no alarm was needed. My relatives refer to this short nap as a *tukje*, and I remember watching her from the hall while she slept with her empty glass resting on her bosom. I was mesmerized seeing this for the first time, wondering if her fingers might loosen their grip, allowing the glass to slide off that voluptuous slope onto her lap. But it never did.

This house was cold, damp, much older, and less spacious than the bungalow back in Canada. I shared one of the back bedrooms with my sisters and slept in a wall bed, which I thought was quite cool until I didn't anymore. My parents slept in the other backroom, and my grandparents' bedroom was at the top of the hallway just inside the front vestibule. There was a two-piece bathroom mid-way down the hall.

The day we arrived, I had to pee, and after taking a few minutes to figure out how to flush the toilet with the long cord hanging from the ceiling plumbing, I noticed there was no bathtub in the washroom. Walking back into the hall, I searched for a stairwell that would surely take me to a second floor with another bathroom accommodating a tub and shower. But there wasn't one because the house only had one level. A shiver of anxiety slid down my spine as I wondered how I was ever going to wash myself. When I returned to the dining room where everyone had gathered for supper, I nervously entered the start of seat assignment around the table.

Everyone stood chatting except my oma and my mother, who bustled back and forth from the kitchen to the dining room with bowls of vegetables and potatoes. A gravy boat was filled to the rim with a rich dark brown sauce and thoughtfully placed beside a platter of thinly-sliced roast beef. The old heavy maple table was round rather than rectangular like the one we had back home, and I glanced at the various place settings of cutlery carefully laid out on Oma's white linen for a possible clue as to where I would sit. Strangely, I tried to picture where my father would have been seated as a young boy—there were four brothers, but I didn't know where he landed in the lineup.

Panic elevated from the base of my pelvis as I noted that Opa had stoically seated himself at what appeared to be the head of the table. But was it? The shape of the table created uncertainty because I wasn't able to assess the positioning of family members without the distinct corners and sides. I also needed to consider the added element of grandparents; a drawing would have helped. Nevertheless,

Around The Table

because it was their house and he was older, I deducted that Opa ranked over my father and automatically assumed head of the household. Thankfully, he was already seated, and I knew that Oma would sit opposite him. This also made sense because she sat closest to the kitchen. But where did that place my mother and father? Since I figured out my grandparents, I decided to go back to the place settings as visual guideposts to determine where everyone should sit. I placed my father beside my opa and my mother across from my father; that took up one corner. Next came my sisters and me, with the eldest going beside my father, which also placed her beside my oma on the other side; this made sense because she was the eldest grandchild. The middle daughter, also the second-eldest grandchild in the room, sat on Oma's other side. And me being the youngest got what was left over—the extra one on one side, which created less room and more risk to spill my milk…just like at home. Also, just because I thought I had it all figured out didn't mean I was courageous enough to make the bold move to sit there. So, I remained standing, anxiously waiting for the others to take their seats.

Before my anxiety became entirely derailed, Oma gave me a soft place to land by telling me where my seat was between my sister and mother; I was right. Her voice was sing-songy yet decisive, directing everyone to their seat, one by one. I had figured everyone's seat out, having been taught the same law of familial hierarchy that my ancestors had. I was relieved she jumped in at the right moment because I did not want to decide on my own for fear of being wrong.

I sat as patiently as my empty stomach would allow, waiting for the food to come around to me—that was the rule. I was starving in my mind, even though I was reminded many times throughout my childhood how disrespectful it was to use that term, given the starving children in the world. I didn't say it out loud, and I was mindful of being submissive, honouring the etiquette of food being passed to me from the right side, beginning with the family's patriarch, my opa. I would never think of disturbing this ritual for a few reasons; one, because I would land in deep shit if I reached out into the centre of the table to help myself; and two, because I understood that the proper step-by-step dinner process provided me with the confidence I needed to move through this meal, keeping my hands where they needed to be without spilling my milk or anything else.

Unfortunately, my hoped-for smooth flow of our first meal in my grandparents' house was suddenly disrupted by my oma who began the right-to-left foodservice procession but omitted a prayer beforehand. I watched the platter of meat move from my opa to my father and on and on in my direction, and it took everything in my power not to call out to her *you forgot to pray!* Or did she? Maybe they did it after the food was served. Seeking validation, I looked up at my mother, but she didn't seem concerned and was in deep conversation, reminiscing with my oma. So, I did what I had to do and reneged on my vow to never look up at Jesus again. In preparation to pray, I clasped my hands together under the table without anyone knowing. I then took a deep breath and looked above the dining room door, but nothing was there. So, I searched above the doorway leading to the hall where there was no bathroom...still nothing. Where was He? Scanning the room, every archway within my view was free of a crucifix. God was not in this house. Yet everyone acted as if this was normal. We never made the sign of the cross.

I was at the end of the food line. However, even though I was the one to receive the last serving bowl, I was the first to finish every morsel on my plate. For a moment, I was free of the nervous constriction in the pit of my stomach, savouring Oma's delicious meal. Briefly, no one spoke, and I let my guard down, taking advantage of the silence to innocently get my mother's attention and ask her for another piece of roast beef. Within seconds, the room vibrated with adult laughter. I glanced around and saw my opa pointing to the empty meat platter sitting in the middle of the table. My mother looked over at me and quietly told me that we could only have one serving of meat because it was very costly in Holland. I felt the heat rise in my cheeks and sheepishly looked down at my lap as everyone resumed their conversation before the women cleared the table. My opa spoke to me only once that first day when I stood up to take my plate to the kitchen, *Waarom hep je niet je melk gedronken?—Why didn't you drink your milk?* Although I knew the answer, I just stood there staring at him and kept my mouth shut. He made me visibly tremble.

In contrast, I basked in my oma's love, and our conversations flowed as easily as the stories I listened to under my favourite tree. I was carefree and self-assured when I was with her, following her zest for adventure and living in the moment. She was a typical jovial grandmother with the same uncontainable sense of humour portrayed by the heroine in movies. She also allowed her heart to lead when nurturing my sisters and me. If I could have been with her all the time, I would have lived there forever. I loved my oma.

But my opa lived there too. And from the moment I pushed my chair away from the dinner table that first day, the same energy I sometimes encountered in my house back in Canada came tumbling down around me. I noted how amplified his strict demeanour was compared to my father's, which scared me even more. It was familiar—the patriarch controlling the helm and the matriarch balancing the push-pull and varying degrees of contentment and anguish. I can't sugar-coat how much my opa squashed my spirit. He smiled sporadically through that initial dinner, but there was something about him that told me I should not upset him—ever. There were glimpses of normalcy, but I learned very early that I should never cross the line of potentially setting off men like him. He had the same personality as my father, but when I was with my opa, the uncertainty of when the ball might drop was amplified.

So, I followed my instincts, aware of the adage *like father, like son* and kept a discreet distance from him—as much as any adrenally-charged child with a wild imagination could. This was difficult because I had an inner enthusiasm that begged to be released, even though I tried hard to be quiet to avoid being reprimanded. As a result, it was not easy for me to abide by the rule of never walking in front of my opa's new TV. It was a set-in-stone rule, and he was adamant that no one come between him and his shows. Opa had health issues, suffering from blood clots in his legs, so he sat for long periods in front of his distraction from chronic pain. Looking back, I empathize with his exhausting discomfort, but that is as far as my compassion goes. Similar to having trouble excusing my father's unreasonable moods, I found it impossible to rationalize my grandfather's tormenting disposition. I was a free-spirited child who could not imagine any possible reason for his disgruntled way of being. Nor could I always think ahead to determine how to avoid it.

One day, when I heard the clip-clop of horse's hooves prancing down the old cobblestone street outside my grandparent's front window, I spontaneously ran to get a closer view of the horse. Unfortunately, the chair my opa sat in to watch TV was directly inside that view, and as I headed towards it, there was a brief moment when the rule about staying away from the TV flashed before me. But the memory was fleeting, and it was much too late for me to physically retreat, already being in motion between my opa and his TV. Before I knew it, I received a hard blow to my left shin that made me fall to my knees. He was quick, strategically taking his cane and whacking me as I passed by his view of the show he was watching; it was like he had been practicing just in case I lost my senses and did exactly what transpired. I laid in the fetal position, pressing my hands firmly on the welt on my leg to take the sting away. When I looked up, he glared at me and sternly raised his voice, slowly articulating each word, *Ga - nooit - voor - mijn - televisie—Never - go - in - front - of - my - television!* His face was distorted, with his glasses sitting low and askew on his nose from the kickback he received when striking me. I was in shock that anyone would do such a thing. From that day on, the amplified fear this man instilled in me was a guarantee I would never go near him or his TV again. In fact, I never looked at or spoke to him from then on. I hated my grandfather.

I lay in bed that night, shaking from the after-shock of being attacked by him. And then, I was triggered by a disturbing memory from our first house in Canada that I had tucked away and compartmentalized almost as soon as it happened. Although my grandfather physically abused me, my father never did, and my mother often reminded me of that as if compensating for his verbal insults. And she was right, he was definitely skilled at hurting us with his words, but his go-to was not physical force. Other than the one incident I bore witness to back in Canada...

I was walking down the hall with my wee bare feet padding the hardwood floor my mother kept shiny clean and heard my father and one of my sisters talking in the back hall. I was on my way to my bedroom from the bathroom when I noticed an edge in my sister's voice when she said something to my father that I couldn't make out. Her tone was argumentative, and I knew that would not end well. They were on the landing of the stairs that led to the basement from the back door, and just as I peeked around the corner in their direction, I saw my father lift his right arm from behind him and swing it forward with his hand landing squarely on her left cheek. I could not help but gasp, and my father instantly looked

Escaping the Cycle of Authority

over at me at the exact moment my sister began sobbing in pain and shock. His stare startled me because he looked like a wild animal. I wanted to protect my sister, but instinct told me to get the hell of there. So, I ran down the hall to my room, where my stuffed animals and dolls remained lined up on my bed, silently witnessing the horror that had occurred from a distance. I quickly shut the door to protect their innocence from the other side of it. To this day, neither my sister nor I discussed what happened in that hall. It was our first big secret. The kind that is made by never speaking about it.

While still living in Holland, I moved on from my opa's beating by strategically dodging him, other than at mealtimes around the table where I had no choice—*three peas, three carrots, four peas, four carrots...* My methodology was to avoid eye contact with him at all costs. I did what I had to because there were other things to deal with, like attending an all-girls school that I was initially enthusiastic about until my teacher told me I was wrong one day. The all-girl part did not bother me because I had no interest in boys at this point in my life. However, I was overly confident because I could speak Dutch well enough to get by, and I was excited to show off my English in class. But that arrogance did not serve me well when my teacher began challenging my pronunciation during our daily English lessons. She persistently corrected me because my Canadian pronunciation was obviously different from the British one that they used. So, one day, I told her she was wrong, insisting that either was correct, and I was sent to the back of the room and instructed to face the corner for fifteen minutes. I was mortified, embarrassed, and ashamed. However, it wasn't the first time I was called out within the school system, and it wouldn't be the last. The difference was that I genuinely believed I was right, and I would be damned if someone else in my life was going to determine I wasn't. So, at that moment, sitting with my nose to the wall, I decided I wanted to go back home to Canada.

From that day on, when my mother tucked me into the wall bed each night, I cried and begged her to take me back to Canada. Of course, I had no influence over that decision, so I countered my unhappiness by spending as much time with my oma as I could. She was so much fun, and I had never been with anyone who encouraged me to freely explore unleashing my spirit the way she did. She was also a practical joker, inviting me to plan and execute several pranks with her. One involved my father, and her proposal initially terrified me. Oma called me into the bedroom that she and my grandfather shared. I had never been in there, and I took a moment to look around at the bed in which I later found out my father and his three brothers were born. There were heavy wool blankets folded at the foot of the bed, the same kind my mother brought over from Holland when they moved to Canada. Her mother had handed them down to her, and I hated them because they made me itchy. My eyes wandered over to the dark navy, thick velvet curtains that framed the incredibly tall glass panes in the windows; they were covered with Dutch eyelet sheers to welcome the sun while also providing privacy from passersby. For a moment, I went to a long-ago time I didn't know or understand but was somehow familiar with. Then suddenly, my oma interrupted my trance by tapping me on the shoulder. She pointed to the closed bedroom door and put her finger up to her puckered lips in a gesture to be quiet.

At the beginning of the long hallway to the kitchen, right outside that bedroom door was the inner door to the vestibule entrance leading to the outer door of their row house. As if giving me a preview, Oma opened the bedroom door a crack and looked up above and to the right of that inner door on the hall-side of the vestibule. I followed her gaze that landed on a large antique iron bell attached to a cord leading through the foyer all the way to the outside of the exterior wall, where a handle dangled freely. This was the original doorbell from when my father was a small boy growing up in this house. When someone pulled the handle, the rope became taut, drawing on the bell, which clanged clearly and loudly throughout the house—I was fascinated by its old-school aura. She softly shut the door again.

I hid behind my oma and clung onto her apron as I looked up in giddy anticipation. I had no idea what she was up to because each adventure was a surprise. She leaned down and whispered, *Wees stil*—*Be quiet* because, on this particular day, my father expected a potential boss to come to the house to meet him for a job interview. It was a critical meeting because if he got the job, it would be the first time in 14 years he would be allowed to work in the career he was certified for. I already knew this because I heard my parents talking about it earlier, and I knew it was serious. She told me that my dad was in the back room getting his suit on in preparation for the interview. As soon as I realized her little adventure included my father, my enthusiasm diminished, and I began to tremble. I feared my father being the brunt of this joke; my intuition told me that his response would not be favourable at all. But I was also curious, and my trust in my oma began to outweigh my trepidation. At this point, I couldn't retreat from the impending exhilaration she was about to introduce me to.

My oma also had a cane she used from time to time. I never asked why, and it didn't slow her down. I remember thinking she waddled like a duck when she was in a rush. She was a heavy-set woman, and I savoured the many times she pulled me into her folds of fat and ample bosom while whispering how much she loved me. She smelled like a mixture of the peppermints she sucked on throughout the day and some sort of spicy scent, perhaps from the soap she used. She always greeted me with a smile when I came around the corner towards her, and she was never too busy for me. So, I was all in when she told me she had an idea and asked me to come into her bedroom.

Once we took a few deep breaths and calmed down, Oma slowly opened the bedroom door again. She looked to the left down that long hallway where the back rooms were, including my parent's bedroom where my father was dressing for his meeting. I remember thinking that the wool runner on the long hall floor was damaged and worn. I later asked her why it hadn't been replaced, and she gently

Escaping the Cycle of Authority

told me, *Het is niet nodig om oude dingen weg te doen als ze nog werken, schat—There's no need to get rid of old things if they still work, dear.* She was very wise, and her decisions mirrored every profound statement she made.

I was fascinated by the preservation of antiquity in my grandparents' home. As with the old bell, my grandmother was adamant about hanging onto things from long ago. Perhaps they reminded her of when her four young sons lived with her and their father in this house. I was told they were wild, constantly running through the house, laughing as she chased them until they finally flew out the back door behind her simple kitchen; she never caught them. My oma did not indulge in modern conveniences, and until the day she left this earth, she refused to get a stove, fridge, or telephone. I used to think she was pretty stubborn and unreasonable, but now I realize she was just practical and grateful for what she had. She felt no need to have things that complicated her life.

The bathroom where I had my first pee didn't have a shower or tub for many years. And when we lived there, I learned a new way of bathing, having sponge baths at the kitchen sink and strutting behind her to the local bathhouse twice a week. She also avoided the need for a fridge by getting up early every morning and walking to the market with her grocery bag to purchase food for the day. She used a two-burner portable hot plate to cook supper for seven. This was the early 70s, and I had never been in anyone's kitchen that didn't have a fridge or stove, so I asked her why she didn't; she smiled and said simply, *Ik heb ze niet nodig—I don't need them* and then turned around, continuing to peel the potatoes for that evening's supper. I was in awe of her decisiveness; no matter how hard people tried to get her to change her old ways, she refused.

Oma included me in her traditional rituals and, along with her pranks and cuddles, they were what I resonated with the most. It was a simple life, and to this day, I know she is still a part of me, having carried on those old Dutch customs and even some of her idiosyncrasies. She loved having us with her for the short time we lived there, embracing each family meal and conversation we had around the dinner table. I took those memories back with me to Canada and used them as inspiration to connect with my father, even though I failed miserably.

Standing inside that bedroom doorway filled with anticipation of what was coming next, I followed her lead and looked down the vacant hall, wondering what my Oma was up to. Affirming all was clear, she nodded at me and handed me her cane. She told me to use it to hit the bell as hard as I could. I thought about how hard my Opa had hit me with his cane, and I began shaking, knowing how loud that bell would ring if I hit it with the same force. I also knew it would alert my father, who was waiting for the gentleman to come to ring that same bell from the outside of the house. Within moments, I quickly put all the pieces together, understanding how this prank on my father would play out. My jitters were intense, but my oma's excitement was contagious, and I knew there was no turning back—her plan was in place, and it was happening. With every passing second, my adrenaline increased and surged through me, motivating me to hold that cane up high, aim it at the bell, and whack it with all my might. Bam!!

Oma was quick and right on cue because, as soon as I struck the bell, she grabbed my vibrating body by the waist and swiftly swooped me into the bedroom, shutting the door ever so quietly behind me. I'm sure my feet left the ground, and the endorphin rush was as intense as a tsunami. She had composed herself by the time I landed beside her shaking uncontrollably. I looked up at her, and her eyes locked with mine when I almost shrieked out loud, so she pulled me into her dirty apron to muffle any peeps that might slip out. She knew I needed some grounding from the rush of energy surging through my body. Just moments later, I heard the sure and steady step of my father's leather dress shoes padding the old carpet runner. I distracted myself by becoming obsessed with the state of the runner again, thinking my oma really should replace it—*five peas, five carrots, six peas, six carrots...*

But suddenly, I moved on and held my breath, counting his footsteps instead and took note of how fast they were heading towards the front door, his potential boss, or us and our possible demise! I released my breath when I heard the inner vestibule door open—thankfully, he was answering the door and not coming to us. My heart pounded from both the excitement of playing a joke on my dad and the angst of being part of it. I knew the polar outcome; one was the fun of playing an innocent prank on someone, and the other was the worry of possible reprimand. I felt the conflict of each outcome but also the security of the cushion of my grandmother's confident leadership. Because she was the seasoned captain of this adventure's helm, I intuitively knew there was less risk for me as the obedient young sailor within the possible negative consequence. I instantly developed an immense sense of security, sitting at the bottom of the hierarchy I so detested, ironically being guided by a matriarch. I have replayed this intimate moment with my oma hundreds of times in my mind, and at one point, I had the revelation that my father's response would have likely been very different had I endeavoured to play this prank on my own.

We didn't stop after the first wack at the bell. Oma urged me to move through the process three more times, with my father repeatedly walking back to the bedroom and then down the hall towards the door again. I counted his steps every time and imagined him nervously adjusting his tie with every few strides. My oma and I silently laughed so hard that I thought I would burst. Other than the intimacy we shared that day, I also remember an unspoken understanding that she knew there was potential my father would be upset about our innocent prank. However, I had a deep knowing she believed it was worth the trade-off to provide me with the joy I craved while living there. She also implemented a strategic after-plan, choosing not to tell my father what we had done until many days later. Once he finished venting about the kids on the street who played Nicky Nine Doors on him and also celebrating having been offered the job, Oma shared our story with him as if it had been part of any other day.

Escaping the Cycle of Authority

She was patient, and her timing was impeccable because she knew to wait for the right moment to disclose our mischievous act with as little chance as possible he would be upset. My oma was accustomed to managing the men in her life and keeping them content. Because she ranked higher than her son on the familial ladder, she knew that my dad would not challenge her, and that is what she banked on and precisely what happened. She taught me patience, along with how to manipulate this pyramid scheme of authority, and these became life-long skills for a little girl at the bottom of the pecking order. This was the beginning of a very long fight for the same respect those at the top who controlled everything and everyone received.

III

~ Escaping the Cycle of Jealousy ~

Experiencing the dichotomy of my grandparent's intentions for their canes was complex for a young girl to absorb but also extraordinarily enlightening. Oma used hers to fulfill spontaneous adventure and to inspire joy through the unconditional provision of love. In contrast, Opa used his to perform a pre-meditated violation that sent a message of hate. I was told he loved me and that I needed to understand he was a little grumpy because he lived with a lot of pain. It was due to the blood clots in his legs, and his expression of distain towards me was justified by his suffering. And yet, Oma's obvious display of love needed no explanation at all. I wondered what physical pain my father experienced when annoyed with me.

Integrating pain and pleasure within receiving and expressing love became a life-long conflict for me. The confusion of it nearly drove me crazy. However, fortunately, I had some positive forces guiding me towards the clarity of what it could be like when love is fully embraced within that full spectrum. My oma inspired me to take a step toward achieving that. She taught me that ignoring the complexity of love was avoiding the inevitable yearning to understand the good and evil within it. In other words, it would always come back to haunt and tempt me to figure it out, so it was futile to stop trying to find clarity. With just over one decade under my belt, I had no idea what Oma's underlying intention was. Still, she planted a seed that motivated me to discover what I would eventually accept as my truth—understanding what love really means to me and that it didn't always encompass feel-goods. She sowed that seed of acceptance, but it was very slow-growing—50 years in the making.

I will never know if my grandparents were conscious of the lessons they each gave to me. Still, I am grateful for the comparison that became obvious much later, eventually echoing how I wanted love to prevail in my world. I also discovered that just having clarity about what love means to me was not enough; I needed to put it into action to move it from a state of fantasy to reality.

Looking back, I believe my grandmother recognized that my father's limited expression of love was similar to her husband's. She also saw that, along with intellect, humour was the gateway to connect with him. Perhaps my opa was the same at one time. I'm guessing this was the same way she learned how to give and receive love from her husband. Although I never saw the possible lighter side of my grandfather, he and his son presented with other similar complementary and not so complementary personality characteristics. The day of the practical joke, my grandmother tapped into a minuscule glimmer of how my father and I might bond by bringing his lighter side to the forefront. It was another challenge I spent many years attempting to succeed at but to no avail.

I believe the chemistry Oma and I shared was as close to pure unconditional love between a child and her matriarch as one can achieve. It was similar to when I was little and had those precious early morning moments in bed with my mother. They naturally arose with no explanation—these were the kind of moments I spent decades expecting from my dad. If only I had known earlier that humour was the conduit of light to connect with him. Oma wanted me to feel both ends of that spectrum, so her son's light would stand out against the dark. Perhaps she thought she could instill the compassion I needed to overlook darkness and find his light. Sadly, the darkness was far more prevalent, and that's what I ended up focusing on.

A few bright sparks ignited during the seven months we lived overseas because my grandmother became my buffer, allowing my curiosity about how my father expressed love to expand a little. With that cushion, I gained a bit of confidence to push his limits ever so slightly, hoping he would step into his love light, and I might be drawn into it. However, decades passed before we surrendered to a superficial connection whereby our darkness blocked any hint of light from each other. Although my grandmother's shining influence continued to be present in the recesses of my mind, it faded with time, overpowered by the weight of my perception of my father's repetitive control, which was amplified by the additional layer of my mother's.

Control and manipulation became tools I learned to use as protection from truths modelled to ignore. Unaware, the great masters of discipline taught me how to use power to block anything painful. With a great deal of practice, I became highly skilled at emotional detachment through extreme self-discipline. I developed the mindset that I could only move forward if emotional pain was stored safely in a forgotten section of my brain so that I couldn't be hurt by it. I became skilled at living in what I later believed was a fantasy world that many women from my mother's generation lived in and were programmed to adhere to. Unfortunately, this talent became detrimental, leaving no space or hope for me to process my fears, acknowledge my emotions, or be guided by my truth. Being strong became my motivation to enact a fake existence that catered to men and the authority they took advantage of having over women. By the age of 40, my soul was as close to death as possible.

I suffered through the grieving process that comes with self-detachment. It eventually resulted in my ability to sense when someone turns their back on their essence. My mother never admitted her soul's demise to me because her commitment to self-control would not allow her to. However, I witnessed and absorbed her pain long before accepting my self-deceit. Due to my lack of awareness, I did not understand the complexity of what she might have gone through, but the counterfeit joy she exuded was much too obvious to pull the wool over my eyes—something always felt off.

Ironically or not, my mother was in her 40th year when her mother passed away while we were still in Holland. Because my oma passed away, she became emotionally detached from her homeland. I believe the initial draw to return home manifested from the guilt of having left her mother 15 years earlier; that hardwired Catholic remorse wore her down. Once her mother passed, the responsibility for her mother's happiness no longer served her; there was no reason to stay. Even though five of her sisters and an older brother still lived in Holland, her mother's death left a deep void that they could not fill. Because the matriarchal tie was severed, she yearned to go back to Canada, where she had established a level of familiarity she missed. She realized it was now her home, and once the honeymoon of visiting everyone in Holland ended, she needed to go back to normal. The thrill of being there was gone without the added purpose of spending time with her mother. Her other siblings immigrated to Canada back in the fifties around the same time as my parents. As a result, she wanted to reunite with them and the unique bond they had created.

From the day I met my oma on my mother's side, she called me *Janje*, short for Diana. Dutch people put *je* on the end of words to attach an element of sentiment. Given she gave all her children nicknames, I perceived this as one of the ways she expressed her love to me. My mother had a nickname, and now I did too, so I felt special. Everyone called her *Puckje*—it had something to do with being tiny. Oma always invited me to sit on her knee whenever we visited her, and she sang a song to me—I remember the tune, but not the words. Like my other Oma, she smelled of mint and often slipped me an entire roll of King Peppermints when no one was looking. I didn't think anyone else knew, and I liked that it was our secret because secrets seemed to be valued on this side of my family. I don't remember meeting her as a very small child when she and Opa came to visit us in Canada when I was just one but reconnecting with her when we went to Holland was a gift. She was 75, and she died not long after we arrived.

I was blessed with a few magical moments with her while living there. She had the demeanour of a monk, and although her smile was contagious, there was a shadow of past adversity behind it. I only ever saw her when we visited my aunts, uncles, and cousins, so I don't know exactly where she lived. She was never standing up, always sitting on an angle nestled in a comfy chair in the corner with her legs leaning to one side and her ankles crossed. Like my father's mother, she was a larger woman; having lived a tough life; I'm sure being thin was her last priority.

Both of my grandmothers consistently wore dark dresses, black stockings, and short-heeled tie-up dress shoes, which I found fascinating. I often thought about how uncomfortable they must be. One time, while living at my father's parents' house, I walked by something resembling a horse bridle standing upright in the back room. I wondered what the heck it was. My mother explained that both my grandmothers wore leather girdles to support their damaged backs after years of heavy lifting void of modern conveniences. I asked her what kind of work they did that warranted such physical deterioration. She told me life was different when she was a child because everything inside and outside the house had to be done by hand, including laundry without a washing machine or dryer. She asked me to imagine a home filled with fourteen children. Her mother was pregnant off and on for twenty years, giving birth to eleven girls and three boys, and they lived in a small two-story row house with an attic in a small village. That attic was eventually converted into a third-floor bedroom for the three youngest girls, including my mother. I was told that a few secrets were hidden there—some that should have been shared but were kept buried as if they never happened.

One of Oma's youngest children was born two years after my mother. He passed away at four with an undiagnosed condition. My mother was only six when he died, but she remembers her older sisters taking turns caring for him and feeding him with a tiny spoon to accommodate his cleft palette. He never grew past the physical or mental age of a baby. My mother's grandmother died when my oma was just 30 years old and pregnant with this little boy. Some believed that his disease manifested through Oma's burden of grief over the loss of her mother during her pregnancy. Coincidentally, my mother was also 30 when I was born. And when I became pregnant for the first time at the age of 30, she shared this story with me and how anxious she was during her pregnancy with me. She thought history could repeat itself, and her mother might die, but she did not. She told me not worry about her dying because the curse had been broken.

My grandparents survived the adversities that came with having a large family, along with the added burden of living through World War II. My mother told me many stories about growing up, emphasizing the high degree of effort it took for a family of this size to accomplish what had to be done in a day. She reiterated how much love they had for each other and that they all did their part, working together and abiding by rigid schedules set by their mother. A strong allegiance was reinforced along with each newly born child. Many nights, my mother and her sisters and brothers went to bed hungry during the war. No one was allowed to help themselves to food unless given permission because it was rationed according to what was available. One night, one of her sisters was so famished she was found sleepwalking and eating the crusted end of a mouldy loaf of bread meant for the entire family's breakfast the following day. This was a serious situation because they had to walk many miles to stand in a food line for a new loaf. Somehow, with a lot of resilience and perseverance, Oma and Opa managed to feed and clothe their children and keep a roof over their heads in an integral way.

My opa had a secure job delivering mail one house at a time as a postal worker, and my grandmother stayed home to care for their children and run the house. Everything was made from scratch and by hand, including darning socks every day—throwing out socks was never considered. They grew all their vegetables in the

Escaping the Cycle of Jealousy

backyard, and my mother has vivid memories of her father tending to the garden after coming home from delivering the mail in the village where they lived. Each child found a job to contribute financially to the household when they reached the working age of 16, leaving the others at home to help their mother cook, clean, and care for the younger children. My mother worked in a delicatessen for a while and then as a nanny for a well-to-do family. She became close with this family and kept in touch with the couple until they passed away. She connected with their son for many years into his adulthood.

Oma had to run a tight ship from sun-up to sun-down for her household to function with the least amount of chaos possible. There were very stringent rules to follow to maintain any sense of order and morality. For example, most Friday nights, my mother and her sisters went to dances for fun and possibly meet future husbands. Any ounce of makeup was forbidden. But my mother was a bit of a rebel, so once she and her sisters turned the corner from the street where they lived, she stood under the lamp post and applied her lipstick. One evening, while putting on her glossy red lips, her father suddenly appeared. With no discussion, she was told to go home and wash her face. It was likely she was ratted out, or her father was sharper than she thought, given he had 11 daughters to keep track of and protect.

When my mother repeatedly told me how incredibly loved she was, I wondered what this meant and how it was possible given the limited number of hours in each day and what her parents needed to accomplish. How could each child possibly receive the attention they required? Perhaps this was achieved through their learned acceptable level of being nurtured and how it was provided. Maybe they adapted to their interpretation of love, given what they received. With a family that size, did my grandparents have the capacity to provide enough affection to each child? Or, in the end, even with that intention, did they just get through each day with the goal of tucking everyone in at night? I wondered if they took the time to say, *I love you*.

Perhaps over time, the children succumbed to the normalcy of the amount of attention they received due to the overriding necessity of being cared for. Maybe they knew it wasn't worth making a fuss over because pragmatically surviving ranked higher than sorting out emotions. Since my mother was the fifth-last born, I asked how her mother possibly provided the emotional support she needed with nine children preceding her. She always assured me that her mother made the time, and her older sisters took up the slack. I translated that into my mother protecting her mother from any kind of judgment because her sisters likely raised her out of necessity.

I often shared my amazement at how many children my oma had. My mother quickly defended her, telling me that her parents were criticized for their family's size by those living in the village. The gossip included the belief that they had too much sex and my grandfather should leave his wife alone. My mother maintained that whenever her parents had sex, my grandmother happened to get pregnant. They didn't have birth control back then, and even if they did, Catholics did not believe in inhibiting the creation of children—having this many children was considered God's will. Unfortunately, some of the townspeople found their situation shameful, and my mother protected her mother—after all, this was God's will, and His message to my opa was for *Mankind To Be Fruitful and Multiply... in His own image*—His not Hers. Along with being subjected to many years of societal and religious misogyny, this later translated into one of the many pieces of my programming...

Psalm 128:3

*Your wife shall be like a fruitful vine
Within your house,
Your children like olive plants
Around your table.*

I hated that they shamed my grandmother for obeying her spiritual guide and that my mother felt the need to find an acceptable reason for my grandmother's rate of reproduction when this was what her faith summoned her to do. I wondered what Oma's perception of this story would have been, but I'm sure there was never an invitation for her to share it.

She had a laborious life, and my mother reminded me how difficult it was to keep up with the expectations for women at that time. For example, with 11 girls who eventually became women, there was a continual necessity to have cloth sanitary napkins on hand, with someone always moving through their menstrual cycle. Disposable pads were not yet invented, so they had a large barrel in the back shed filled with a mixture of ammonia and water where the daughters deposited their cloth strips as the first step of cleaning them for reuse. Each girl was assigned a job within this process; once the cloths had soaked for a specific period of time, they needed to be rinsed, wrung out, and hung to dry. This was a never-ending task and only one of many to be completed.

Once their father finished in the garden at the end of each day, the whole family sat around a large table and had dinner together. My mother told me how much she respected her father, sharing what a hard-working and kind man he was. I cannot count how many times she expressed how much he loved and doted on my grandmother. She also told me that when one of the children spoke out of turn at the dinner table, as the head of the household, he reached over and poked their hand with his fork. My mother recognized this as a necessity, *Can you imagine 16 people all talking at the same time?!* But, again, rules were an unavoidable requirement, and my mother believed my Opa had no choice; no matter what he did or said, he was respected, whether she agreed or not.

In 1939, the outbreak of World War II escalated destructive hierarchy to an unfathomable level with the looming fear of Hitler at the apex of governing Germany. It began with the invasion of 11 countries, beginning with Poland and included Holland, then known as The Netherlands or Nederland in Dutch. The adversities of everyday living were nothing compared to the hardships of extreme immorality during wartime. My mother's siblings depended on each other for emotional and physical survival. There were so many right and wrong things they had to understand and abide by to protect themselves and their family. Being responsible was first and foremost, and they needed to be clear about what that entailed. My mother remembers often being summoned to instantly hide under the dining room table that doubled as the place where her family gathered every day to thank God for his gifts, including the little bit of food they had to share. At the age of nine, she found herself silently crouching down, trembling, huddled up against her sisters while listening to the shooting planes overhead—no one asked any questions; they did what they were told. Their family dinner table became protection while Germany invaded their country. Holland was occupied for five years, with over a quarter of a million Dutch people dying. When I heard this for the first time, I thought being pricked by a fork didn't seem so bad.

There was a rumour that my opa used his position with the post office to hide a Jewish neighbour from the Nazis. One day, he took his mail cart after completing most of his deliveries, and he stopped at a house and hid a man in it. He then took him somewhere, never to be seen again. My mother remembers the Nazi soldiers going door-to-door, asking if anyone had seen their neighbour. When they came to their house, her father told the children not to speak, and he addressed the soldiers' questions one-by-one with short yes or no answers, protecting the whereabouts of the hidden man. My opa sacrificed himself for his family, country, and anyone in need, and I believe that is something to be respected for. Unfortunately, no one was told if this man was ever found or if he managed to remain safe from his possible downfall.

When my mother recounted this story to me, she was sure to mention that her father had no choice but to lie to protect this innocent soul. I discovered that God bends the rules, permitting people to lie and keep secrets when it comes to saving someone's life—there is no guilt attached to deceptive acts of kindness. I concluded that, even if someone does a nasty thing, their good deeds balance out the bad, and they are still considered worthy of God's love. I loved this side of God. I also observed that this was especially true if those keeping the secrets were men. I hated this side of God.

This deviation in the religious theory of worthiness was a grey area for me because I was raised in a very black or white mindset—right or wrong, superior or inferior. The fact that men seemed to benefit the most from it annoyed the hell out of me. As a result, equality became the main topic of any argument I engaged in, and I argued it well. It also became a frustrating value to live by in the world of amplified hierarchy I was raised in, with men landing on the right and superior end of the system and women defaulting on the wrong and inferior end. Obtaining clarity usually decreased the ambiguity but seldom changed the prevalent patriarchal environment, which remained inconsistent with my obsession with equality.

In 1945, the Canadian army liberated Holland from German occupation. My mother and her sisters and brothers once again listened for planes, but when they heard them coming this time, they were summoned to come out from under the table and encouraged to run out onto the street. Looking up to the sun with their arms reaching for the sky, they caught food and medical supplies dropped from Canadian planes. Their freedom was unprecedented, even though they all became ill from eating so much because their stomachs needed time to adjust to the abundance of food. This was the sign of the end of the Second World War, and Princess Juliana of Holland gifted Canada with 100,000 tulip bulbs as a gesture of gratitude. The tulip has become a symbol representing the friendship between these two countries. Since then, any Canadian who visits Holland has been considered a welcome visitor by the Dutch.

Through the war and after, my oma went to church at six o'clock every morning before anyone else got up. My mother told me it was her time to reflect with God before beginning a long day. At the end of the week, she and my opa took their children to church for Sunday mass. They were devout, God-loving, God-fearing Catholics who taught their children to be the same. When I was young, I believed that trusting and following God's word magically translated into love and peace for all. However, this confused me because I saw hate being added to the mix. Most of the time, being in the company of my mother's sisters provided a tranquil connection—*gezeligheid*. However, I discovered that God has no control over the dissonance created when jealousy rears its ugly head. Eighty percent of the time, my aunts followed God's guidance, but harmony took a back seat when the green-eyed monster of envy knocked on the door.

Just as my mother was deeply devoted to her matriarch, the loyalty to the rest of her family was well-established from birth on—sibling devotion that many wish they could achieve. However, as they grew into adulthood, it was often countered by deep-seated resentment that often surfaced as damaging hostility. I craved being around the unique camaraderie of the familial cord that profoundly tied them together, and yet, I was repulsed by the large knots of jealousy that blocked that tight line of love. When any one sister became triggered by temptation, I envisioned God shaking His head in condemnation. I cringed when I envisioned Him sitting on his throne, looking down upon their antics and prayed that He didn't think I was part of this sinister side of them. Witnessing them tearing each other's souls apart moved me to heart-breaking tears as I reflected on what could have brought them to this state of good versus evil. What could override the powerful parental love my mother said they grew up with and the leadership of their almighty God? My aunts' see-saw behaviour made me skeptical of the words of the Roman poet Virgil, *Love conquers all*.

Escaping the Cycle of Jealousy

As adults, whether in Holland or Canada, my mother's brothers and sisters all appeared to get along when gathering at birthday parties and reunions, playing cards, or spending the day at the beach. However, I heard some horrible accusations woven in between that familial allegiance. Some of the sisters talked behind each other's backs and had long-term feuds with one another. I listened to their endless bickering for so many years that it became one of my inherited characteristics. Yet, they managed to carry on as if nothing ever happened, boomeranging back and forth from love to hate.

Outwardly apologizing was done sparingly, disingenuously, and only if they were caught in the discomfort of a lie and the inevitability of having to admit to their indiscretion. Saying *sorry* was a last resort to the admittance of guilt. They were brought up to repent their sins in the confidential housing of the confessional, but their egos dissuaded them from admitting them to their adversary if at all possible.

The families of the five sisters and one brother living in Canada and the United States often vacationed together at each other's homes. When I was very young, I often opened my bedroom door a crack after going to bed and watched my aunts and uncles singing old Dutch songs together. I was drawn to that magical *gezelligheid* as it danced around the room along with the music, and I longed to be a part of it. They created a welcoming place to embrace their culture gathered within the haven of four walls; it reminded me of laying under my willow tree.

They also drank a lot of alcohol, and their conversations included things they would not normally speak of. So, when sober in the days and weeks to follow, I witnessed them pair off, using bits of information previously shared in confidence as ammunition to stab each other in the back. This provided them with a level of self-righteousness that made them somehow better than the others. They seemed to naturally divide into two camps, which reminded me of the kids on the playground at school. The outgoing, more confident sisters were on one side, and the quiet, less confident ones were on the other. But no matter what side they landed on, they all worked equally hard to build their team and strengthen their defence. However, no matter the scenario, every team and player had a breaking point, and when reached, it was not pretty; the superior always beat out the inferior.

Before my oma died, she told her children never to stay angry with each other and to always keep the peace. Her youngest son remained faithful to this commandment by guiding his sisters towards a truce when necessary. He is the third son and youngest child born into this family. He was pretty easy-going until the poor behaviour of one or two of his sisters got way out of hand, and an intervention was required to maintain his mother's request for familial peace.

My mother and her younger brother's wife engaged in a lifetime of back and forth bickering and amends. My aunt met my uncle when he came to Canada to live as a young man. She is a fiery French woman who does not like anyone telling her what to do. Neither do I. I don't think anyone does, including my mother, but that does not stop her. And so, the games began when my aunt wanted my mother to respect her decisions, and my mother often told her she was wrong.

I love my aunt. She is younger than the other aunts, and she always took the time to chat with me. I thought she and my uncle were so hip and cool the way they danced the jive as if they were in a competition; at family weddings, they were front and centre, with everyone clapping and watching in awe. They were magical on the dance floor together, and they remained madly in love.

However, back then, things got complicated when my mother began interfering in their marriage. As if out of a soap opera, she appeared to be jealous of his relationship with his wife. I did not witness the beginning stages of my mother and my aunt's dysfunction, but the first time I experienced one of their fallouts was when our family visited my aunt and uncle for dinner in their new house in a near-by small town. I was a little kid, and at some point, during our visit, my mother flipped a switch into her being right mode and took it upon herself to tell my aunt when she should get her son into his pyjamas. My mother didn't bank on meeting her match when her sister-in-law told my mother not to tell her what to do with her child—in so many words. My mother underestimated my aunt's confidence, and I instantly sensed the intensity as their voices elevated. I looked around the room to see if any other players would join in; my father sat on the sofa with his trademark smirk; he definitely enjoyed this shit. My uncle sat upright to get ready to defend his wife, knowing this was just the beginning of an intense battle. My sisters and I intuitively took several steps back while my aunt and uncle's son continued playing with his toys. It did not end well.

This kind of thing happened all the time; even visitors from Holland found themselves in the mix of my mother's dramatic scenes. Her eldest brother and his wife came over from Holland one year, and my parents were invited over for a game of cards during their stay with this same aunt and uncle. When the evening ended, my mother suggested that the visiting relatives come home with them one day early as they were to begin their stay at our house the next night anyway—why take another trip back to pick them up the next day? My mother was told that they had plans organized for the next day, so leaving early wasn't possible, and they would arrive as planned. My mother went ballistic!! While sitting at the card table, she could not contain herself, seeing her two brothers and their wives getting along. She screamed in response to my aunt, telling her she was unreasonable. My mother had made her mind up; she wanted her visiting brother and wife to come that night, and that was that. When her adversary continued to refuse, my mother grabbed her coat and stormed out the front door only to trip and fall into their big mud puddle of a lawn, which did not have sod yet. When I heard this story years later, I could not help but laugh but also empathized with my mother and wondered if she would ever release herself from this insane cage. I believe she came close many times.

These two women spent decades feuding, with my uncle bringing them back to a somewhat amicable place each time. As exhausting as I'm sure it was, he finally managed to get them to a neutral state of co-existence whereby they agreed not to argue. He succeeded at honouring his mother's wishes by being the peace-keeper in the family; he is an integral man. And he was able to manage this reconciliation by moving him and his wife miles and hours away from my mother. He discovered that distance provided the needed space for their relationship to survive past trauma.

His wife was not my mother's only nemesis. She had an older sister, and she and her husband lived with their four children in the other side of the duplex my parents lived in—the one that was home to my willow tree. She was my Godmother, and every year, she gave me a birthday card with ten dollars in it. When this aunt drank too much Martini and Rossi, she told me how much she loved me and that I was her favourite. Then, when I turned 16, she told me I was too old for cards and not to expect one anymore. Some 50 years later, she went into a nursing home when her husband died. She missed him terribly, so I visited her a few times to give her manicures. I wanted her to know I cared about her, even though her message to a young girl was that being loved and someone's favourite wasn't worth the cost of a card.

No matter how much they wanted, my mother and this sister simply could not keep their mother's promise of serenity. They had a tumultuous relationship, and there were many times when I came home from school to find my mother and aunt arguing, screaming at the top of their lungs. At times, they were exceptionally verbally abusive towards one another. During one incident, I saw them standing in the back hall at the top of the stairs, pointing their fingers at each other and yelling about my sister's bike. It usually stood leaning up against the side of the house, and apparently, my cousin used the bike that day without asking for permission. When my mother didn't see it there, she thought it had been stolen. My aunt was furious because my mother reprimanded him when he returned it. My aunt refused to see her son's accountability in the incident, claiming he innocently borrowed the bike. Likewise, my mother refused to release him of any blame and demanded he apologize—neither would let it go. The episode ended with my aunt kicking our cat's food dish down the basement stairs with kibble flying down after it like remnants from a volcanic eruption. She then walked away, slamming the screen door behind her. My mother heaved a huge sigh of anger, stomped up the four steps from the landing, and looked up to see me watching. Stopping dead in her tracks while I froze in the same spot I was when my father slapped my sister across the face, she stared at me, and I saw the same piercing glare my father gave me the day I caught him. Once again, I ran terrified to my bedroom. Sitting on my bed, catching my breath, I told myself to avoid the back hall whenever possible—it seemed to be where violence flourished. I wondered where God was when these things happened.

This same aunt spent the last few years of her life in a nursing home a few blocks from my parents' apartment. She enjoyed the company of another resident at the home at dinner, playing cards, and riding around the neighbourhood together on their scooters. One year, our family celebrated my mother's birthday at my parents' apartment. My aunt and her friend rode to my parents' building to wish her a happy birthday. They buzzed from the lobby, wanting to come up for a visit, but when my mother heard they had their scooters, she told them they could not come up. I stood there in disbelief and asked my mother why she would turn them away like that. She told me there was no room for the scooters, but I told her we could move things around to make room, and she dismissed me and walked away. My aunt looked happy with her new companion, which triggered my mother's uncontrolled jealousy.

My aunt could be equally hostile, finding fault in my mother. Who knows who started the ping pong pattern that began so many years ago? It seemed that each time either of them witnessed the other experiencing happiness, they immediately reacted, sabotaging it by creating drama. I saw my mother going into panic mode when she noticed her sisters sharing a special moment, a knee-jerk reaction created by feeling left out. All I know is they fought off and on until my aunt was weeks away from dying. My mother suddenly decided her sister was her best friend, and she walked to the nursing home several times a week to sit by her bedside. I'm sure my oma's words were ringing in my mother's ears, telling her to keep the peace, and the guilt she experienced would not allow her to be on the outs with her sister during her dying days. My Godmother passed away at the age of 86, and my mother told everyone how often she visited her sister and how close they were.

My mother had two younger sisters, and although she craved the camaraderie of multiple sisters bonding, she enjoyed having one of them to herself more—to have a unique singular connection. I believe this developed from having a tight bond with them since they were little girls, but the two sisters were not as connected to my mother as they were to each other; they were best friends, and they still are. They are two years apart with one still residing in the United States. She is my deep-thinking aunt, who always took the time to talk things out. We had many telephone conversations over the years, and her advice always left me a bit wiser. She divorced the father of their three children and married the love of her life years later. After spending time with her family at their home, I always considered their son one of my very dear friends. They had a pet pig and dirt bikes, and they lived beside a cemetery that we were forbidden to explore. But we did anyway.

The other sister has always lived in Holland. She outlived my uncle, who she was madly in love with. I know her to be kind, fun-loving, and filled with enthusiasm; she's always up for an adventure and a good meal around the table. Both of these sisters are peacemakers, eager for everyone to get along. They also value loyalty to their family but not without advocating for themselves and others by using diplomacy and rules for a fair outcome. They are my kind of people.

Escaping the Cycle of Jealousy

Unfortunately, my mother defaulted to arguing and using rules to win to the point that both of my aunts would throw up their arms in frustration.

During one of their visits to my parents' place, they wanted to thank them by making a traditional Dutch dish they all loved called *poffertjes*—mini pancakes sprinkled with icing sugar. My one aunt bought the ingredients and even brought the special pan and a particular spatula she swore made the best *poffertjes*; she liked it so much that she bought one for her bestie years before when she was visiting her in the States. After they all enjoyed their *poffertjes'* meal, they decided to go shopping, and my mother said she wanted to buy the same spatula they had. One might think it was because it worked so well scooping the *poffertjes* out from the small indentations in the pan. But by the end of the shopping expedition, it was evident that my mother simply wanted the special spatula—they shared a commonality that my mother did not.

So, wanting to keep my mother happy by being part of this spatula club to make *poffertjes* with as much ease as her sisters did, they went downtown to a kitchen specialty shop to find one for her. After scanning the racks, one aunt told my mother that the store didn't have that spatula. Things suddenly turned for the worst because my mother wanted that spatula no matter what. So much that she was determined to make it happen, so she turned around and took the first spatula she saw off the rack and triumphantly announced that she had found one. That same aunt looked over and told her it was not the right spatula. My mother responded that it was. My other aunt remained quiet, choosing just to listen, knowing what was likely coming next. Back to my other aunt, who explained that the spatula in her hand was not the same; it was a different style, width, length, and so on. But my mother was adamant that it was the same spatula, and a major fight ensued with a disastrous rift to follow.

I was not there, but hearing the story and knowing my mother, I would bet my life that this was exactly how it happened. Not many in this family readily concede because the battle must be fought for the purpose of winning, thereby declaring the other the loser. Both ends of the spectrum must be accounted for at all costs, and they must get to this end no matter what. The name-calling and verbal abuse I grew up around was so extensive that I thought it was normal for the longest time. There were days when it felt like a competition to determine who could be the most consciously cruel and had the fortitudinous endurance to not emotionally break down. In the end, the entire clan's hard-headedness became a major problem, with all having the strength and stamina of leopards. Each used frightening elements of control and manipulation. My mother often pursed her lips when getting into this state of being. When I saw that look on her face, I knew we were in for a good one. Sometimes, she scared me. The irony is that, at one point in my life, my daughter told me I sometimes scared her. And I understand because, even now, I feel my lips start to purse like my mother's when I get upset about something. I refuse to look in the mirror when it happens because I don't want to be reminded that I have that part of her in me.

Around The Table

My life was not only riddled with my mother's family's drama. I also have fond memories of visiting many of my aunts and uncles, especially those who lived in Canada. My mother's older sister by a year and her husband invited me to their farm almost every summer. This aunt was one of the sweetest, most loving people. She never rocked the boat, being more like her younger brother. With six children of her own, she was skilled at putting on a meal for a large crowd. My favourite times on the farm included celebrating Thanksgiving with her family. I have never seen turkeys as big as those she prepared, and they were always cooked to perfection. The men always got the legs, and everyone else was handed the platter of sliced white and dark meat as it went around the table—I love the legs. My aunt had a hard life as a farmer's wife but never complained, always eager to meet the needs of her husband and children. They were a dedicated Catholic family and committed to a significant role in the church choir, playing instruments and singing every Sunday at mass; they were very talented. After my uncle died, my aunt freed herself from the burden of farm life, and she spent time with friends, going out for lunch and playing slots at the casino. Sadly, she died young at the age of 76, the youngest of all her sisters. She had a massive stroke while playing a slot machine, and her children said she died doing something she loved.

I cherished going to the farm, and it was positive for the most part, with a few uncomfortable moments woven in. I was an urban gal, so it was a big deal for me to get up at five in the morning to help milk the cows. My uncle wasn't afraid to show me anything, and in fact, I think he enjoyed my horror when he killed a chicken right in front of me. We were all standing around feeding the chickens, and he suddenly asked me if I knew how he accomplished its fate of being dinner on his table. I told him I did not, and I wanted to walk away. But I didn't. He immediately grabbed a chicken's neck just under its beak and began twirling it around. Its body flew around in circles in the air, with the neck simultaneously twisting tighter and tighter. With very few rotations, it resembled a rope used to secure a boat to a dock. I froze in my tracks, not believing what was happening, and my uncle suddenly yanked up on the chicken's head. I heard a loud snap, and he immediately let it drop to the ground. To make it worse, the poor animal ran around in circles, its head repeatedly bouncing off the ground until it finally fell over—dead. I stared at that chicken, barely hearing my six cousins' melody of laughter in the background, sounding like an uplifting hymn sung at a funeral. But I knew they were laughing at the shock on my face created by the cruelty I witnessed. I instinctively made a sign of the cross.

As much as this left me traumatized, I soon realized this was their reality. It didn't make my uncle a horrible person but rather someone surviving a gruelling life on a farm. I understood that animals were food for their table and provided an income, similar to the corn and potato crops. However, that night as I lay awake with visions of the chicken's head bopping around above me, I wondered why my uncle thought it was a good idea to show me that. Not only did I find the way he killed the chicken inhumane, but I didn't understand what possessed him to upset me. Many years later, I recognized this as part of the long subliminal male power message that continued to feed my growing emotional trauma.

My cousins were integral players in their farm's sustainability. I was welcomed as part of their family and their farm when I was there. My cousins were very different from the kids I went to school with because they treated me as I believed true friends do. One of them was the closest to my age and my cousin-bestie. We all jumped off the ladders into the barn hayloft, played see-saw on the trailer, and she and her older sister spent many hours with me, swinging back and forth on the swing set, singing *On The Good Ship Lollipop*. My aunt and uncle had one boy, and he was a prankster. I did my best to stay clear of him after seeing one of his sisters get saturated by a manure bomb he set above the mudroom door. It was triggered while rushing out the door to begin her chores. Everyone laughed, but again, I did not find this funny—it didn't feel the same as when my oma and I played the joke on my father. Even though I loved my cousin, my distrust in male counterparts continued to grow and embed further into my psyche.

In this same mudroom, a long row of various-sized rubber boots sat waiting to be worn by anyone on the day-to-day chore schedule. My aunt asked if I wanted to help, and I was excited to be part of their daily ritual of slipping my feet into someone else's boots. I may have been a hindrance as a farmhand, but no one complained about my ignorance while fulfilling each task; they just taught me as they had each other, and when I made a mistake, we all carried on. As a result, I developed a deep kinship with my cousins on the farm. And when my visit ended there, I moved on to another aunt and uncle's place one city over.

They had five children, and their second-last and I became fast friends. Every night, we talked and giggled after saying goodnight to her parents, not stopping until we heard them turn off the Johnny Carson Show and walk up the stairs to go to bed. She had two older sisters who had bedrooms in the basement. One played the guitar and often listened and sang along to the Carpenters on her record player in the rec room outside the bedrooms. She was also a baseball player, and I thought she was incredible, having both musical and athletic abilities. I was not athletic— well, I was told I wasn't by one of my gym teachers, so I never bothered putting much effort into it.

I remember her being so kind and patient, letting us go downstairs to join her to listen to music. She was around the same age as my oldest sister, who wasn't as inviting, asking my mother for a lock on her bedroom door so I wouldn't bug her. At some point, this cousin became a nun and did mission work in Africa, and I always thought that was so intriguing. Her relationship with God ended up being much more positive than mine, and I wished I saw Him the same way she did, but I didn't know how to make that happen.

Their mother worked hard and ran her household the way her sisters did by utilizing my oma's many teachings. When I was a young girl, this aunt provided me

Around The Table

with a sense of ease. Then, as I got older, I had meaningful conversations with her, and I recognized that she had a sort of deep knowing; she always looked directly into my eyes, listened intently, and nodded with reassurance. I could count on her being calm, confident, decisive, and wise, never saying more than was necessary. I was never afraid that she would react, but instead, naturally came up with solutions to my problems after chatting with her. And yet, she never outwardly gave me advice. I remember her as my patient aunt, who was filled with wisdom.

I'm sure my mother confided in her for the same reason, knowing she would not be judged. My mother never started an argument with her older sister but instead respected her as much as I did. Several times, she told me, *She tells it like it is. She never talks behind my back, and I know I can trust her.* I found this interesting because my mother often spoke behind most of her sisters' backs to gain camaraderie with the sister she was sharing with. So, as much as it was a compliment for my aunt, I thought my mother was hypocritical. She disclosed many secrets to those she shared confidences with, but this did not include her older sister because this aunt would not put up with my mother's betrayal of others. My mother often sought her advice, but she never tried to manipulate my aunt because she was too sharp for that nonsense. I often thought she was kind and calm like my oma and reasonable and pragmatic like my opa. In her presence, she did not allow gossip or the team-against-team model that some of the other sisters engaged in, some to a higher degree than others. But definitely not with her.

She passed away at the age of 96 after being lovingly cared for by her daughters. I reflected on how devoted they were to their mother, and my soul tells me that my aunt earned the matriarchal respect conducive to this level of dedication. My decades-long hierarchal trauma created a repeated pattern of being sucked into hopeful confidence, only to be followed by damaging doubt—layers upon layers of gaslighting that completely wore me down. The frustration began within the glimmers of confident attempts I made while sharing how I felt, only to receive the horror they exhibited in response to my vulnerability. My father continued to say, *Just forget about it*, and my mother acted shocked that I felt the way I did. I felt invalidated and believed I was some sort of weirdo. She would start to cry, saying I ruined everything, and then doubt enveloped me. I was always left wondering how my emotions could be wrong when the tables suddenly turned during my well-rehearsed conversation. My courageous soul ended up seeming to be responsible for their anguish, and I landed in the deep discomfort of shame. Was it possible that I was guilty because I made them feel uncomfortable? Maybe, my father was right, and I was too sensitive. Maybe, I fabricated the emotions that coursed through my veins.

I often thought about the possibility of taking care of my parents later in their hour of need, but this bubbled up traumatic incompetence and unworthiness, prohibiting me from placing myself at that level of vulnerability. My suit of armour was immediately triggered by the fear of being beaten down, which in turn inhibited

Escaping the Cycle of Jealousy

the compassion required to care for them with the unconditional love they would need. Now and then, I took the chance and offered small tokens of support, only to receive the message that it was not enough or the right way. My therapist gave me permission to stop torturing myself.

A humble reverence transpires when I consistently trust another person, and they trust me. Sadly, my mother and I have only ever achieved a sliver of that genuine confidence, and my father and I never came close. So, when I receive the threat of shame, I immediately remind myself that my misperception of their trust is almost always followed by betrayal. It keeps me on my toes and provides the opportunity for me to step back and protect my soul from jumping into the insanity of guilt. I began feeling this red flag very early on in my life, but it took a long time before I knew how to interpret and use its warning to shift the process from harming me to protecting me.

I didn't spend a lot of time with or get to know some of my aunts, but shared stories by others provided both positive and negative lights on them—I will never know which are true or false. I met one of my older aunts and uncle when I was very young and another time in my twenties. I don't remember much about their children, but one son and I connected as adults. She divorced her husband after he cheated on her for years. I called her a couple of times during the last few years of her life because she was quite ill, and I wanted her to know I was thinking of her. She passed away at the age of 95.

I met four of my older aunts for the first time when I lived in Holland. One was six years older than my mother, and she was energetic and always smiling. She was a beautiful person from the inside out and was unlike most of the others because she was consistently kind. I think this is why mother treated her differently from the others, never speaking an ill word about her. The third and fourth eldest seemed very reserved and looked like my oma. They were a mix of her welcoming demeanor and stoic stature as they sat poised with their legs crossed in front of them in their chairs.

The eldest lived in Holland her whole life. She came to Canada a few times, and I enjoyed some happy moments with her when we lived in Holland. She was spontaneous and always full of energy. My favourite memory with her is when she and her daughter took me for a walk with my mother on the famous Scheveningen beach. My mother was so carefree, walking along the shoreline that day; she respected this sister, and I don't recall them ever fighting. That beach walk will be forever etched in my mind as a time when my mother showed up as the genuine person I know she truly is.

Like most of my aunts, she was a hard-working woman and very independent. She divorced her husband who cheated on her after having three of his children. She was emotionally and physically strong, running her grocery store and taking care of her children on her own. Everyone loved her, but she also had that superior side to her that no one wanted to cross. She passed away at the age of 92, and I heard that she did not speak to one or more of her sisters for many years before. That made me sad.

Verbal ammunition was a powerful asset when it came to the love-hate dynamics the majority of these sisters engaged in, and I often tried to figure out how they evolved to this state. I eventually concluded that jealousy was the common thread and the catalyst for most of their altercations. I do not know why it was prevalent for some and not others. These intricate familial relationships filled with good, evil, and everything in between had both healing and traumatic imprints on me. Each aunt influenced me in some of the most positive ways. However, simultaneously, their interactions created adverse conclusions about what I believed love was. I cared deeply for my aunts, but my perception was also slanted in paradoxical ways by my mother's stories, the arguments I witnessed, and the hostile feuds they moved through, with some never being resolved.

When I think about them now, I consciously focus on their positive attributes rather than the uncomplimentary characteristics they sometimes showed up with. However, I found it difficult to erase the distressing memories ingrained in my mind through the lens of a small child who saw and heard many nasty things. They blocked me from tapping into compassion for the people I loved because they seemed to make it their mission to inflict misery on those who loved them. For a long time, I could not get past how a family brought up with the guidance of the love of God and their parents could land in such a catastrophic state. Why did they inflict such pain on each other? Was it just so they could prove they were right or prove the other wrong? How did their jealousy for each other manifest in a lifetime of animosity for some?

Asking these torturous questions was necessary because I inherited the legacy of my family's trauma. I needed to be clear about why they became who they did before choosing to step in or out of their shoes. For me, ambiguity becomes a punishment of torment alongside residual guilt that washes over me as I struggle to empathize with the people I love so much—my family. Why do they treat each other with the level of disdain they do? Can I accept them no matter how they show up? That's what God preaches—forgive others no matter what. And is that what my father was trying to teach me when he repeatedly told me to *Just forget about it?* Because the message I received was that the anarchy he created through his ambivalence avoided addressing my emotional distress. Everyone above me in my familial army taught me that the ability to control my and others' emotions is powerful ammunition when surviving a war between the superior and inferior Gods, especially when the master manipulators of truth are my commanders-in-chief.

IV

⋄⋰⋄ Escaping the Cycle of Shame ⋄⋱⋄

When my mother decided it was time to pack up and go home, it didn't take long to come to fruition. After living in Holland for a mere seven months, our family was boarding a plane on a return flight. I was sad to say goodbye to all my cousins, aunts, uncles, and one close friend I made at the all-girls school. My mother carried the added shame of changing her mind and believing she needed to use a combination of tears and drama to persuade my father to go back home. It worked because her presentation required either an empathetic response or a dispassionate shut-down. He did the latter and agreed to leave his new career and pack up to fly back to Canada. I chose to take advantage of my mother's misery because I was no longer thrilled about living in Holland. Although I had struggled to fit in with my peers back in Canada, I managed to make a few friends before we moved and looked forward to reconnecting with them. My paternal oma introduced me to flashes of comfort. Still, I was willing to sacrifice them and looked forward to being freed from anticipating my grandfather's anger around every corner of their house.

I begged my mother every night to take me back home long before she decided we were going. For months after we arrived in Canada, there was a part of me wanting to believe I somehow influenced her decision; that she might have done something like that because she loved me so much. Tucking me in night after night, she asked me why I was so upset and wanted to leave. I never told her that my grandfather terrified me because I didn't want to disappoint her or disrespect my father or grandmother; I couldn't share how the man of the house kept me awake at night because I worried about what he might do to me the next day. I knew she would excuse his behaviour, *He's not well. He's old. He doesn't understand English.* It was the same way she justified my father's sporadic irritability back home and part of her peace-keeping process, justifying the patriarch's harmful conduct, *He's tired. He worked the night shift. He doesn't mean it.* She never acknowledged the impact I'm sure she saw it had on me. Instead, she constantly overrode uncomfortable truths to justify the emotional anguish I went through. Her rationale supported her loyalty for him and always included a final statement, *He's your father.* It was a non-negotiable message, indicating no further discussion.

Although everything she said was true, she used those truths to disguise her husband's intolerance as something justifiable, *He works hard to put food on the table. He's a good man. He loves you.* My mother presented each excuse as if they were a good reason to treat me disrespectfully. I could not articulate the doubt that sat in the pit of my stomach. To my emotional detriment, it emphasized my father's superiority and my mother's inferiority, which I interpreted as more concerning than comforting. I never disputed what she said because she was groomed to honour her husband, and I was groomed to honour her. And that entailed avoiding disrupting the hierarchy way of thinking.

So, the day my mother announced we were returning to Canada, I went along with her and didn't ask any questions. I knew how to play the good girl game by now: be quiet, act like everything is fine, and *just forget about it*. I wasn't told why we were going home, and I didn't care. I simply wanted to go. I thought about how my sisters would miss their friends in Holland, and I remember briefly thinking I was selfish. But that didn't last long as I easily pushed that aside. And just as I was initially excited to move to Holland, I was over-the-moon relieved to leave. The young girl who sat on a plane seven months before in eager anticipation of a fresh start in Europe now sat quietly in her seat, flying home, hoping everything would be the same as when she left. Albeit far from perfect, I knew everything would be alright if I kept my mouth shut, didn't ask any questions, and did what I was told. That was the unwritten rule I followed. Unfortunately, my manifestation of a happy-ever-after friends' reunion was as short-lived as the eight-hour flight home.

We didn't have a house to move into upon our arrival, so my parents stayed with their friends until we got one. They arranged for my sisters and me to stay with our girlfriend's families until everything was organized. I began grade seven that September at the Catholic school near my friend's house where I stayed. It was the same school I left before our Holland adventure, and the first day presented a déjà vu of my grade one experience. Although I was not bullied, I was excluded by the few close friends I thought I had before leaving less than a year ago. Those girls did not welcome me back as I expected they would because they had moved on, creating new alliances. This reinforced my perception that loyalty is unsustainable over time without in-person connection. My saving grace was the family, who agreed I could stay with them and welcomed me into their home. My friend introduced me to some of her friends, and I became a part of their group by default.

Another blessed soul welcomed me with open arms and has since passed on. I regret not having kept in touch with her through the years. My memory of her is that she exuded an inviting warmth from within her, and she had a smile that melted even the most disgruntled individual. I remember a local shopping trip with her and a spontaneous photoshoot in one of those booths at the mall—we laughed until we cried. I will never forget her with the fondness of a true friend. These two girls provided the confidence I needed to get through that school year, and I am indebted to their kindness.

The family who I temporarily stayed with was what my mother would describe as real Canadian. They ate a lot of healthy food, but they also introduced me to white Wonder Bread with peanut butter and jam, French fries with ketchup, hot dogs on buns, and chocolate cake with Canadian icing that my mother said had far too much sugar. Other than European cake with buttercream icing, our family did not eat these things. In reflection, having long since moved through parenting my children, I respect my mother's adamancy for providing hers with what was considered healthy food in the early 70s. It wasn't until I was in my teens that my mother started buying a treat meal like Hamburger Helper and Kraft Dinner for supper on Wednesdays. I'm pretty sure it was a function of self-survival because life got busier, and she had more to manage. We did eat some typical Canadian meals like meatloaf, but traditional Dutch meals graced our table for the most part. Still, when I was at my friend's house, I ate food my mother would never have served us, which provided an adrenaline rush of both freedom and rebellion.

Dutch people of that generation ate a simple meal of meat, vegetables, and potatoes with gravy. Holland is a centuries-old farming country, and this was a hearty meal that the farmers' wives made from the fruits of their husbands' labour. Like my uncle, they didn't have the modern machinery farmers have today, so manual work began very early in the morning and ended late in the evening. They replenished their energy with the simple, rustic food their wives cooked for them from the crops they sowed and the livestock they raised. Breakfast usually began with homemade, dark rye bread topped with butter and gouda cheese. This was followed by a sandwich with thinly sliced cold cuts for lunch. Dinner included meats like *gehaktballen*—pork and beef meatballs, *paarderookvlees*—smoked horse meat, or *sudderlapjes*—slowcooked beef, along with any vegetable grown in their fields: green beans, peas, carrots, red cabbage, brussels sprouts, endive, and spinach. Potatoes were served every night, and many meals like *stamppot boerenkool* and *zuurkool* included a mixture of mashed kale or sauerkraut and potatoes with *rookworst*—smoked sausage placed on top. They also made the most delicious homemade soups and *hutspot*—potato and carrot stew. Besides my maternal grandfather's backyard vegetable garden, neither of my parents were born into farmers' families. Still, they, along with most Dutch people in general, adapted their farming ancestors' traditional way of cooking.

They also added various recipes brought home by the soldiers, including my father, who fought during the Indonesian War of Independence between 1945 and 1949. He never spoke of his time there, and I always figured he didn't want to talk about it. However, until not long ago, the hand-carved mortar and pestle made from maple wood he brought back with him still sat on the bookshelf in my parents' apartment. It was the one I used as a microphone while standing on the ottoman to sing after church. All I knew was that this armed and diplomatic struggle between the Republic of Indonesia and the Dutch Empire provided us with delicious recipes like *Bami Goreng*—stir-fried noodles with pork and veggies, *Nasi Goreng*—fried rice with chicken and veggies, and the traditional *Rijstaffle*—rice table, including over 40 Indonesian dishes. The soldiers brought home the spices to accompany the elaborate meals they loved, and their wives learned how to cook the dishes that took a lot of time to prepare. It included making various sauces and marinating the chicken, beef, and pork for days. For the Dutch, this cuisine became what Chinese food is to Canadians, with Indonesian restaurants scattered in every city around Holland.

Aside from their adaptation of Indonesian food, the old Dutch farmer's diet became unhealthy in a more modern age with high levels of carbohydrates and fats. In addition, they were not automatically worked off due to more efficient equipment requiring less physical exertion. But, when my parents and many other Dutch people immigrated to Canada, these time-honoured meals became part of their way of connecting with their homeland and each other. Cooking and eating together with their extended family were how they maintained their heritage. And as my mother and her sisters moved into their 40s and 50s, along with perimenopause, they struggled with their weight and started and failed every diet that ever existed: Ayds, Atkins, Scarsdale, and Weight Watchers, among others. I watched the ups and downs of weight loss and weight gain in awe, and it slowly became a part of my daily mindset as well.

The realization that someone's body was not accepted as it came out of the womb was well-engrained before I reached the age of twelve. I quickly learned that I had to meet specific societal standards of weight and shape. I was a skinny little thing, and everyone brought this to my mother's attention, *She's so thin. Does she eat enough? Is she a picky eater? I can see her ribs. Have you had her checked?* I heard it all, and this constant chatter, along with my mother's endless talk about food and those last five pounds, gradually created my adult obsession with weight loss. Whether eating too much or too little, diets, and exercise became critical but dangerous tools for me to detach from my trauma.

The truth is, I ate a lot when I was a child and liked most of my mother's cooking, but there were a few things that I couldn't stomach. One of the Dutch dishes was the beef tongue she boiled in a large pot of water on the top of the stove. That whole cow's tongue was the most disgusting piece of meat I have ever seen, with a thick layer of skin left on the top, goosebumps, and all. But my mother proudly sliced it up and placed it on a platter with the carrots, peas, onions, and potatoes that were boiled along with the meat and piled beside it as if it was one of her best roast chicken meals. Every time I saw that tongue lying in the centre of the table after being called to dinner, I immediately started to gag. I couldn't help it. My repulsion was so apparent that she eventually stopped the madness by only making me eat the tongue broth with the added boiled vegetables. I managed to force a bowl down if I didn't look at the tongue sitting in the middle of the table in front of me.

Liver and onions for dinner and *griesmeel*—Cream of Wheat—for breakfast were two other dishes I had the same physical response to. But my mother was adamant I eat them. My father was particularly strict about this, and I remember sitting in front of my plate one night long after everyone left the table with my liver

Escaping the Cycle of Shame

and onions still untouched before me. After hours of sitting before me, the liver was cold and shrivelled, so it was even less appetizing. My father finally walked in and told me, *You can sit there all night if you want, but you'll be eating everything on that plate, so you may as well get started. Think of the poor African children!* So, I did think of them and concluded that they would not want to eat this no matter how hungry they were. But I didn't say it out loud, knowing what would come of that. Instead, I choked it down. This was a torturous process and repeated with a bowl of *griesmeel* one Saturday morning. My mother refused to put a tablespoon of sugar in it like my oma did, making it even more bland and disgusting. This time, I refused and sat there for over an hour while my sisters and father laughed at the cartoons on TV in the living room; my father loved the Roadrunner, and it actually made him laugh out loud. Then just when my humiliation peaked, and I wondered how many more hours I could endure, my mother snuck in and took the bowl away. She didn't look at me as she emptied its contents into the trash. Without saying a word, she walked by the table as if I wasn't there and went out to join the others again. I sat there stunned for a moment, yet thankful for her empathy and the release of my misery. However, I also interpreted her silence as avoiding my father's retribution if he knew what she was doing. She would never confess that to a child. So, I did what my father advocated and forgot about it, got up, and went down the hall to my room.

Then one day, not long after, my mother came to tell me that I had a doctor's appointment, and she would pick me up from school to take me for a physical. I thought it was just a regular checkup and gave the note to be excused to my teacher. I left class when it was time to meet my mother at the school's main door. When we got to the doctor, my mother accompanied me into the patient room. She explained that I eat a lot of food but never seemed to be satiated and wondered if something was wrong with me because I was so skinny. It felt like I wasn't even there while they chatted back and forth. Listening to their conversation, I began to wonder if there was something wrong with me. She was right, I rarely felt satiated, and when I did, I was hungry an hour later. I still am to this day.

The doctor examined me and poked at my tummy as I lay on the examining table. When he was done, he indicated that I might have a tapeworm. *What?!* Still ignoring me, he asked my mother if I ever ate raw hamburger meat, and she told him that she often gave me a bit when she was rolling her *gehaakballen* because I really liked it and asked for it. The way she said it made it sound like I had done something wrong. And it was true, I loved raw ground beef, but my mother willingly gave it to me, so I didn't think there was anything wrong with that. Wasn't she supposed to say, *No* when I asked for something that wasn't good for me? Shame built up inside me, and I was annoyed she made me look like a bad girl.

He told her to take me home and have me lay on my bed without my underwear on and hold a piece of raw beef in front of my anus. I couldn't believe what he suggested and what he said next, *If there is a tapeworm in her, it will come out.* I

Around The Table

remember being confused and nervous, thinking that I must be in some sort of horror show. I then wondered if he was Catholic, and this was one of their rituals I hadn't heard about yet. He finally looked at me and told me not to worry because I was probably too thin due to my high energy and metabolism. My mother laughed and told him, *She's just like me.*

My mother acted like this was all very normal, so I was quiet all the way home. When we got to the house, she told me to go to my bedroom, and she got the beef. She walked in and sat down beside me on the bed. She held the plate with a small piece of steak on it and pulled down my underwear. She then asked me to bend my knees, and once I did, she took the beef and held it in front of my bum and told me it wouldn't take long. After 15 minutes and no evidence of a worm, she put the meat back on the plate and told me I didn't have a tapeworm as if it was just something else to get done that day. I said, *Thank God* out loud and prayed we were not eating that beef for dinner. She told me not to use God's name in vain, and after she left and shut the door, I swore I would never ask her for raw meat again.

Staying with my friend's family expanded my awareness of what mealtime could encompass. They introduced me to the possibility of having a non-confrontational experience at the dinner table. Of course, they sat together for meals just like we did, but just like at my oma's, I was initially stumped, unable to figure out the order of their seating plan. It didn't make any sense because other than their mother and father, they were scattered here and there with ages and sexes all mixed up. Most prevalent, the boys didn't assume the patriarchal position beside their father. The food was set in the centre of the table as a free-for-all, first come, first served extravaganza, rather than passed around in a specific order; I didn't realize it then, but I was experiencing equality. And, I wasn't expecting the pleasurable chaos that accompanied it, especially with the added noise level of so many people talking at the same time. There was inviting energy around their table—possibly joy?

After a few days of hesitantly submerging myself into the extreme opposite of organized quiet I was used to, I caught myself laughing out loud. I quickly checked myself, feeling a shiver of anxiety run down my spine—*seven peas, seven carrots, eight peas, eight carrots...* However, it didn't take me long to realize that everyone else was laughing as well, so I joined back in. The father of his household smiled and winked at me when I looked up at him, encouraging me to enjoy the connection he inspired around his family's table. I glanced above him and noticed the absence of a crucifix over the door behind him.

Regrettably, my father was forced to repeat history when we returned to Canada by forfeiting his professional career and going back to Dupont to work on the line. If I learned anything about him, it was his strong sense of duty to fulfill his role as husband and father by providing for his family. My mother reminded me many times that he was integral and sacrificed his career to take care of us. I used to feel bad that he carried such an immense sense of responsibility towards me. As a parent of two, I realize the normalcy of this obligation; I am saddened that as a little girl I carried the burden of his unhappiness after my mother reminded me of his sacrifice, *He is a good man.*

For the first time in her married life, my mother went to work full-time at a Woolco department store. I'm sure it was an agreement my parents made to help with their financial setback from the move overseas. Initially, I didn't think about how my mother's extended work hours would affect my father's moods or the amount of attention I would receive from her, but it did. When I was younger, and my sisters and I were all in school full-time, her small part-time gig as an Avon lady only took a few hours a day, but this was different. Now that we were older, she left in the morning when we did and got home after an eight-hour shift right at supper time. She assigned jobs to her daughters just like her mother did when she was my age: peeling potatoes, cleaning the vegetables, and preparing the meat. I noticed my father's agitation towards me, my sisters, and my mother increased in frequency and intensity the more hours she worked. I suddenly missed what I didn't realize I had before—the security of my mother's presence when my father was home.

After school, I always knew when he was home from the midnight to four shift because his lunchbox stood on the counter with his thermos open by the sink; its base and cup were filled with soapy dishwater inside them. I knew to be quiet because I heard him snoring in the living room. When I was a very wee girl at home every day with my mother, I remember hearing that same rhythmic heavy breathing accompanied by my mother's shushing me. She did that a lot because my mind would wander, and I forgot about not waking my father, just like later in Holland when I ran in front of my opa. Coming home from kindergarten with her, she put her index finger up to her lips as soon as we walked in the side door where my sister got slapped and my aunt kicked the cat food down the stairs.

Along with the chill that went down my spine, I knew that I needed to do what she asked. Not just because I was mindful of doing the right thing, but because I was fearful of doing something wrong and causing grief for my mother; it would be my fault if I woke him. Then, by the time I reached my pre-teens, I didn't need a reminder because I knew to tone myself down a few octaves when I arrived home and saw my father lying on the sofa. My mother was confident she could go to work and leave me home without her because I was well-programmed by then.

There were moments when I believed my mother understood me from my soul's core and even more often when my father did not. I focused on the positive attributes my mother and I shared while distancing myself from the ones my father and I didn't. Over time, my mother and I drifted apart because our similarities weren't enough to hold us tightly together. However, I hung on to a bit of a bond and sense of trust we maintained between us. I yearned for the same with my father when I was with him, but he could not provide what I needed to feel emotionally secure in his presence. I used my mother for that kind of protection and watched how she modelled, detaching from insecurities and fears. To this day, my mother tells me that I was daddy's little girl, but I don't recall experiencing her interpretation of that. My confusion increased when I wondered if I missed something and finally concluded that she must have been trying to manifest what she wished for by saying it over and over again.

I'm not sure the kind of love I sought from my father was ever meant to be because we were complete opposites right from the beginning. I developed an understanding that experiencing love meant always allowing my father the honour of being right even if I thought he wasn't. From the start, our mindsets were misaligned. At the age of 12, I began to cognitively process if and how he loved me—I wanted proof. That's a lot for a young child to manage on her own, knowing she could never share what she discovered with anyone because she didn't trust them. I quickly learned that life can be hard, and I wouldn't always get what I wanted.

I didn't stay with my beautiful friend for long because, within a few months, my parents bought a bungalow in another subdivision on the west side of town. I was transferred to the first public school I ever attended in grade eight. The kids there were no different from those at the Catholic schools I attended; religion didn't seem to make anyone a better person. I remember one girl in particular, cute, well-dressed, and very popular. She knew she was special, and she hand-picked each of her apostles based on how much they drooled over her. I wanted to be a part of that—being either the drooler or the droolee—and began emulating her and her entourage.

High leather, wedged boots were all the rage back then, and everyone in her pack wore them. I decided I needed a pair, along with the trendy Farrah Fawcette hairstyle: long, feathered, and flowy. I grew my hair out and bought a curling iron in an attempt to look like the most famous Charlie's Angel. My mother told me I looked better with short hair like her. I ignored her comment and somehow convinced her I needed a new pair of boots. So, off we went to the store, and when I showed her what I wanted, she disapproved of the boots with absolutely no function other than looking good, and she was right. Inwardly, I agreed because they were God-awful ugly, and I did not explain why I could not live without those boots. I could not tell her that if she didn't buy them for me, I had absolutely no chance of ever making a friend at this school. I begged and begged and finally wore her down. She hesitantly purchased the boots, and I think she knew there was more to why I was so desperate to have them, but she never asked. I carried the large Aldo box to the car and placed it gently in the trunk. I was smiling; she was not. And although making me happy over her went against my grain, I boldly made that move.

I wore the expensive boots my parents could not afford for 14 days straight. I received compliments from everyone except those I wanted to impress; they may have noticed the boots, but they didn't give me the time of day. That mean girl never took a second glance at me—I was still the nerd, even when I wore nice boots. After those two weeks, I placed them back in the box they came in and tucked them in my closet out of sight. I detested those boots, and I hated those girls. Going to school the following Monday, fancy boots or not, nothing had changed. I stood with the other invisible girls in the schoolyard and watched the self-involved egotists giggle and toss their hair off their pretty faces while their lip gloss shone in the sun.

I cut my hair up short that night, and my mother told me it was cute. Then, she asked me where my new boots were. I told her I didn't like them anymore, and the argument of the century ensued, *How dare you convince me to buy the most expensive boots on the shelf and only wear them for two weeks! Do you think money grows on trees?!* I glared at her and thought, *No, but happiness grows under willow trees!!* Filled with shame, I could not bring myself to tell her I was not worthy of those boots—I never was. It was my mistake. I began agonizing over my upcoming graduation months ahead, not wanting to attend. When the day finally arrived, I faked being sick. I was so relieved to finish that part of my life, but high school was fast-approaching, and I fretted about it all summer long. That spring, the boots were brought to the second-hand store.

Although these are haunting memories, my childhood had glimmers of happiness. Unfortunately, they almost always seemed to transition into disappointment with the shadow of a dark cloud. As each year passed, I learned that joy was not a given because I would get so close to experiencing it, only to have it somehow ripped out from under me. Even at such a young age, gaslighting became part of my day-to-day without even knowing it was happening. I discovered what this term meant 30 years later while chatting with a friend who left her husband after years of emotional abuse. She described all the beautiful things he used to do for her: bring her coffee in the morning, tell her how beautiful she was, and buy her gifts, only to make a complete 360 by verbally insulting her and returning everything he ever gave her. He intentionally raised her up to make her feel extraordinarily special. And then, just as deliberately, he made her feel as insignificant as he could by pointing out her flaws and taking away the gifts that she believed were expressions of love.

As she shared her horrible past with this man, I realized that I had experienced the same thing she had but with my parents. However, even as a mature adult in my 40s, I could not accept that they were capable of such a strategic ploy. I still don't believe they were aware of the damage they did, using age-old learned manipulative behaviours. Unfortunately, their lack of awareness created lifelong psychological consequences for us all.

One of the girls in my class lived two doors down from me, and we had our parents' Dutch heritage in common. She was also the brain of the class and incredibly funny. She had a dog who got out of the house one day and came back pregnant. Sixty days later, she had her litter, and my friend's parents wanted them out of the house as soon as possible. I wanted one of the puppies so badly that I came up with every reason people get dogs: they bring joy, they are lovable, they are fun… But my parents came up with all the reasons that people don't get dogs: they are work, they pee inside, they need obedience training, they have to be fed and cleaned. Although these were all valid, I wore my mother down with tears and the same drama I watched her use with my father. Finally, she convinced him and reiterated that I promised to do all the work. I agreed that the dog would have to go if I was irresponsible. I thought this was very reasonable, except that they set me up for failure by never once offering to help me. It was as if they wanted to teach me a lesson. They gave me the gift of receiving the high of getting a dog, only to jolt me down to the low of having to give it away.

I named my puppy Kishu-Kali; Kishu is a beautiful Japanese dog breed I thought she resembled, and Kali is the Japanese black goddess of time, doomsday, and death. I believe her name symbolized the duality of events I intuitively knew was about to unfold. In hindsight, I should never have been allowed to have this dog. She peed all over the house when she was home alone during the day and when she jumped up to greet us as we came through the door. She was hyper, and although I tried to teach her to come, sit, and stay, I knew nothing about training her. I discovered that my parents did not like dogs. Years later, this made sense when I learned that people who love conditionally are uncomfortable receiving unconditional love—the kind that dogs provide. In the case of Kishu-Kali, my parents only focused on the inconvenience she created and refused to absorb her enthusiasm for life and the love she gave so freely. Instead, they let me have the dog to prove that I could not take care of her.

When they rejected her, I also experienced rejection. They only saw her poor behaviour, and I was to blame because I promised to keep her out of trouble. Not once did they support me to train the one who gave me the kind of love I needed. After six months, they indicated their intolerance of my dog's hindrance and made it quite clear that she must go to another home. I snuggled in my bed with Kishu one more night, and they took her to a farm the following day. My mother told me it was the right thing to do. I was tricked into a teaching moment that felt like a punishment.

Later in my 50s, while working with another therapist, I tried desperately to make sense of why I managed to repel joy from my life; why I filled every moment of my day with getting things done rather than making space for whatever sheer bliss might be like. She asked me to reflect on a time before the age of ten when I experienced what I thought joy felt like. Other than memories with my paternal oma, I couldn't answer at that moment, and she told me to go home to take time to contemplate her question. It was a little disconcerting that I had to think that hard to come up with a joyful moment. Was the purpose of the question to get me to realize that my childhood was void of joy? That felt wrong. Or was it to encourage me to dig deep to bring hidden joyful memories to the surface so that they might become more prevalent than the sad ones? That felt right. Maybe it was

Escaping the Cycle of Shame

a combination of both. Looking back, I think she just wanted me to discover the truth, no matter if my life encompassed either more joy or misery, so I could choose which I wanted to manifest into my life.

At the time, I simply did what she asked because I was too confused to figure it out on my own, and I trusted her process. She asked me if I had a photo album with pictures of when I was young. I remembered the photo of my grandparents sitting with our family on the side of the road having a picnic and answered, *Yes, my mother recently gave it to me, along with the photos of my children I gave her over the years; she was downsizing and told me she didn't have room for them anymore.* My therapist seemed subtly taken aback, and she didn't answer right away and stopped writing. She looked at me over her glasses, frowned, and then asked me to go home and look through my baby album to see if any photos might prompt a joyful memory. And it worked—sort of.

Placing the tattered book on my lap, it was the first time I noticed that the cover was light blue, opposed to the pink ones sold for baby girls. When I opened it, the binding on the spine fell apart; it had clearly been opened and closed many times. There were twenty-odd pages of photos and just as many with cards celebrating my birth from my mother's and father's relatives and friends. All the cards included sentiments written by the women in their families. I read each one and smiled, reflecting on how each of the authors had possibly joyfully impacted me through my life. Given my assignment, I did this intentionally to establish past joy, even though my therapist wanted that sensation to be inspired naturally. But I was determined to achieve the goal and make it happen. Subconsciously, I believed I would be considered normal then.

Right after the section of cards, there was a lock of my baby hair glued under a piece of clear plastic that had turned yellow with age. Beside it was a list of six chronological dates with a section to write my weight beside each. I weighed seven pounds, seven ounces the day I was born. Within six months, I had gained an additional seven pounds, six ounces. Beside the first entry, it was noted I was 22 inches, and beside the November entry, I was 25 inches; the other four were left blank. I wondered who the hell cared about all that anyway.

There was a page with a heading: *Bestemd voor een min of meer geregeld verhaal— Designated for a little or a lot of my story.* My mother definitely went for the little bit because it only encompassed half a page of my mother's Dutch handwriting, and more baby cards covered the other half. I found it interesting that my mother's first line described me as a happy baby, sitting like a princess in my carriage all day. Indeed, she often made me feel like the special one, while other times, she treated me like the third and last child I was. The rest was pretty much about how well I ate and slept, along with how much I smiled—I was a good baby. She said that my dad was a good father. What did good mean?

My mother would be the first to say that her handwriting is awful, so it took me a while to read it; I was grateful to be fluent in Dutch, both written and spoken. Turning the page, I came upon the heading: *In beeld gebrachte grote en kleine gebeurtenissen uit mijn verdere levenjaren—Snippits of large and small events from later years in my life.* The first line on this page began with *January 19,* and my mother shared how well-behaved I was getting a vaccination; she noted that the doctor was proud because, again, I was so good. The following line began with *February 3.* I was five months old: *Het is een heel lief, vriendelijk meiske—It is a very loving, friendly, girl.* On February 22, she wrote that I graduated to the playpen and loved it; when I was older, my mother told me that I was content in the playpen for hours. Next, she wrote that I got my third vaccine a few days later and listed the foods I was now eating. The rest of the page was blank. I sat there, ashamed of believing I was so hard done by, comparing the lack of content with the pages and pages I saw she wrote in my sisters' photo albums. I remembered my mother joking about how little she wrote in mine, given how busy she was with three little ones. I understood, but I couldn't deny that I felt slighted.

    I moved on to the photos of my baptism with my aunt—the one who later kicked the cat kibble down the stairs—holding me beside the holy water font and the priest making the sign of the cross on my forehead. I found it interesting that my mother chose her to be my Godmother; maybe they weren't fighting yet. The last photo in the book is of me at the age of eight, posing in front of our church's altar with the Archbishop at my Confirmation. I wondered where the rest of my childhood photos were. Understandably, I had no memory of events before the age of five, but I was in awe that I didn't recall experiencing anything in the photos after that. It felt like I was looking at someone else's life, and I became distracted from the task my therapist gave me to find any sparked joy in the photos. Instead, I focused on sorrow and deprivation, asking myself, *Why don't I remember certain events or periods of time in my childhood?* I heard that people block out uncomfortable memories as a coping mechanism. Did I do that? I was smiling in every picture, which indicated I was happy, yet I didn't understand why I wasn't emotionally connecting to them. Even at that young age, was I just impersonating a joyful child for the person taking the picture? The images portrayed a carefree little girl, but I did not resonate with the persona of happiness they depicted. It made me think there was much more behind that smile, that I had possibly interpreted my life differently from others and compartmentalized perceptions that needed to be excavated and brought to the surface. So far, I was not successful in establishing whether or not joy was prevalent in my childhood.

    Turning each page, I noticed the beautifully-embossed filament paper that separated them. I then came across an image of me sitting on my paternal oma's knee on a swing at the beach my family went to almost every Sunday. This photo was carefully secured with four black triangular corners like all the other photos. My sisters were on their own swing on either side of Oma and me. Below the photo, it read: *Zomer 1962 Oma blijft jong met haar kleinkinderen—Summer 1962 Oma stays young with her grandchildren.* This photo stirred up a calm ripple. There was no way I would have remembered this moment because I was only two at the time, but it prompted a heightened response, unlike the others—I thought it might have been joy.

Through this process, it became evident that the amount of connection I developed with the people in my life determined how moved I was when I looked at each of them in the photos. This particular photo immediately brought me back to Holland when I was 11. I became enveloped by my oma's love simply by looking at her holding me tightly on the swing, nestled in her bosom. I was sure I was experiencing what joy might be when that photo was taken. I believe this is how Oma would define love—as something that inspires the freedom to express joy. I reflected deeper about why my connection with the people in the other photos had dissipated over the years and concluded that their definition of love did not mirror the expression of joy that Oma and I shared within our love for each other—not that I saw anyway. I don't think my therapist was entirely sure where this project would take me, but we both discovered that it entailed more than simply finding a moment of joy in a book filled with memories I couldn't recall. As an adult, I concluded that joy was not prevalent in my life, and much more detrimental, I didn't realize how much I yearned for it.

The beach in this photo was on the property where my father worked. The plant had taken the lake's shoreline and made an incredible spot for their employees to bring their families. It had a sandy beachfront, an expansive grassy area with playground equipment, and a large canteen. I loved that beach, and my parents rightfully reminded us how privileged we were being able to enjoy this member-only sanctuary. However, along with experiencing gratitude for this haven in nature, I sadly continued learning the dysfunction of wanting to be regarded as the special one and the need for attention.

My mother always packed a picnic, and we wore our bathing suits under our clothes so we could tear them off upon arrival and go directly down to the beach. It was shallow and gradually deepened the further I walked out. I used my toes to grasp the hard, rippled sand until the water reached my neck, and my mother yelled out not to go any further. I was often still out in the water when my father decided to go into the lake to cool off after lying in the sun. He would suddenly get up out of his lawn chair and walk down to the water without saying a word. He never volunteered to play with me, but since he was heading my way, my mother called after him to let me jump off his shoulders into the water. She always took the opportunity to create a memory that would not necessarily have happened had she not; she was forever working on creating a photo to place in the album and remember years later. Without turning around, he always said, *Yes* less enthusiastically than my mother and I would have liked. Years after, my mother repeatedly told me how wonderful my father was, *Do you remember how you loved jumping off your dad's shoulders?! He's a good father.* I often wondered why she didn't share all the other wonderful things he did with me.

Around The Table

Although my father told me he didn't know how to train my dog, there were times when it seemed he did to train me. However, he wasn't consistent, sometimes not rewarding me for no reason. And his reasons to punish me felt self-serving. In this case, I respectfully waited for him to initiate the reward process once standing beside me, *Do you want to jump into the water?* I responded with an instantaneous, *Yes!!!* Once on his shoulders, I was thrilled to stand up tall and feel the sun beat down on my face and the breeze flow through my hair. He then grabbed my ankles, counted to three, and threw me up and forward into the air. I was flying—I'm pretty sure that's what joy felt like. I shrieked just before tucking my legs into a cannonball and hitting the water with a mighty splash; that was my reward. When I came up from under the water, I went back to him and obediently waited for his command. He submerged himself under the water, head, and all without saying anything. That was my cue, and I climbed back up on his shoulders—over and over again, repetitive joy.

Then one day, out of the blue, he changed the gig, adding a punishment to our ritual that negated any euphoria I was experiencing. After exactly three launches, he suddenly swam away towards, what I believed, was the end of the earth until I couldn't see him anymore. He didn't say anything, just turned around and left me standing there in the shallow water alone. My attention immediately went to the rippled sand as my toes nervously curled around the ridges—*nine peas, nine carrots, ten peas, ten carrots...* Within a moment, my father erased the reward while simultaneously taking away my joy.

I watched him do this the first time and thought he was playing a little trick on me. I was sure he would turn around after a few moments and come back, and we would laugh at his silly joke. After all, my oma taught me that the way to his heart was through humour; maybe he was doing that with me. But he kept going, and the further he went, the more terrified I became. It wasn't funny anymore. I heard my mother call me from our spot on the grassy bank and turned to see her waving me in; she knew his dramatic take-off probably upset me. When I got back to her, I told her that Daddy was swimming far away, and I couldn't see him anymore. My mother acted as if it was normal and assured me that he would be back, *Daddy works hard and needs some time to himself.* I thought, *Okay, but he could have told me*—this didn't feel right. I had that re-occurring icky feeling in my stomach while sitting on the blanket with my towel wrapped around me. It provided a bit of security like a cocoon as I waited for him to return. I reminded myself that he was a good father. My mother gave me an apple and smiled. She seemed pleased that I was worried about my father as if that validated my love for him.

The next time we went to the beach and my father went into the lake, she did the same thing and called after him asking him to let me jump off his shoulders. I wished she hadn't because I didn't want to anymore. So, when he asked me if I was ready, I looked up at him and said, *If you want to go swim, that's okay, Daddy.* He did. Without a word, he turned around and swam towards the horizon. My

Escaping the Cycle of Shame

mother never asked my father to play with me in the water again, and he didn't offer. I spent more time on the swings near the canteen and never learned how to swim. It wasn't fun anymore.

Then one summer, my parents decided to rent a cottage and off we went. I was so excited because my mother told me that we had a whole piece of the lake to ourselves with a dock and a shoreline beach. After driving for two hours, we arrived mid-afternoon and stood at the door as my father fumbled around looking for the keys. Unfortunately, he left them at home and had to drive all the way back to get them. I watched my mother jump into the peace-maker mode, overcompensating by soothing him to shift his demeanour, *It's okay. We'll be fine here. Take your time.* She kept nervously blurting things out, and I could see it was annoying him, and he was about to blow a fuse. He had come off the night shift that morning and got in the car without sleeping. Growing up, I witnessed my mother anxiously navigate my father's volatility. It slowly instilled the amplified angst I lived with as I watched his irritability build and then erupt in verbal attacks. That day, he abruptly turned around and yelled, *Godverdomme—Goddam it, didn't you see the keys on the counter?* Suddenly, it was her fault, and my heart sank. Shame.

Feeling her shame and watching her scramble to accommodate him was much more difficult for me to manage than the physical and mental vibration that ran through me when my father yelled at us. We all became quiet as my mother quickly took the coolers and food out of the car before my father stormed away, taking any bit of joy that had been ignited along with him. He didn't arrive back until after dark. We didn't have time to unload the rest of the car before he left, and he didn't think to do so. As a result, we had nothing to amuse ourselves with. However, my mother put on her happy face and reminded us that we wore our bathing suits there, so my sisters were happy to go into the water. I had not gone into a lake since the last time I jumped off my father's shoulders, but when my mother saw me looking at the water and not going in, she assumed I was upset about my father. She smiled and told me, *Daddy will be fine. He's just a little upset because I forgot to give him the keys.* She took full responsibility, and I'm sure she apologized to him later. I walked away from her and found a quiet spot under a tree by the water's edge and pretended it was my willow tree. Sitting on a massive piece of limestone, staring out into the water, I could hear my father yelling *Godverdomme* repeatedly in my head. Each time I saw his gnarled face glaring at my mother with such intensity that I could have sworn he hated her. My father scared me.

When I was little, I didn't know my mother's smile was a front, making it look like how he spoke to her didn't matter. I thought she was positive, brave, and confident, but all those things comprised her fake armour. At the cottage that day, I wanted to fight my fear, be strong like her, and learn not to let what he said bother me; she was good at that. I thought I could conquer my fear of him. I ignored that he was much more powerful than me and began walking into the water towards his stern voice echoing off the waves. *Be strong*, I told myself. Taking a few steps into the lake, I was doing well until my feet sank into something incredibly slippery and slimy. The muck came up to my knees within seconds. Thinking I was in quicksand, I screamed so hard that my mother was by my side before I had a chance to inhale and scream again. Like a superhero, she pulled me out of the water, sat me on the rock, and then ran away from me up to our food bins. I didn't understand why she was running away from me. Then, looking down at my legs, I saw what she did; my legs were full of leeches sucking the life out of me from my knees down! Ten seconds seemed like ten minutes, but suddenly, my mother stood before me, pouring salt up and down my legs out of the Morton's Salt box. I focused on the leeches falling off my legs—*one leech, two leeches, three leeches...* I was in shock, but my mother was calm and composed, getting shit done. Within moments, the box of salt was empty, and the leeches lay in a pile before me. I'm sure my mouth was open as wide as my mother's as she sat back exhausted, staring at me on a rock, *Never go in that part of the lake again.* I never did.

My father came back and acted like nothing ever happened. He had time to cool off. *Just forget about it.* Everyone else went on as if everything was fine without acknowledging the impact of my father's verbal rant. But I could not get over the residual turmoil of my father's erratic behaviour. With each similar event, my mother ignored or defended the trauma that occurred and manifested in me. This spiralled into an acute perception of being deprived of my emotional needs. In turn, this lack of support further developed my ongoing yearning to be seen and heard. Ironically, I believe my mother doted on me more than my sisters because I began demanding her attention with sudden emotional outbursts. I listened to my parents discuss my bouts of crying with my father saying that I was too sensitive.

The leeches did not defeat me, but my father's words motivated me to survive emotionally through detachment. As I grew older, there were subsequent times when I pumped up my chest and said what I thought. But that also motivated my father to do the same, using his native tongue and overbearing voice, *Hou je mond dicht onders sla ik em dicht*—*Shut your mouth, or I'll slap it shut.* I wanted to believe my mother when she told me that his threats meant nothing. However, I think he did this because he didn't know how to respond to my newfound confidence. Control became his default when he felt powerless. For a while, I clung to the hope that my mother wanted me to believe every time he lashed out at me, *Your father loves you.* After a while, her mantra didn't work anymore because his kind of love made me feel ashamed. My child's mind interpreted his hurtful one-liners as criticism, which outweighed my ability to rationalize why someone who loved me could so freely fire them at me as if I was a target in a firing squad. There were times when I understood his seamless way of verbally assaulting me as acute disdain for who I was.

As I transitioned into my teenage years, my further-developed story of not belonging and being unloved became my reality. I listened to his banter for years, and I was not a child anymore. I became more curious about why my mother didn't speak up to tell him not to treat us the way he did. I had a deep knowing my mother was not convinced that the things her husband said to us were okay. But she was invincibly trained as the submissive wife, forever pardoning my father's rule while simultaneously sculpting his verbal judgments into something morally passable. She accomplished this by accusing us of setting him off, thus justifying his reaction within the altercation. If we were guilty, he could not be; only one side could be right and one wrong. At her insistence, we always ended up apologizing to him, and if she was the victim of the verbal assault, she quickly said she was sorry to make peace, *I should have reminded you to remember the keys to the cottage.* My father always calmed down with someone else's admittance of guilt. His response included that smirk, followed by that infamous line. Over time, I interpreted all apologies he received as bonus points for him in the game of being right.

As a teenager, I saw what being conditionally loved looked like for a wife through the disconnection of emotional detachment. I witnessed dutiful reverence in response to psychological control while simultaneously developing a protective personality that shielded her from unimportance. My perception of this unbalanced state of loyalty indicated a shift around her mid-forties when she went to work full-time. She stepped into her power like a chameleon and learned to recalibrate to achieve worthiness. I think a switch flipped in her head, along with an awareness prompting her to believe she was valued. A soul can only be robbed of connection for so long before it catapults into an awakening.

This epiphany generated action with the caveat that she had to figure out how to self-fulfill outside of meeting my father's needs. This was a massive endeavour. The astonishing part is that she was victorious. Whether she knows it or not, my mother took the first step towards attempting to break a generational misogynistic pattern by not sweeping past matriarchs' unworthiness and degradation under the rug—a subconscious bold move. To compensate for feelings of disconnection, she worked on acquiring the same value my father had—the matriarchal equivalent of the patriarch. She began juggling loving herself without depriving him of what he believed he deserved.

My mother continued on this crusade for several years. And she was smart, having learned the effectiveness of centuries-old manipulation from the patriarchs before her—let him think he's right, even if it harms others. So, just as my father achieved the gratification of self-importance by controlling her, she used the same tactic by upping the control of her youngest rebellious daughter. I became the chosen one because my response to the world at this point needed controlling in her mind—and it probably did. I was a young teen, and although I felt a drastic shift in my mother's response to me, I was not aware of what she was up to yet. But it didn't take long to see that control was a useful tool in her mind. Thankfully, I dodged the bullet of falling into the power trap and chose to fight her every step of the way. However, I definitely had my moments because next-level manipulation was a mind-fuck I was unprepared for as a 14-year-old getting ready to go to high school.

Around The Table

I was striving for autonomy within the pressures of a conformist society, and I noticed that my older sisters did not seem to have this compulsion for individuality. That confused me and confirmed I must be an alien within this family of five. While I desperately tried to discover who I was outside of what society dictated, my mother's timing, using me as a token in her game of self-worth, made my goal of achieving the same much more difficult. She got in my way by amplifying her guilt strategy to the degree that heightened my determination to take control of my life—big time. I gave her a run for her money, so she began using passive-aggressive behaviour to reign me in.

I fought being submissive with every ounce of resilience I had built up and put on the armour she gave me so long ago. Finally, I decided I was ready. But it was one of the biggest fights of my life, given my opponent was a tough Dutch damsel in distress whose mandate was to shape me into another version of her. The reason she needed me? No chief achieves victory without competent soldiers by their side—strength is made in numbers!! But, again, I had no clue what her objective was, and I don't think this was a deliberate plan within her desperate state of wanting to save her own unique identity. She simply and suddenly went to war and decided I would go to battle with her. What I now know is that she was in the same emotional survival mode I was: classic flight or fight that sent her into preserving any morsel of authenticity she could, in any way she could. We both used control as a weapon to detach from the darkness of our inherited obedient roles.

While she fought for self-preservation, I did the same. Unfortunately, neither one of us realized that our self-serving mandates created the perception that we were manipulating each other, which was not untrue. I discovered that conversation is not encouraged when emotions, opinions, and values are not honoured, and the result was a battle of control, with no hope of a peace treaty. She tried to convince me that I was just like her, which prompted me to engage in yet another round of rebellious detachment from her pull that triggered my push. And yet, she still had an advantage because no matter how hard I pushed my mother away, I could not fully commit to the strength I needed as I struggled to tear myself away from her. She had the advantage of being the adult, so it never quite balanced out, and, inevitably, she succeeded by using her go-to of guilt, which always maintained enough control over me to keep me coming back. I couldn't seem to break away from my youngest-female-child-lowest-family-ranking because she used all those things to make me feel special…and then pushed me off my pedestal as soon as I stood in the light of glory. Not only was this emotionally damaging, but it also just didn't feel good. My truth about familial love became an extraordinary discomfort that I knew was very bad.

The year before I went to high school, I remember lying in my bed one night with overwhelming thoughts creating chaos in my mind. Sometimes, I embraced being special when I was with my mother, only to feel insignificant a moment later. I became lonely and frightened, not understanding what was happening to me. My

Escaping the Cycle of Shame

chest became tight, and my neck tingled from multiple sharp chills darting up from the bottom of my spine. My heart began to race when I realized the possibility that my mother was using me as a scapegoat for her happiness. I became so overcome with alienation that my breathing quickened and became shallow. The fear was suffocating, and my body and mind eventually slowed down as I counted each breath. I instinctively made each inhale and exhale a little longer. While reining in my adrenaline, I slid my right hand over one of my breasts and grazed my fingers over its nipple. Moving down, my hand cupped my entire breast, meditatively caressing it with larger circles in a more rhythmic motion. My breathing became slow and steady, soothing me into a light sleep. Sinking a little deeper, I found myself envisioning a mother pacifying her baby in a rocking chair. When the chair swayed back, the face of the mother was a child—it was me. And when the chair came forward, the face of the baby was my mother's. Subliminally, it only took a moment for the clarity of this vision's message to surface; my life's work was to nurture my mother.

Fear returned with my heart racing and my breath becoming shallow again. Then, just when I thought I could not calm my angst, I was jolted awake by a knock at my bedroom door. *Yoo-Hoo,* my mother called. I pulled up my sheets and nervously said, *Come in.* She told me she wanted to say goodnight, but I was sure she knew I was committing a sin. I looked over her head at Jesus hanging above my door and said, *Goodnight, Mom.* This was the first and only time I utilized my own physical touch to quiet the chaos that constantly enveloped me. So many times, over the years, a flash of that evening reminded me of a little girl who did something very naughty. I wished I had stuck to counting peas and carrots.

A few months later, I found myself in a situation I was sure I was going to hell for. I met a girl in grade eight who asked me to come for a sleepover one Friday night. We had just started hanging out a few weeks before, and she seemed nice, but I was leery because my track record with trusting others was not great. She lived around the corner from us, so I reassured myself, knowing I could walk home if something went wrong. We went to my house after school to grab the overnight bag I packed in the morning and headed over to her place. Her mother was there when we arrived, and she was a very well put-together woman, June Cleaver style, but without the flared skirt. I thought my mother took special care to get dressed and made up every day, but this mom upped the ante. She wore a navy dress with a tight bodice and thinly-cinched belt, showing off her large breasts and tiny waist. It had a pencil skirt that modestly landed just below her knees and emphasized her long, slender legs. I looked down at her stiletto high heels clicking along the floor and wondered if she knew they could damage the hardwood; we weren't allowed to wear our shoes in the house. Her hair was styled in loose, shoulder-length curls, and she had perfectly-applied bright red lipstick.

A plate of cheese, Ritz Crackers, and grapes sat on a tray on the kitchen table beside her designer purse. I was mesmerized by the bag's beauty and equally startled when she noticed my eyes resting on it a little too long. She suddenly grabbed it as if saving it from the hands of a thief. I had never seen one quite like it, and, as she placed it up on the counter behind the toaster, my tummy made an anxious flip, sensing her distrust in me. I felt like a criminal, innocent before proven guilty.

My friend noticed my discomfort and swiftly took the snack tray by the handles and told me to follow her. When we got to her room, I couldn't help but notice how beautiful it was. She had white lace curtains and a matching bedspread on a large bed. I thought double beds were only for married couples, but she had one, and there were no stuffed animals on it. There were two extra pillows with different kinds of cases that I found out later were not for sleeping on; their ruffled edges indicated they were just for show. I figured out very quickly that this room must have cost a lot of money, and yet I found it super boring. Why would anyone want everything in white? I was also very nervous eating off the snack tray while sitting on the bed; that's what tables were for. My friend told me not to worry when I spilled some crumbs on the bedspread, *My mom will clean it up.* I was thankful she didn't offer me any milk.

We finished our snack, chatted for a while, then went out to the living room and watched TV. I heard her mother in the kitchen making supper, and then her father came home from work. He wore a three-piece business suit with a tie, so I knew he made more money than my father; my friend's high-end bedroom décor all made sense now. He went into the kitchen, and I saw him kiss his wife through a crack in the door—that was nice. He then came out and took off his jacket, placing it on the railing in the hall and came to the living room and said, *Hello* as he settled in his La-Z-Boy. He then reached over to one of the knobs on the TV and changed the channel to the news without saying anything more. Two minutes later, his wife arrived with a whisky on the rocks, placed it on the side table beside his chair, and walked back towards the kitchen. On the way, she picked up his jacket and hung it in the front hall closet before she finished preparing supper. Since our show was interrupted, my friend jumped up and said, *Let's go to my room.* I briefly had a revelation, noticing an even higher level of patriarchal control than my family followed. My mother served my father his food and drinks, but he was not averse to hanging up his coat. My mother would never have needed to hang up my father's coat, but I know she hung up mine many times—my father did not. These seemed like little things, but they made me realize that my family wasn't the only strange one out there. Maybe this was just the way everyone was, and some were weirder than others.

Her mother called us to dinner at six o'clock on the nose. I experienced a sense of ease when I noticed the table was tucked in a corner. Her father sat in the same spot my father did, but he was beside the doorway instead of under it. The other difference was that just like at my other friend's house, Jesus wasn't hanging above him. What was similar was that they had a table with corners, and my friend's mom sat across from her husband closest to the counter and food. There were two

Escaping the Cycle of Shame

other placemats, both with glasses of milk already poured, and my friend assumed her position on one side in between her parents. I breathed a quiet sigh of relief, confident that my spot was opposite hers, where the other glass of milk was. Besides the absence of Jesus, another difference was that her mother served the food on our plates at the counter and brought them over to us. I was happy because I didn't need to worry about knocking anything over while serving myself.

I grew up in the era when most parents believed children should be seen and not heard, and my new friend's mother and father were no different. After everyone finished eating, her mother excused us, and they retired to the living room to finish their coffee. We went back to her bedroom, chatting all evening and listening to records; I could not believe she had a record player. At precisely nine o'clock, her mom tapped on the door and told us it was time to turn off the music and get into bed. I went to the bathroom, put on my flannel nightie, and brushed my teeth. When I got back, my friend was already in bed on the side closest to the wall, so I jumped in beside her. She showed me where the flashlight was on the nightstand beside the bed on my side just in case I had to go pee during the night. We spent some time gossiping about the other kids in my class before I eventually drifted off to sleep. Apparently, she did not because I woke up to find my friend over top of me under a tent of sheets and blankets. She had pulled the front of my nightie up to my belly button, and her finger was in my vagina! Shocked, I jumped up to a seated position and saw her crouched down with the flashlight pointing at my private parts. My underwear was resting down around my ankles.

Once I came to my senses, I pulled up my panties and, even though I knew, I asked her what she was doing down there. She told me quite casually that it was good to explore your body parts; her mother told her so. Well then, I thought, sarcastically, *If your mother said so, it must be true!!* But I didn't say it out loud. She asked me if I wanted to check her out, and I emphatically answered, *No, I want to go home.* Her parents were watching Mannix when she went to her mother to tell her I wasn't feeling well and wanted to go home. *Umm*, I thought, *if your mom thinks it's okay to touch me down there, then why didn't you just tell her that I didn't like what you did?* She then turned to her dad and asked him to drive me home. I didn't want him to, so I stood with my head hanging down in front of him and told him I could walk. He was adamant that I did not walk home in the dark, and his wife got his coat out of the closet. He heaved a big sigh and got up, and I wondered why he was so tired, having been catered to all night. That terrible icky feeling surfaced again as tears began rolling down my face.

As we got ready to leave, my mind was racing, questioning if he thought it was okay for his daughter to touch me while I was sleeping, and if so, would he do something like that to me in the car. Finally, her mother came over and led me into the kitchen. She had a purple fluffy housecoat on and curlers in her hair, and she had already removed her makeup; she didn't look as good as when I first met her just hours before. My face got increasingly hot and sweaty, and I wanted

73

Around The Table

to make a run for the front door but instead remained standing frozen in front of her. She asked me if something had happened, was her daughter mean to me? I shook my head from side to side because I was filled with shame for something I didn't do. I knew what my friend did to me wasn't right, but I didn't think she was mean to me, and yet, it was very, very wrong. Maybe this was how they expressed their love for each other—but that didn't feel right either. I couldn't find any words to explain that her daughter had sexually molested me because I had never heard of that before. And did I even want to tell her what her daughter did to me? No, because then I would have to tell my parents, and I intuitively knew that Jesus and my father would believe I must have some part in the blame for this, and my mother would back them up. So, I needed to keep my mouth shut and *just forget about it*. I looked up at her mother, and all I said was, *I want to go home, please.* In the end, I was disappointed in myself for not telling someone what happened. However, it ended up being the right thing to do because, when I was older, my father announced that women who dress provocatively are asking to be raped. My intuition was correct, protecting me from further shame because I knew how he would have reacted if I had told him what happened to me. That also made me ashamed of my father.

My friend's mother said, *Alright, dear* and told her husband I was ready to go home. However, before we left, I managed to squeak some final words out, asking if my friend could come along for the ride. Everything inside me said I should protect myself, and if she was there, the chances of him doing something to me were less. I was the least important person in their house, and my mother would tell me to be strong. So, I was, and my friend's mother told her she could go with us. When I got out of the car, I enthusiastically said, *Thank you* as if I meant it. My mother always told me to be polite, no matter what, and they did give me snacks and supper after all. I thought it was the right thing to do, and yet it was like I was expressing gratitude for being raped. Her father told me to come back any time, and I replied, *Okay,* but once home, I swore on my bible that would never happen. When I went inside my house, I told my mother I felt sick to my stomach. It wasn't a lie because I thought I was going to throw up, and she sent me right to bed and tucked me in with a big bowl on my nightstand just in case. I assumed the fetal position under the wool blanket my mom brought back from Holland and cursed how it made me itch. However, I was comforted by its weight that night. I never told my mother about the girl who decided she could touch me without asking, and I never went to her house or spoke to her ever again.

Over time, I became more and more emotionally distanced from my family, and I know my mother felt me drifting away. She began using my hunger for attention to reel me in with compliments, constantly saying how much I was like her, assuming that was a good thing. This also served to lift her up as a sort of back-handed way to self-admire, *You're strong like me. You look just like me. You have lots of energy like me. You're skinny like me. You're so outgoing like me*—wait, what?! The

Escaping the Cycle of Shame

first three, yes, but that last on, no. I was the girl who spent endless hours lying in solitude under the sky. I was the kid who leaned heavily into a chain-link fence to avoid the bullies on the playground. I was the daughter who kept her mouth shut at the dinner table, fearing that my father and God would send me to hell for spilling my milk. However, as much as I wanted to say, *I am not like you*, I still had one foot on the never-ending roller coaster of making my mother happy. I was addicted to being accepted and continued thinking that's all that love encompassed. Going into grade nine, I was obsessively addicted to needing to belong and believed I was well on the way to going insane from debilitating shame.

V

Escaping the Cycle of Deceit

I sensed a foreboding inkling that my mother's verbal admiration for me was dysfunctional, and I was unable to welcome any good intention, sensing the likelihood of a hidden agenda. I experienced a genuine camaraderie in one moment, only to discover that something was amiss the next. Because I acquired heightened awareness about this misalignment, I became more confused by her complimentary behaviour. It was more challenging to distinguish between the pragmatism of something being either right or wrong and the complexity of something right combined with something wrong. I hadn't been programmed that way, so I didn't really know how to react to the mix of loyalty alongside betrayal.

She complicated things further by throwing in moments when she seemed to genuinely want to get close to me, and although I wanted that connection, I often repelled it. It wasn't because I was opposed to her kinship, but because I suspected an ulterior intention similar to the one that I witnessed between her sisters that accompanied the love they shared. It displayed a darker motivation, supporting a thirst for personal power. Looking back with the clarity of an adult, I realize I was not avoiding my mother's love, but rather the conditions that accompanied it; my soul knew something wasn't right, but my brain wasn't sharp enough to interpret what that was yet. Without that wisdom, I did what any innocent adolescent defaults to, defensively planning to take her power away. Ironically, I chose to do the same thing she was doing to me, and it all came down to control. I began taking advantage of her wanting to get close to me by using her need to feel loved in order to fill my void of the same. I skewed the truth and became a good liar to manipulate her. Unbeknownst to me, I was conforming to who I thought she had become.

I came to realize that my mother could also slant what was true, so she was good at detecting my deception a mile away. And she had no tolerance for me lying to her because she now had to manage me manipulating her. Catching me in an act of duplicity, she used the most effective way to deter me from doing it again by telling my father, who reprimanded me into isolation. I was outcasted to my room, which took away my power and created an alliance between my mother and father—the person I feared the most. I had long ago alienated being consoled by the stuffed animals and dolls on my bed and automatically moved to being devastated that I had lost. When this initially happened, I sat at my desk with my head in my hands, crying my heart out.

However, I was taught to move on from loss and regret. So, I watched my tears

Around The Table

pour down onto my desk blotter into a puddle of self-pity, slowly transitioning into single droplets plopping down until the last one made a final ripple in my pool of emotion. I understood that the duplicity I created was the opposite of what I was trying to achieve, and just as that final tear left my body, so did my remorse. Something took over, and I knew it was time to move on; a sort of resilience transpired from a combination of the guilt of being wrong and the awareness that I believed I was right. But what choice did I have while striving to belong to this herd of sheep? As a team, they passively labelled me the black one by further alienating me to the confines of my room. Should I just forget about it? *No*. Reaching for my pen, I simultaneously ripped the tear-stained piece of paper out of my notepad and threw it in the trash bin. Done—I could forget about that! I retreated inward and immersed myself in the comfort of reflection.

Fourteen years of patterning: infliction, abandonment, isolation, fear, sadness, survival, resilience, fortitude. Fuck them. Getting angry provided bits of enlightenment as I found solace in focusing on managing reality. I refused to dive into the depths of dysfunctional fantasy like she did. However, I did choose to be alone within the fantastical world of writing poetry. It was definitely used as an escape, but I could describe my emotions and thoughts through words and relish the awakenings that came with putting pen to paper. There didn't seem to be anything wrong with this, and yet, I kept it a secret—we were good at that. I wanted to share it because there was a nagging longing for the attention that I thought it and I deserved. However, I was conflicted with wanting to shield my sisters from any attention I believed I should get. I didn't want to be the special one because I knew how that affected them, but I simultaneously yearned for self-importance. There was that push-pull of arrogance versus humility that became an exhausting tug-of-war.

Truth

I want to tell you how I feel,
Yet when I'm near you, nothing's real.
Your speech flows by me like the wind,
Carrying softness, sadness through the sky.

You make me happy, sad, and not,
Because of you, my life is caught.
Reality just disappears,
And leaves me seeking fairy tales.

You will leave some time, I know,
But horoscopes will always grow.
Creating dreams for everyone,
What is real will not be told.

1974 ~ 14 years old

Escaping the Cycle of Deceit

I wrote this poem about the aura presented when I was with my mother. It's a poor piece of writing but reflects the bombardment of attention she created as a contrast between reality and fantasy. The latter brought light to the premonition that I was worthy of bountiful praise even more than my sisters were. I knew I got more than they did, and when I didn't, I subconsciously equated that to a deficit of love. This mindset gradually transpired over time and elevated to a game in itself because I ended up playing a passive-aggressive scheme to fulfill my psychological needs. To top it off, I had a deep knowing that this was the definition of control, but I could not articulate its impact on me or others and pushed it away in the recesses of my mind. I'm sure my sisters were impacted by my mother's over-compensation for my emotional demands, and although I was unaware at the time, there is regret within what was created between my siblings and me. To this day, I question how I managed to supersede their status in our familial lineage because it was against any hierarchy rule that I was taught.

My mother told me I was her favourite many times behind my sisters' backs. When I was young and naïve, I was unable to process the uncomfortableness that bubbled up in the pit of my stomach when she whispered her secret, *You are my favourite, you know.* I actually liked it because it fed my newfound diabolical motivation to control my mother, *Get her on your side and then pull the rug out from under her as she does to you.* I countered this evil side by never sharing what she said with my sisters; my mother may not have been lying about me being her favourite, but I kept it a secret because I knew how damaging those words would be for them. Unfortunately, the innocent girl in me didn't realize that actions speak louder than words, and I discovered much later that I wasn't the only one who fell prey to my and my mother's manipulative behaviour.

After that lonely year in grade eight and lying about being sick to get out of my graduation, I was shocked when my mother called the school to invite all the girls in my class to our house to celebrate it a week later. She kept this all hush, hush from me. Surprise!! What the fuck!! I was faced with the dilemma of bathing in the luxury of being the special one while being equally mortified because I didn't have any friends at that school. It was why I didn't want to go to graduation in the first place, but she didn't know that because I didn't tell her. So, the quandary became to sit in the shame of telling my mother the truth that none of those girls cared if I lived or died or bask in the false pride based on my deceit and her perception that I had friends. I knew every one of them would go anywhere for a place to party, so I chose the latter; pleasure over pain seemed like a no-brainer at the time. They all arrived on a Saturday night, and my mother ushered them down to our basement that we decorated together in streamers and balloons. I sat in the Queen's chair, wearing the long floral dress with capped sleeves she made after guiding me through picking the pattern she thought was suitable for a girl my age. I went with the one she liked to avoid an argument. It was easier, and we couldn't afford a new dress anyway.

Around The Table

The atmosphere of the evening was a replica of the grade eight schoolyard I had just endured and thought I had finally escaped. I sat in the security of my special chair and scanned the room featuring a variety of cliques. The segregation was as evident as the long nose on my face. I noticed the odd singleton standing with their back against one of four walls. They sipped their Coke, eyes simultaneously darting around, checking for any incoming insults they might need to deflect. I wondered why they bothered to come and put themselves through this torture. Perhaps they carried that same bit of hope I did, thinking it might be different outside the schoolyard. But it was not, and I felt their pain, understanding how having my fingers wrapped tightly around a cold glass of pop provides the courage needed to be unnoticed. In later years, that pop became a glass of wine, providing the same resilience required to escape the torment of alienation in the high school cafeteria. I empathized with them, yet even though I was in my basement, where I ranked above anyone else outside of my family, I defaulted to a coward who did not approach them, fearing I would create the illusion I was one of them. Instead, I used my Coke-induced confidence to get off my throne and chat with the popular girls, the mean girls, the athletic girls, and the academic girls who each claimed a corner of the room. I had the advantage of hosting the party, which motivated them to not necessarily be nice to me but not completely discount my existence; they knew their place within the hierarchy of my home. That night, I became one of the special ones, if only for a while. My lifelong aversion to having opulent parties bestowed upon me was birthed that day because I felt like a fraud.

It was like a re-make of Cinderella, except with an 11 o'clock pick-up. Most had a good time, and some, along with me, managed to make it through the night somewhat unscathed. And then I never heard from any of them again. I finally made it to my last summer before high school, and my parents announced that my paternal oma was scheduled to arrive for a visit. Opa had passed away the year before in 1972 from a blood clot that travelled to his heart. The same thing that made him miserable for years managed to kill him. This was my first experience with someone in my life dying, and I don't remember seeing anyone crying like they do in movies. I was not sad or overwhelmed with grief, and I did not pray to God to watch over Opa in heaven.

When I heard that Oma was coming, tiny tears of joy popped up in my little eyes, and I gave God a thumbs up. The whole family drove to Toronto to pick her up at the airport. Wearing seatbelts was not the law until 1976, which was in our favour as we could squeeze everyone into the gold Plymouth Valiant, taking turns on each other's laps. As we drove along with the windows partially open, that exquisite sense of *gezeligheid* entered the front of the car where Oma sat; it wafted to the back seats along with the outdoor breeze, weaving around each of us. I closed my eyes and welcomed her presence washing over me. Everyone was talking while answering Oma's questions about what we had been doing the past two years. And then, during a brief moment of silence, she turned to look out her window and said, *Het is zo duidelijk hoe massief en rond de wereld is als je het op deze manier ziet—It is so apparent how massive and round the world is when you see it this way.* Having lived all her life in a small country with very little wide-open space other than farmland, she was in awe of the expansiveness of land and sky. Still to this day, any time I wonder about how I would describe gratitude, I reflect on that moment. It has nothing to do with what was happening but everything to do with how Oma expressed her awe of the universe. I believe she was describing her God, and this made such an impact on me that I wrote how thankful I was to be alive in my diary before sleeping that night.

Oma stayed with us for a couple of weeks, and one day I was happily alone with her because everyone else was off to work. After lunch, I asked if she would like to sit in the backyard under our patio set's bright yellow umbrella. It was a gorgeous sunny summer day, so she enthusiastically agreed. Oma was just as heavy and waddled even more than when we lived with her just a few years before, so I grabbed her cane, and we headed for the back door. She used it with her left hand while I held her right elbow, supporting her to climb down the three steps to the back hall. Once we got to the screen door, I went outside to hold it open for her. As she began to take her first step through the door, it became awkward for me to hold the door and support her at the same time. As accidents tend to, her fall happened quickly when her legs suddenly buckled underneath her. I gasped in horror to see my oma suddenly lying on the cement slabs outside the door. I immediately jumped to her side. As soon as I sat beside her, I asked her if she was okay, and she started to giggle. Nothing was broken, so she asked me to push her up to a seated position, which I did. Once settled with her legs sprawled out wide in front of her, toes pointing up to the sky, she looked at my terrified expression and laughed hysterically. *Oh my God,* I thought, *If you truly exist, please help me get her up!!!*

We tried everything for over 30 minutes, but my 90-pound body did not have the strength to push or pull her large frame back up onto her feet. Every time we made a bit of headway, she rocked back down, and we found ourselves engulfed in another fit of laughter. So, there we sat, and I realized this was serious; Oma was 76, sitting on the ground in the peak of the mid-afternoon Ontario heat, and no one was due to arrive home from work for several hours. Selfishly, I thought about my consequence within this debacle. What would my father say? What fallout would ensue from this bright idea of mine? And more importantly, what was I going to do to fix this? We didn't have cell phones in 1973, and I wasn't allowed to phone my parents at work unless it was an emergency. I didn't even have a number for my father's work, which was good because calling him made me shutter. Was this an emergency? I thought it was. Should I call my mother? Probably. But before I went that route, I decided to try getting Oma up one more time. I stood in front of her and told her to be serious and really concentrate. She giggled again. I looked Oma in the eyes and said what I thought my mother would say, *Oma, sterk wessen!! Be strong!*

She got serious when I asked her to bend her knees, and when she did, her dress fell down around the top of her thighs, exposing her heavy-duty leather girdle, *Lord, thank you for inventing this device that will likely save her from breaking a hip!!* I placed my feet up against hers and leaned forward, reaching for her hands. *Niet lachin! Don't laugh*, I said to her. And she didn't. I have no idea where my strength came from, except that at that moment, I heard my mother's voice in my head, *You are strong like me*. I told Oma we were going to rock back and forth five times, and on the last rock forward, I would pull her as hard as I could. I asked her to place her feet up against mine and use her legs as leverage on each forward rock. How my body balanced the weight of my oma's is beyond me. But we pushed against each other, and at the count of five, both her and my arms shook like an earthquake, and she suddenly popped up in front of me as I fell backwards. I shook off the reverberating pain in my butt, and then we laughed until our sides hurt.

While Oma sat at the head of the dinner table under Jesus that night—my father automatically got moved beside Emily when Oma arrived—she told our story, sharing how brilliant I was at solving the problem. She told my parents I was courageous and smart. Basking in the glow of Oma's praise, I looked up at my parents, feeling like I had accomplished something extraordinary. My mother smiled and said, *Yes, she is!* My father peered over at me, smiled, and then asked Oma to pass the potatoes. I understood that as having possibly done something right.

I never saw Oma after that visit, but I heard about many of her future shenanigans. She had a sweet neighbour lady who lived beside her, and since Opa died, she checked in on Oma every day. One afternoon, Oma decided to get on a chair to clean the tall old windows in her living room, the ones I was running towards to look through when the horse was trotting by. The next day, her neighbour found her lying on the floor right in front of Opa's chair with a broken hip. When I heard this story, I thought about the significance of where she fell, but then let that go, not wanting to give Opa any more power than he had when he was alive. She remained there overnight and was taken to the hospital after being found. While Oma recovered, my mother arranged to have a telephone connected in her house in case she had an emergency like this again. She still didn't have a fridge or stove, so it was unlikely she was going to take kindly to this modern contraption of a landline being installed behind her back. And she didn't. The day after she arrived home from the hospital, her neighbour found the phone with its cord neatly wrapped around its base sitting outside Oma's front step. And that was that.

Over the next four years, Oma transitioned into the injustice of dementia. But she did so with the dignity and humour she naturally defaulted to in the past. When she turned 80, my parents went back to Holland to visit her. Her extended family organized a big birthday celebration dinner, and one of my relatives picked her up at the nursing home where she now lived and took her to the restaurant to join the rest of the family. Upon arrival, there was a big table for everyone to sit at. My grandmother was the guest of honour, placed at what was deemed the head of the table. Everyone else sat according to their relationship with their beloved matriarch. Each son sat on either side of her, and then their wives, along with their sons and daughters, following the protocol. Oma smiled and chatted throughout the meal, enjoying having her family together at one table. Then without any warning, she reached over to my father's plate, scooped up a spoonful of potatoes and began eating them. My father, who was on her right, simply smiled, and those sitting near her began to chuckle under their breath. Someone else sitting near her gently told her it wasn't appropriate to take food off someone else's plate. She turned to them and jovially said, *Als je gek ben, kan je alles doen! When you're crazy, you can do anything!* No one disputed her profound proclamation, but when I heard this story, I wondered if she really had dementia or if she was pretending to play one last trick on everyone. Oma passed away at the age of 92, and she used joy to bring a little more ease into her and others' lives right to the end.

More than ever, as an innocent young child, I wanted to create the same connection with my parents that I had with my grandmother. My mother used shame to punish me for anything she thought I did wrong, often moving to full-on hysterics about what I did or said and how they negatively affected her. Guilt was her tactic to stop me from creating a more significant upset than was already occurring. If she could end my drama, she could deter the escalation of involving my father at the same time. I believe my mother was protecting me from the consequences of his ill-temper by doing whatever she could to keep him out of issues that needed solving. Tears were an added exclamation mark if I dared to defend myself, and because I did have a connection to my mother, guilt ultimately reduced my drama. The only time she brought my father in for reinforcement was if I was adamant about my position and did not give up. To this day, if I share my feelings or ideas and they are misaligned with hers, she immediately moves to victim mode to end the conversation. My mother's unwillingness to welcome emotional discomfort within our relationship or listen to my side became a considerable roadblock. Her refusal and, ultimately, my resistance to being vulnerable naturally transitioned into a lifelong pattern of emotional detachment.

When my mother needed my father to intercede, his style of punishment was utterly void of emotion and definitely accomplished what they both wanted—for me to stop talking. His method reflected his inability to express empathy as he immediately dismissed me to shut me up. If I did something he disapproved of, I was automatically and abruptly told I was wrong and to be quiet, and then I was sent to my room. Ironically, although his approach was traumatic, it ultimately supported me because being sent into isolation gave birth to the beginning of self-discovery I was meant to experience. It was complicated, arduous, and painful, but it evolved into a 50-year necessary process of understanding and accepting myself. Even though I lost faith in the possibility of an emotional bond with my father, I continued to crave the fantasy of it. Not surprisingly, this never came to fruition. I tediously tried sharing my emotions both outside of and within disputes, but it was never welcomed. His lack of respect to listen to me became a barrier between us as detrimental as the one I had with my mother. His inability to naturally communicate with me in a meaningful way and my incomprehension of that transitioned into meaningless disconnection.

I was a strange duck, well ahead of others my age when it came to being aware of uncomfortable internal sensations that arose from external sources. I know that I am no different from anyone else when it comes to feeling all that moves through me. But I was highly sensitive and well aware of that, having been told this over and over again. And although I was encouraged to squash my sensitivity, I could not ignore the goodness that was sparked along with it. I was a truthsayer from as far back as I can remember, the one who paid attention to her gut without understanding the inner conflict of being misunderstood. So, I used solitude to uncover more layers of that truth when I was shunned to my room for sharing who I was.

The summer before high school, I discovered the security of insightful private writings. I kept my diary under lock and key, hidden in my top underwear drawer, along with anything else I wanted to keep a secret. I still had a child's bedroom and asked my mother for an updated room with new furniture. I actually begged her for it, and she agreed. We painted the walls purple, added a matching bedspread, and she bought me the purple and red psychedelic lamp I wanted. It hung from the ceiling in the corner, shining a light on a brand-new white desk that matched a dresser and bedside table. That desk meant everything to me—much more than the privilege to paint my room purple. I knew my mother had to persuade my father with every ounce of her being to get him to agree to this re-decorating extravaganza, and I thanked her and gave her a hug.

I still see myself sitting at that desk under the window, writing long after my mother asked me to turn off my new hippy lamp. Memories like this remind me why I continued to credit my mother with keeping us connected with just a thread of trust through the next decade. For a time, I carried eternal hope that someday we would reach a balance of repair and disrepair. There were times when things got better, when we both did better, and awakenings were stimulated—healing was attempted. However, some of the damage could not be mended unless we both agreed to participate in the extent of rehabilitation required. Being supported and stitched up is a beautiful experience and meant to be savoured, but when thread gets old and tattered, the sustainability to hold everyone together detaches from the eye of the needle; the worn weave becomes disconnected and falls apart. My mother was right to instill strength in me because no matter the quality of thread, resilience was the only thing that seemed to keep my rope tethered and tight. Even when damaged and repaired over and over again.

My parents chose to send me to an old high school rather than the newly built one I was looking forward to. It was the first open-concept school in our city, and my parents believed I wouldn't be able to cope with the freedom it provided. They were probably right since it was super progressive with no walls or doors in the classrooms, just dividers between each. My parents thought it was a ridiculous concept that advocated too much freedom, and they sent me to the school my sisters attended. It turned out to be quite an experience for me, both positive and negative. Because it was a public school, there was no religion class and no mention of God. I spent the first year in hiding, utilizing my talent of being unheard as a means to be unseen. Balancing being alone and feeling lonely within this new environment was something my soul innately knew how to survive. To avoid falling into the devastation of anxiety, I applied my rehearsed system of managing the duality of being an introvert in an extroverted world. Years of my mother's modelling emotional fortitude came in very handy.

My hope that grade nine would be different from every past school year was squashed the very moment I walked through the front doors. I tried desperately to fit in and, once again, went the route of attempting to fit in by dressing like the popular girls. Seeing Brooke Shields promoting Jordache Jeans on a TV commercial and in magazines, I decided they were the solution to conquering my social alienation. I asked my mother to buy me a pair, but she was still scarred from the boot episode and told me that I should get a job if I wanted 90-dollar jeans—fair enough. I was intrigued by the possible confidence I believed those jeans would provide me, so I began my first job search. I was only 14, with legal working age being 16. However, I discovered that the local library could hire me if I didn't handle the cash register. So, I got a job straightening books after school and walked about two kilometres from the high school to the library three days a week, with my shift starting at four. One of my sisters or parents picked me up at seven to drive me home. I was paid one dollar and seventy-five cents an hour, so I calculated I could buy my Jordache Jeans after about 18 weeks, along with some smaller purchases along the way. People may have noticed my jeans, but my social ostracism remained unchanged.

Unfortunately, I was addicted. I stopped asking my mother to buy me things and substituted human interaction with my self-funded shopping sprees. I was making money, and it didn't take me long to be drawn into the influence of fashion marketing; I had the buying bug. At around 16, I quit the library and got a job at the local K-mart in the shoe department to earn more per hour. I was now in grade ten and made friends with one of the popular girls who worked there and went to the same school I did. We soon became inseparable, and our K-mart manager called us Buck and Dip—I have no idea why. I began spending time with her crowd at school, which included a variety of popular students from stoners to athletes and any other socially approved individual in between. She became my *Oma buffer*, creating a soft landing for me to make friends: kind of like a salesperson's warm call versus a cold one. I stopped counting peas and carrots, yet there was still a deep void in my life.

Around The Table

One day after school, I stood amidst the crowd of students waiting for the school bus, and I experienced a feeling of desperation, realizing how alone I was even with the comfort of my best friend by my side every day. Since I was more creative than athletic, I spent a lot of time smoking weed with my newfound crowd and hung out by myself in the art room during lunch. Being alone was still a significant part of my M.O. I was an introvert by nature, and my father reinforced that because he praised me as a good girl when I was quiet. At school, the art room became my substitute for the solace of my bedroom at home and my willow tree before that; it was my safe place where I could be me, even if that included agonizing times of loneliness. But at one point, desperate to experience more of the camaraderie my friends had, I decided I would be an extrovert. I witnessed their bond, and my motivation became to share the same connection they did. This was a pivotal time in my life because I decided to betray my authentic self in exchange for fabricated acceptance through developed extroversion. I believed I had to change everything about myself to be granted this longed-for gift. It's incredible how 16 years of conditioning influenced my lack of worthiness. I now know that a sense of self, whether positive or negative, comes from perception, and perception is only validated if believed.

The warrior in me chose to de-value being alone and extinguish my incessant loneliness. I decided to adapt my image to find human connection within an extroverted world. Unfortunately, I believed whole-heartedly that I had to abandon the gift of writing in seclusion, where my soul thrived in order to establish relationships with others. During this attempt, I became suddenly aware that this group of friends didn't welcome me into their group because they chose to, but rather as a condition of being half of the Buck and Dip show; I was the sidekick, and Buck was the star.

I wanted to be the star even though I knew she deserved that accolade because she was intelligent, funny, and naturally drew everyone in around her. I would have to work much harder than she did, but I wanted it, so I became super creative in my efforts to be recognized for being as unique as she was. One day after being told a hundred times before how much I looked like Barbra Streisand, it came to me. I loved her, so I decided to emulate her, deciding it would be easier to be someone else rather than work with the insignificant being I was. The fact that I resembled this woman and she looked different from any other famous person considered beautiful, talented, and had superstar status was fascinating. I envisioned myself as her, transforming my inadequacies into her assets. I had a similar likeness of her through facial features, and I permed my hair to resemble her 1976 Star is Born persona.

I imitated her so much with the goal to be popular that I even stood on the bench in the change room after gym, singing her songs to my classmates. They clapped and praised me. I was living a double life, which provided me with the ability to function socially. However, I found myself immersed in a dysfunctional pattern of achieving self-confidence by pretending to be someone else. Mastering being a chameleon got me what I wanted while gaining the attention and shallow approval of others. It took me a long time to realize this triggered a continual spiral of becoming fully immersed in a story of deception. As much as I wanted to genuinely embrace my uniqueness without trying to be like someone else, I just didn't know how. So, I continued with my façade, became stoic like my mother, and concluded that I needed to transform my distinct physical characteristics and use them to my advantage—like Barbra did. The very aspects that caused my lack of self-confidence in the past provided me with strength; my squinty eyes, long nose, and big mouth all suddenly became my allies. I was so starved for the loving energy that comes from meaningful relationships that I did what I needed to get someone to embrace my unique way of being—albeit fake. I was tired of being that unseen little girl alone in the art room instead of being surrounded by many in the cafeteria.

At the time, pretending to be someone else provided me with the safety of superficiality. It was later, entering adulthood, when it became a chaotic whisper in my over-thinking mind; I was not good enough unless I was someone else. My perception of reality became distorted, and more confusion set in. I experienced several failed relationships with guys who cheated on me, who I allowed to take advantage of my people-pleasing nature while seeking their approval—patriarchy continued to prevail. I was sad and incredibly disillusioned about who I had become, where I was headed, and what love entailed within an intimate relationship.

Along with the heartache of several breakups, the question resurfaced about what love is. I eventually concluded there was nothing about me that anyone, including myself, could love because none of me was real. Realizing that I allowed my need for approval to affect every decision I made and how I showed up in the world was an epiphany that came much later. But until then, having no idea what I believed to be my truth became my eventual trauma. It stuck to me like glue well beyond my 40s when I finally dedicated my life to discovering who I am from deep within my essence. I decided to re-discover who that little girl was who experienced joy with her oma and believed in God for a fleeting moment under a tree so long ago.

I was 16 when I stopped going to church for what I thought would be the last time. Leaving mass with my family that day, the priest approached me and asked when I would be attending confession next. I told him I didn't believe in baring my soul to him but shared my sins with God at home before I went to sleep. He told me I could not call myself a Catholic if I did not go to confession regularly. I did not respond immediately but instead looked down at the gaudy marble church floor, taking a moment to calm my mind besieged with thoughts, *I have given you 16 years of Sundays, listening to your sermons, and trusting your guidance, only for you to tell me it's not enough?!*

Suddenly, I saw my father's face staring back at me above the priest's white

Around The Table

collar. It was him, not Him, I was speaking to as I faced the unnegotiable control that I had spent 16 years terrified of. With each passing year, I had become more and more aware that conditional love was not limited to the four walls of my family home. My fear of my father was interchangeable with God, and now this priest stood towering before me—they had all become an extension of each other—an intricate triple threat of intimidation that was far too much for any teenager to process. Every day, my father followed me through the hierarchy of God, and God followed me through the patriarchy of my father with every step I took. On Sundays, the priest became the conduit for each of their roles in my life, reiterating the power of patriarchy.

Standing there that day with the priest representing all three, I knew I would never be free of their hypocritical binding shackles that only ever reiterated my unworthiness. From deep within me, there arose a profound realization that only I could end this madness. So, I slowly lifted my eyes from the black and white marbled swirls on the floor and followed the path of intricate gold embroidery on the silk sashes that lay perfectly flat against the priest's pretentious robe. I looked into the priest's eyes and suddenly found myself speaking to the foreboding trilogy. Then, with the firm voice of any man I ever met, I announced, *Then I am not a Catholic.*

My body began to tremble when I saw the jowls on the trio of bobbleheads start to shake, and their mouths dropped in shock. I had taken the priest, God, and my father off guard, and it instantly occurred to me that they would team up and come at me with a rebuttal within seconds. I knew they would be quick on the draw, and although I had experienced debating one-on-one with my father, I was not equipped to simultaneously take on all three heads of state. So, before they composed themselves, I straightened my back, pivoted around, and walked out of the intricately carved doors. If I had to estimate, I would say this all took two-point-five seconds, with an adrenaline rush like no other I had experienced. Fear motivated me to do what was right for me that day.

Those monumental church doors were opened wide to the massive concrete stairs at the front of the building. This was where the head of this household gathered to bid farewell until the following Sunday when his flock congregated to practice their rituals once again. I walked right by them all, including my family, and headed directly to our car. My mother called after me, *Diana, is everything alright?* Without looking back, I replied, *Ask him,* using my thumb to point to the priest who represented the patriarchy I was terrified of from the first day I noticed the crucifix above the door while sitting around the table at the age of five. It became clear that the blood on His hands that connected religion to authority to the fear of spilling my milk was not imagined.

Although out of breath, I felt safe, standing in the shade under a tree in front of our car. I smiled briefly, noticing it was a weeping willow, *What are the chances of that?* I didn't see it when we parked the car, but now, it was blowing in the wind

Escaping the Cycle of Deceit

as if begging for attention. Looking back at the church, I thanked God one last time that I would never have to return to the opulence of His house and what it represented.

This was the first time I blatantly defied my parents in a way that went against their religious beliefs, particularly my mother's. I'm not really sure my father cared if he went to church or not. Most Sundays, he fell asleep during the sermon, and my mother had to elbow him to wake up. He always told her that he was just resting his eyes. When I was very young, I thought it was funny. Then, as a pre-teen, I found it embarrassing. Finally, as a teenager, I found it downright self-righteous that he thought it was okay to sleep in the house of the Lord. It was like he forgot his place in the line-up. But maybe, he actually thought he was above his maker; I don't think my father feared God the way I did because he didn't grow up with Him, and he also had the added benefit of his positioning as a man.

Surprisingly, my mother told me I didn't have to go to church after my altercation with the priest. I didn't understand why she took it so lightly, but it gave me the confidence to push a few more envelopes a little further. Having lunch with my mother 45 years later, I told her I didn't believe in religion or the God I grew up with. Without hesitating, she told me she didn't either anymore. She had just turned 90. *Wow*, I thought, *maybe it does take a life-time to figure some shit out.*

I moved beyond fearing only adult males on the high end of the patriarchy spectrum to realizing that even boys my age scared the shit out of me—more than even God had, or my father still did. However, my want to belong motivated me to seek a relationship with a boy. I longed to fulfill the fantasy of being with someone who adored me. I had enhanced my looks with makeup, changed my hair, and wore all the latest trends, and of course, I had all the same sexual urges as any other teenager. One day, while walking to the back stockroom during my shift at K-mart, one of the new stock-boys walked by and took the time to nod his head and smile. I felt a flutter and irrationally thought this must be what the beginning of true love feels like. He was a popular boy, so I had to work at shutting down the chatter in my head, telling me that a good-looking guy couldn't possibly be interested in an ugly, shy girl like me. I wanted so much for someone like that to pay attention to me, knowing for sure the validation would be extraordinary. So, the next time he walked by and actually spoke to me, saying, *Hi*, I dug deep and looked directly into his eyes. I said hello in return, and he smiled at me and walked on. *Yes!! I did it.*

Over time, we talked a lot and became Kmart friends. He was so funny and made me laugh. I found out later that he was high most of the time, but I didn't care because he paid attention to me, and in my mind, that was an extension of love. I wasn't an idiot, knowing that love was measured on a sliding scale with friendship at the bottom and lovers at the top, and there were many other stages in between. I quickly figured out and chose to be grateful for where I ended up on that scale, somewhere in the muck of ambiguity. To compensate for where I landed, I began imagining what it would be like if he were my boyfriend, dreaming up incredible adventures with him. Before I knew it, I found myself at my family's dinner table, sharing made-up stories of us, moving through hilarious escapades together. In real life, he was a country boy with an easy-going twang when he spoke, so when I narrated his parts of the story, I exaggerated his drawl; my father laughed every time. Night after night, I shared and entertained my father. Oma wasn't wrong when she taught me that humour was the key to connecting ever so slightly to my dad, and I became obsessed with his laughter—belonging. As a result, I told a story around the table every evening until I realized that my relationship with this boy was nothing more than an imaginary series of dead-end fairy tales.

However, I did discover that sharing a story provided a gateway to connecting with others, and I used it more and more with every piece of positive feedback I received. I began telling stories to my friends, sisters, aunts, uncles, and anyone else who would listen. Whether true or made up, my stories became my shock-absorber for developing the confidence I needed to live in a world where extroverts were valued, and introverts were not—I found another substitute for peas and carrots. As my self-confidence grew, I became more comfortable in crowds and more of a party girl who was up for almost anything. That same year in grade 11, one of the guys in my group of friends asked me to go out with him; extroversion proved to be successful, even if it was coated with deceit. He was okay, nothing out of the ordinary or an athlete, but popular as one of the stoners. I said yes because someone actually asked me out. Of course, I settled because I was thrilled that I was even considered worthy enough to be asked.

He asked me to go steady after a few weeks going with him to the parties that I would have gone to with our friends anyway. I wondered if anything would change, and I found out one day when he and I went to his house alone during our lunch break from school. His parents were both at work, and when we got there, he put on the fireplace in the living room, laid down a blanket, and got some food out for a picnic. I found it all very romantic, and we began kissing once we finished eating. He pulled out a condom as if he had done it a million times before, and it didn't take me long to figure out where this was heading. I went along, ready to finally experience the intimate part of love I had been waiting for, and … well, the adoration I was supposed to receive with said love. It was over in all of five minutes and was nothing like I had anticipated, nothing like in the movies, nothing like in the books I had read. It was nothing at all. And as much as I knew he went to a lot of trouble to make it something, in the end, it was far from anything.

But I never said that. I told him that he was amazing. He didn't tell me I was and looked as pleased as punch. It was my first time, and I was sore and embarrassed that I got blood all over the blanket. He told me not to worry about it; he would take care of it. I pretended I was fine; I should be happy someone wanted me enough to go to the trouble he did. We had sex, so I was sure we were in it for the long haul and went to my doctor to get birth control. I didn't want to be the girl who got pregnant in the middle of grade 11. I hid them in my underwear drawer

Escaping the Cycle of Deceit

along with my diary, knowing my father would not laugh at this story at family dinner. I took one pill faithfully every morning. And then, months later, I arrived home from school to my father standing at the top of the hall stairs. My mother was behind him, crying at the kitchen table. I thought someone had died, so I was ready to console them after asking what was wrong.

But instead, my father held the long, plastic, pink birth control package up in the air, and I watched his face shift from stern to scary. It was that same demonstrative expression he had just before slapping my sister's face years ago; what was it with our family's obsession with halls and freaking out? For a moment, I thought maybe he needed to trap people in the foyer to enhance his authority. I stepped back but couldn't go anywhere other than out the door. Holding one end of the package between his fingers and thumb, he waved it back and forth and told me my mother found this in my dresser drawer. I looked at him and wondered if that was a question…should I say something like, *Yes, sir?* Or was it an accusation? Yes, it was, so I should say, *I'm sorry,* or *I thought I was doing the right thing?* Nothing seemed appropriate, and everything I thought of saying screamed back, *If you say that, he might slap you!!* I decided to be a good girl and not speak, *Just forget about it, allow him to be right, and it will all be okay.*

I knew that I was not about to be praised for being responsible, which was why I hid them in the first place. However, I knew this had everything to do with losing my virginity when my mother wailed dramatically in the background, *My little girl had sex!* I looked past my father to my mother and in that instant, I hated her for going in my drawer, finding the pills, and especially going to my father with them. She had secrets with so many people, but she couldn't keep this between her and me. And why was she carrying on and making it worse right now?! The distrust I had for her and had been fighting for years suddenly peaked and transitioned into immense disdain. I looked back at my father as he threw the pills at me, called me a slut, and walked down the hall towards the master bedroom. Boom!! Default—shame. Standing there in the middle of the hall, I was initially relieved that I didn't get a hand across my face like my sister, and I briefly contemplated what she had said back then that was worse than taking birth control.

Then my mother broke the silence by standing up. She had stopped wailing and was composed now that my father had completed his tantrum and disappeared. I was sure I was going to get an earful about how I had ruined her day, but instead, she walked up to me and quietly told me not to worry, *Dad will calm down by supper time.* Okay, that was good to know, nice chat. I looked down at my birth control package teetering awkwardly on one of the stairs and leaned over to pick it up because I needed them. My mother went to the sink and started cleaning potatoes. I walked to my room, putting the pills back in my underwear drawer. No one talked to me about them again.

By spring break, my boyfriend dumped me for one of the popular girls as quickly and easily as he took away my virginity. And before the end of the school year, she threw him to the curb to date someone else who was more popular than him. He came back in a drunken state one night, driving his old Buick up on our lawn and yelled at the top of his lungs how much he loved and needed me. My father was livid, and my mother begged me to go out and tell him to leave, *He's upsetting your father.* I had no problem telling him to piss off. He sped off, and I saw him the next day at school with the rest of our gang out in the smoking area like nothing ever happened. I guess he was brought up with the same *forget about it* rulebook.

My mother had transitioned from Woolco to working at Ziggy's, the delicatessen section of Loblaws. All the women had to wear the most horrible outfits and looked like they had jumped out of the Hansel and Gretel fairy tale, with their short plaid skirts, puffy-sleeved white blouses, and aprons to match. The men got to wear regular pants and shirts—interesting. Every morning, my mother got up, showered, and put on her little Edelweiss outfit before driving to work. She was in charge of the cheese cooler, ensuring that all the varieties were cut up in different sizes for customers to grab and throw into their shopping carts. She was very proud to have a job where she could use the skills she learned while working in the deli in Holland many years ago. If my mother is anything, she is one of the hardest workers I know. She was passionate about doing the best job possible, and she went out of her way to make every customer happy. I know that she took that position, sexist outfit, and all, because it was an opportunity to make more money and benefits than she received at Woolco. This, in turn, supported our family. I cannot think of any other reason for anyone to subject themself to the humiliation of wearing that getup day in and day out. I don't think I would have done it.

I've also never understood the allure of a negligee, the skimpiness of it, and the price tag that goes along with it. My mother had at least one that I know of, and she had it on the day she was suddenly inflicted with a gallbladder attack. My father was working the day shift, and I don't know where my sisters were, but it was just my mother and me at home. She didn't get up that morning and told me she wasn't feeling well. After several hours, she called me into her room, where I witnessed her writhing in pain. She begged me to call our GP, so I ran to the kitchen and called his office and explained her symptoms to the receptionist: intense pain in her abdomen, vomiting, high fever. Terrified, I told her that my mother could not get up to come in, and I was afraid she was going to die. I was so upset that the receptionist convinced the doctor to make a house call.

I ran back to my mother's bedroom and immediately went to her dresser to retrieve her flannel pyjamas. She was groaning from the pain but stopped to ask me what I was doing. I told her, *The doctor is coming, so I'm going to help you change into your pyjamas, Mom.* I was in full get ur done mode, wanting to help my mother; I would be her hero. But, as soon as I got to her bedside with the pyjamas in my hand, she locked eyes with me and with lips pursed, she asked, *Why are you making me feel bad for what I am wearing? I am not changing!* Whoa! I was so taken aback and filled with shame for making my mother feel equally ashamed by assuming she would want to take off her see-through negligee. Without saying anything, I stepped back and put the flannels back in where I found them and walked out of the room. She called out to me, *Where are you going?* But I kept going and sat on the stairs in the front hall, crying and waiting for the doctor. My tears reflected my frustration, wanting desperately to do the right thing by taking care of her but never seeming to be able to. She had her negligee on through his examination, and he determined she had a gallstone and needed her gallbladder removed. I heard her giggling with him, and I wondered how she managed to muster that up through her suffering. I thought my mother hated me that day.

But she never talked about it again, let alone apologized for how she spoke to me. She had her gallbladder removed, and everyone treated her like a queen through her recovery. And then, one day not long after she got back on her feet, she discovered that a well-established local Dutch delicatessen was for sale. Growing up, my sisters and I frequented this deli every Friday evening before doing our groceries with my mother. Each of us received a dime, and we could pick anything we wanted. Holland is known for its black licorice, both salty and sweet, and because I love savoury, I always chose my favourite—two large, black, salted diamonds at a nickel apiece. If I licked it for a while first, it lasted a lot longer than the smaller pieces, so I thought I was smart. Originally, it was a small store tucked in the corner of one of our town malls and was owned by a Dutchman. He later relocated the store to a larger space in the same mall. He had immigrated from Holland with his wife, and he did well and was well-liked as a business owner and entrepreneur. Like many Dutch people, he and his wife were members of the Christian Reform Church, and they had a few cute little blonde-haired kids. He was always very friendly when we went into the store, but I didn't think much of him when I found out he cheated on his wife with one of his employees. I remember being shocked that he gave up his perfect little family to be with someone much younger; I found it quite creepy, actually. Maybe the Christian Reform God was more lenient when it came to adultery.

This would become my mother's store, with my father working there on his days off. After returning home from a year attending a college in Toronto, my middle sister became the full-time manager. My mother told me she was homesick, *She's not outgoing like you and me.* She offered me a part-time job there after school and on weekends, so I quit my job at Kmart and went to work for my mother. By now, my eldest sister was married and worked as a medical secretary. I found it exciting that my mother took on this endeavour, owning and running a store loaded from ceiling to floor with all things Dutch. It seemed like the perfect fit given her past experience working in a deli in Holland as a young woman. I was thrilled I could work amidst the ambiance of my heritage with Dutch music playing all day long. I also got to speak Dutch quite often because, like my parents, the customers were immigrants from Holland for the most part. As a result, I experienced that feeling of *gezeligheid* I remembered from so long ago, and that was what I enjoyed the most working there. I was also surrounded by all the food I grew up with lined up on the shelves and stocked up in the coolers. The store was very popular because our city had a large Dutch and German community, and they too felt connected to the culture of their homeland when visiting the store.

But things weren't always rosy on the deli front. We sliced a lot of meat and cheese, and at Christmas time, we worked 10 to 12 hours a day with very little time to rest. My sister and I often didn't get a break during this busy season because we were the daughters, and my mother could get away with bending the labour laws with us. We would grab something quickly behind the counter to eat or drink on the run, but it was never a restful 15-minute break like the other staff were told to take. Work became an addiction from the day I was taken under my mother's wing at the store, *You're a hard worker like me!!* Crazily, I experienced a sense of camaraderie with her when she made a statement like that. I wanted to please her, so I became the hard worker she wanted me to be. Along with being a workaholic, perfectionism became a scary struggle that haunts me to this day. The two go hand-in-hand, and as much as I enjoy my work, striving to maintain the highest standard in everything I do can be torturous and self-destructive. As one of my dearest friends tells me, *You are such a Virgo, darling!!*

My mother was indeed the epitome of hard work and perfectionism, and as a result, she was super tough on her employees. I was often embarrassed by how she spoke to them with condescending questions and comments like, *Why did you do it that way? It must have been busy last night for the cooler to be so empty. Do you not see a customer up there?* There were many times when she walked right up to a customer and took over from the employee already serving them. Without saying anything, they received the message loud and clear that they were not doing it right. Later, she took them aside to tell them everything they had done wrong and nothing about what they did right.

My mother got so frustrated with her employees that she often huffed around as if she was the only one who could meet her own expectations. Except for the few who somehow managed to take the abuse, including my mother's right-hand person who did a lot of the cooking, the employees left as fast as they came. I recently chatted with a friend who briefly worked for my mother, and I asked her what she experienced. She answered with only two words, *Shear fear.*

Along with the pressure of the fast-paced, physical work, most did not take kindly to being shamed in front of the rest of fellow staff members or customers. For the most part, my sister and I were definitely spoken to more kindly, which was obvious and uncomfortable for me. My mother still expected certain standards, but she was definitely much more patient with us for the most part. Around this time, I realized I did not want to be the special daughter who was treated differently. I began shifting how I responded to her by not taking advantage of my situation, and I was mindful of doing the same that the others were asked to do.

Escaping the Cycle of Deceit

I also compensated for how they were treated when my mother went home while working with them in the evening; I provided a less strict, fun environment. We always got everything done without feeling as stressed about it. I figured we could enjoy our shift together as long as we got the work done.

One Christmas Eve Day, my mother took her demand of customer service to an all-time ridiculous abusive high. We had a line-up out the door, and my mother was on one slicer, and I was on the other. Side-by-side, we sliced at a fast, rhythmic pace: pounds and pounds of salami, ham, and turkey, as well as gouda, edam, and Jarlsberg cheese. Hours went by, and I suddenly felt the tampon I had put in at the beginning of my shift drop down, along with a swoosh of blood. I knew this meant it was beyond full and needed to be replaced. I thought it was a no-brainer, so I side-stepped over to my mom and told her that my tampon was full; I needed to go to the bathroom. Without missing a slice, she first looked back at the line-up behind us and then bent her knees as if analyzing the height of the glass in the cooler. Then, she turned to see where my pelvis landed in relation to it. To my surprise, she continued slicing and told me to carry on with my customer. She whispered, *No one can see your pants through the cooler, so you can wait until all the customers have been served.*

Remarkably, I did what she said without question, turning around and going back to my slicer to finish my customer's order and then take the next one, and the next one, and the next one… I waited until the line died down and went to the washroom. My underwear and pants were soaked through, and I had no extras to change into. Luckily, my pants were black, so nothing showed through. My mother never asked me if I was okay, and I finished my shift in my bloody pants, washing them when I went home hours later. I have often wondered how low my self-esteem must have been for me to let her do that to me.

My mother also basked in the glow of a good sale and encouraged whatever it took for me to achieve the same. This included serving and striking up conversations with the older couples, especially the husbands. Many of them were dirty old men who got off on a young girl who paid a little more attention to them than their wives did. My mother bragged about how I could get them to buy another half-pound of ham if I flirted with them, *You're just like me; you can sell anyone anything!!* I actually agreed with her because I was a good salesperson. It's incredible in a demeaning way just how programmed I was to use promiscuity to get what I wanted and to please my mother. If I happened to be working the snack bar at the front of the store and any elderly Dutch couple came in, she would run up to me and tell me to go to the meat counter to serve them. *He likes you,* she would say. That was my cue to be a little tease and make the husband feel special. She continued to put me up on a pedestal while using me to achieve a better sales total at the end of the day. I let these men say anything they wanted, and it was almost always inappropriate. I laughed and chatted away but always read the room and drew the line when their wives looked displeased, responding to my banter. Nine times out of ten, the men

Around The Table

conceded to buying the extra meat I suggested. My mother was right—it worked. At the time, I thought this was all normal, and I was oblivious to how she used my naivety to her advantage. I actually felt good about it all—useful, valued, loved.

When my father came in on his day off from the plant, he did the bookkeeping and sat upstairs in the office overlooking the store through a wide window opening with no glass. He was semi-hidden behind a Dutch white lace curtain similar to what my oma had hanging on her bedroom windows. I know he saw everything that happened below on the floor because he often hollered rudely at the girls to go to the cash or the meat cooler if a customer was waiting for more than a moment. He interrupted their conversations if he disagreed with what they said when serving someone. If he happened to stop by right after working a night shift without going home to sleep first, he was even more blunt; his lack of sleep the night before dictated the degree of his verbal agitation. He never once came down to tell me I didn't have to subject myself to the demeaning banter I engaged in. It never occurred to me to ask a customer not to speak to me like I was a sex object because I encouraged them to do so, and my mother congratulated me with every extra sale I made—I felt special. When I look back at myself as a young woman prostituting myself for the sake of earning an extra five dollars for my parents, I am disgusted with my promiscuous behaviour. I cannot imagine using my child's need for belonging to my advantage and their emotional detriment.

Being used and thrown away like a piece of trash aligned with a required function of the misogynistic algorithm I fit into. Men created the rules, and I followed them like a little puppy, motivated by the treat in their hand. Rewards included glancing my way, smiling at me, buying me a drink, touching my hand, asking me out, and eventually, granting me the big prize of sleeping with me. I discovered it wasn't as difficult as I thought because I was good at pushing the pain of degradation aside. After being cast aside in grade 11 by the guy who fucked me once and pitched me aside, I waited for the next one who might deem me worthy of more than one. I thought he might be the one who arrived just before the end of grade 13. He didn't go to the school I did and, in fact, had already graduated and lived in another part of town. I met him through a sister of one of my girlfriends and was told he was a little wild. But I was attracted to that side of him, thinking I must be quite something for someone like him to notice me. He was intelligent and liked to drink, dance, and have sex. Unfortunately, he was also manipulative and didn't use his brains for anyone's greater good, including his own. He got into fights when he drank, was the best dancer in the room until he couldn't stand up, and he was not a bad lover until he passed out in the middle of it. At this point, I had left home and lived in an apartment downtown with my sister and had abandoned my dream of going to university to be engaged to him. I got a job at Bell Canada as a long-distance operator to support myself. I was adulting and being a good woman.

His mother was quite something, and, although mine was too, they were the exact opposite of each other. I was intrigued by his mother's laissez-faire attitude, letting her children make their own choices and living with any consequences as a result. It didn't mean she didn't care about them, but for the most part, she stayed out of their business. It also didn't mean she kept her point of view to herself; the exact opposite, actually, as she discussed each of her children and their situations with their siblings. Although she and I were also very different, we established a mutual respect for one another, and I believed her husband liked me as well. He was a hard-working man and was always kind towards me. They both welcomed me into their home any time of the day or night. She didn't work outside of the house, so she was usually there when I came to visit her son. Unfortunately, she was often drunk before dinner because she drank...a lot.

I remember arriving late one afternoon for my first Christmas dinner at their home, and she was already three sheets to the wind. For the most part, she was a happy drunk, and I could tell she was pleased her family was all there. I took a seat and a glass of wine. I didn't question that no one was setting the table because they had a small home with a kitchen but no dining room, and any time I ate there, it was very informal with all five kids, their spouses, and children grabbing a plate and sitting in the living room. I loved this relaxed approach to mealtime because it seemed to focus less on doing things a certain way, with no expectation to sit anywhere in particular; there was much less pressure to do things right. I often noted that everyone said exactly what they thought, and in between uncomfortable disagreements, there were a lot of lighthearted moments and laughter. Opinions were part of the process to support decision-making, but everyone's solution was theirs to make without criticism.

On this particular day, after a couple of hours of socializing in the living room, it occurred to me that it was getting close to dinner time. There was no familiar smell of a turkey roasting that I was used to at my house, so I wondered what dinner would be. My boyfriend's mother was slouched in the corner of the sofa with a glass of rye in one hand and a cigarette in the other. I was curious how long it would take for someone to notice the two-inch end of ash that grew more with every second she sloppily held it between her fingers. It was everything I could do not to jump up and place an ashtray underneath her hand, but something told me that would not be welcomed. So instead, I asked her if there was anything I could do to help with dinner. She looked over at me, smiled, and told me not to worry, *Everything is under control.* I turned to one of the sisters who then looked at the others; it was like we all suddenly realized that Christmas dinner might not have been started. One of them jumped up and went to the kitchen, where she found the raw turkey sitting in the sink. To my surprise, no one got upset when she came back out and told us we were having Chinese food for dinner. No one ever mentioned the uncooked turkey again. This was their normal, and although very different from mine, I liked it because it didn't include any drama and a whole lot of grace. No matter how much someone messed up, they were forgiven, and a memory was created to share many years later.

Around The Table

Sometimes, under the influence, this matriarch had no filter for saying what was on her mind. I remember her sitting in her usual spot on the sofa after a few too many one day. She suddenly turned and looked me square in the eye, smiled, and, in her heavily slurred tongue, told me, *You can be replaced, you know!* She giggled at the end, and I was confused, not understanding why she would say something like that to me. In the literal sense, her words were cruel, but they didn't feel heartless. If anything, I thought about a possible hidden meaning behind them. Many years later, it came to me that she wasn't being mean but was trying to passively protect me from her son by driving me away without outwardly betraying him. She had a unique patriarchal loyalty to him and would never say anything against him, her only son. But the more I saw them together, the more verbal storms I witnessed him bestow upon her. I believe her disguised communication to me was, *Leave while you can.*

I can still hear her saying, *Oh, for Christ's sake,* and I smiled every time, knowing my family considered this was taking the Lord's name in vain. Although it had been a few years since I abandoned my obligation to God, I often chuckled, wondering what He would think of this woman who drank too much, swore like a trooper, and said what she thought with a smile and not a second thought. I loved that she didn't hide who she was—no airs about her—most of the time. She and her husband attended a few of my family's events, and I was surprised that his mother actually curtailed her drinking at them. This was unusual, and I knew she was probably reminded by her son and husband to behave. I also noted that this reflected where my future in-laws perceived they landed within life's pretentious chain of command, affecting how they presented themselves when in my parents' presence. It made me sad to think they felt the need to change their way of being to accommodate my parents' approval and perception of their status. On the other hand, I appreciated their kindness because they saved me from listening to even more judgment by my parents about my boyfriend's family. I knew they did this because they cared about me, but it upset me that they were intimidated by my parents, who were no better than anyone else.

My family can be kind, accepting, fun, and hospitable to those who are like them. Those who are not are judged. It took me a long time to understand that my father put others down so he wouldn't have to admit his own perceived shortfalls. I know this because, at my worst, there were many times when I followed suit to compensate for my flaws. My father found a weakness in every person I dated—in anyone, really. My father's friends were husbands of my mother's girlfriends who got together with them for coffee or to have drinks and play cards. One by one, these couples dropped off from their circle due to my father's distasteful, off-colour remarks and the altercations he created while disputing someone's opinion in the room. My mother always defended him, becoming very obstinate that he was right when he was obviously trying to stir up shit. Eventually, she lost almost every girlfriend she ever had. Once in their eighties, I only knew of one couple who went to their place to visit. They met in their apartment building, and I'm positive this relationship lasted because my father couldn't argue what was being said because he suffered from hearing loss.

Throughout his life, whether favourable or not, if someone showed up the least bit different from my father, he commented negatively about the contrasting characteristic. He often judged someone without explaining what he found particularly adverse about them; simply pointing out where they lived, their nationality or their financial status was sufficient criticism. It was his tone that made these statements accusatory, *He lives on the north side of town.* My father was a racist. He was the guy who used labels like *Blackies, Wops,* and *Chinks.* He had a stereotype for everyone: *Pakis smell, Jews are cheap, Newfies are stupid.* He loved the joke that went around years ago: *How many Newfies does it take to change a lightbulb?* I grew up with this mindset, and I used his off-putting jokes as a conduit to connect with him, laughing at them even though they made me cringe. However, the trade-off was too dear once I had children, and I asked him to check his bigotry at the door because I didn't want my kids to feed into their grandfather's discrimination. *Well, it's the truth,* he would answer with that same smirk he had on his face. There was no doubt that my father sought the shock factor by putting others down and wanted others to agree with his slander to establish camaraderie. I got to know when my father was preparing to blurt out something derogatory because he shifted his shoulders up and down in a jerky sort of way just before announcing his proclamation. It was like a nervous tick he developed while mustering up the courage to say something he knew had shock value. There was a time when I felt sorry for him, realizing that he judged others to compensate for his low self-esteem, trying to build himself up in a sick sort of way.

He seemed to enjoy diminishing this particular boyfriend of mine by pointing out every flaw he saw in him: *He lives in that part of town. He doesn't have an education. He can't handle his liquor. He still lives at home. He has a temper.* Everything my father said about him was true, but what disappointed me was that he used accusations as reasons for me to leave him rather than finding reasons to support the person I cared about to be better. I believe he saw some things he hated about himself in this boy, including his own fiery temperament. But my father would never admit to seeing in this young man what he himself needed to change because that would require acknowledging his own imperfections and possibly stepping up to support my fiancé through his. Instead, his defence was to stigmatize him as an outcast, as someone not good enough for me or my family to be affiliated with. This, in turn, took the onus off anyone possibly recognizing how alike they were.

After a while, my sister decided to move out to live with her future husband. My boyfriend and I were still dating, and I moved in with his sister, who became a lifelong cherished friend. We recently reconnected after many years, and it was as if we were back in our twenties again. She will always hold a place in my heart as someone I trusted and was always there for me. She was a single mom, and we had a lot of fun together, making dinners, going out for drinks, and spending time with her beautiful daughter. All the while, I was managing my boyfriend's alcohol induced Jekyll and Hyde personality. My parents ended up being right about him, but I was in love and didn't welcome what came across as judgement rather than advice. When he drank, he became diabolical, spewing hurtful words at me.

Before we got engaged, he only showed me tiny glimpses of this side, and I tolerated them because I was used to the uncomfortableness that comes hand-in-hand with the verbal authoritative posturing of a man. In the beginning, he showed me his gentle and kind side much more often. I remember when he approached my father and asked him for permission to marry me. I thought it was so chivalrous, and I was embarrassed when my father looked up at him from his easy chair, peered over his glasses and simply said, *No*. I accepted his proposal anyway. However, once he got a ring on my finger, I learned that I loved him when he was sober but much less when he was drunk, which became more frequent than not. Surprisingly, I also loved myself enough to walk away when I realized he found himself and alcohol far more important than me. I painfully relate to the degradation that surfaces through the egoic upper hand of another.

After breaking up with him, I briefly reflected on my father's response to this man's marriage proposal in a different light. Perhaps I had a glimmer of hope because, just as his mother attempted to protect me, I thought maybe my father tried to do the same. Was this how my father showed his love for me? I hung onto this misguided faith until I realized that both my father and my ex used verbal abuse as part of their recipe for control and had difficulty saying, *I love you*. Both also had no problem calling me a slut; it easily rolled off their tongues. The battle of expressions of love versus hate continued to mess with my head and heart for many years to come.

When I left him, I fell swiftly back into my pattern of seeking my forever-after guy. Friday night was when I went out to the bars with his sister, and once after drinking too much, I got into one of our neighbour's Corvette with him and drove around town. Alcohol clearly takes away one's safety filter because I had no problem going in his car with him, knowing he was a drug dealer and could be dangerous. At around two in the morning, he stopped at a local donut shop, told me to stay in the car and went inside. When he got out of the car, I looked down at the console and saw a gun. I immediately sobered up, got out and walked a few miles down the road to a friend's house. I passed out on her porch and woke up when the sun came up. Remembering the night before, I started to shake, wondering what I was thinking. Walking to the nearest phone booth at that same donut shop—still no cell phones—I called a cab to take me home. That was a huge red flag for me, but I continued to find myself in several risky situations.

My ex was very determined to keep me in his life, and he came around a few times after drinking too much, yelling, and carrying on outside my and his sister's apartment. I didn't want to create a wedge between my friend and her brother, so I decided to move out. I was 21 and had never lived alone, and although I didn't

Escaping the Cycle of Deceit

recognize it at the time, I had become quite a co-dependent gal. Still emotionally traumatized, I did an incredible job compartmentalizing it all. I used alcohol to block any memory of the degradation I had experienced with the first two men in my life. Subconsciously, I blocked negative memories and focused on the few positive experiences that had even a hint of what I thought happiness was—any level of joy seemed entirely out of the realm of acquiring. I was overwhelmed with not knowing who I could go to, accepting I couldn't tell my parents what had happened because they disapproved of my relationship from the start. I was sure they would go on and on with, *I told you so*, and the last thing I needed was more shame—my cup runneth over in that area. So, I called my cousin, who had moved from Pennsylvania to Florida during his transition into adulthood and asked him if I could come for a visit. I needed some space from what had happened, and I knew he would be there for me. He did not fail me. I never told him what happened, but I'm sure he sensed something was up. Respecting my privacy, he knew that just holding space for me was enough.

After a few weeks soaking up the sun and spending time with my cousin, it was time for me to go home. And oddly, home meant my parents' house. Somehow, I was drawn to the familiarity of my parents, and I sank into my mother's home cooked-meals, clean sheets, and admiration for me. I knew it was fueled by a combination of her need for self-fulfillment and genuine nurturing for her daughter, but I didn't care because she was who I knew better than anyone, including the functional and dysfunctional parts—my yearning and hope for what connected us kept me coming back to her. It was also self-fulfilling for me because it turned out to be a safe place to briefly land. Unfortunately, we both quickly returned to competing for the position of being the special one, and my glorious perception bubble popped.

My trip to Florida gave me distance from my trauma but distracted me from working through it. Living back home with my parents also impeded me from putting all the pieces together, finding myself right back where I started. I was defensive at every turn, with my mother suggesting what I needed to do and who I needed in my life. Finally, I did what I knew best and blocked my pain by finding an escape; I began seeking the fantastical love of my life again. And, while standing in a bar one night with my friend, I took a sip of my drink and glanced to the right. There he was—a beautiful specimen of a man who made my heart race. He was of Swedish descent and gorgeous: tall, blonde, blue-eyed, and very charismatic. I dated him for about six months, and what felt like adoration for me was something I had never experienced before. He wined and dined me and treated me like a prized possession, often inviting me to his apartment, putting candles and music on. Everything seemed genuine, slow, and intentional. I believed he loved me, although he never told me so, and I would never have said that first—women don't do that. We didn't go out with other couples, and I just thought I was unique, and he wanted me all to himself. When I invited him to my sister's wedding, he agreed, and I had the best time, dancing and singing with all my Dutch relatives while he stood back watching. He smiled when I looked over at him, but I sensed something was off. A big red flag appeared when someone lifted their camera, and he refused to have his picture taken. I understood his hesitancy to join the family group photos, thinking he likely felt awkward having just met my relatives. But he also declined having our picture taken as a couple. My stomach did its usual flip, and the hair on the back of my neck stood up. I began digging.

It was 1982, and there was still no social media on the horizon, so I did what we did back then and started mentioning him to people I knew. Then one day, I happened to be chatting with some friends, and I told them about my boyfriend. One of them looked me square in the eye and said, *I know him; you know he's married, right?!* Uh, no!! I thought my uterus would fall out of my vagina, and I ran to the washroom and got sick in the toilet. Cleaning my face, I looked in the mirror and stared at each of the features I so abhorred: my squinty eyes, my endless nose, and that large mouth. But as much as I still believed they had caused me grief, I refused to deceive them this time. How did I not see any sign that he had another life? Was I that desperate that I denied what was right in front of me? Yes, I was.

When I came out of the washroom, I asked my informant who this person I loved was married to. She shared the name of a prominent businesswoman in the community, and I immediately decided I would save her from a lifetime with this adulterer. I was angry, and I would rescue her by disclosing his discretions, which would double as my redemption for what he did. My plan was to be a hero and release her from further dishonour. I was on it like a fly on shit.

So, off I went to his wife's storefront. Walking in with my head held high, I bravely asked if I could speak to the owner in private, *It's important.* I was escorted to a back room and introduced to her. She was beautiful and smiled when I entered the room. A shiver ran down my spine, with my heart aching for her. I almost turned and ran out because I didn't want to be the one to hurt her. Then, in a quiet, soothing voice, she asked how she could help me. I knew she deserved to know the truth, so I immediately blurted it out, *Your husband is cheating on you. I'm so sorry; I didn't know he was married. We have been seeing each other for six months.*

This was when I wished someone had slapped me across the face instead of being put through the humiliation I was not expecting. Her smile grew wider in a condescending sort of way, and she didn't seem as kind as she did before. She put her hand on my shoulder and gripped it tightly as she told me not to worry about it; they had an open relationship, and she was okay with her husband seeing other women and having sex with them. And just to confirm that I wouldn't have anything to argue, she added that they had an agreement; that's what the extra apartment was for. The conversation continued, but only in my head as she took my elbow and led me to the front door, *Okay, that's weird. But wait a minute, I'm not okay with it; no one let me in on this plan…because I would not have agreed to it. I don't share my men; that I know for sure.* She gave me a gentle shove through the door, and from the moment I stepped across the threshold onto the sidewalk, my value of monogamy was implanted more solidly in my soul.

VI

⸻ Escaping the Cycle of Naivety ⸻

Staying at my parents' house with no plan during the summer of 1982 was safe because it was familiar. However, it wasn't ideal because it took me back to old patterns that didn't serve me well. I was stuck in the betrayal of trauma, unable to think ahead and needing space to think. My mother gave me the time and space to sort myself out, but she also believed I needed to move forward from whatever it was that had me sitting in stagnation. And yet, she never asked me what was wrong. In her defence, years of responding to her with barriers of steel likely stopped her from trying to support me. I have moments when I wish she would have persisted and been the person to hold space for my emotions rather than being the one trying to fix me.

In this case, she was neutral, not attempting either, so I, naively, spent my days lying by the pool. At the same time, she busied herself, justifiably reaping the financial rewards of a successful business and having convinced my father to buy a house that some well-to-do people in a newer neighbourhood were selling. The owners were going through a sordid divorce, and the splitting of assets warranted getting rid of their family home. Hearing about yet another man's cheating, I was reminded of my last boyfriend's deceptive scheme. I still don't understand how a scammer's mind works, which is likely why I have been victimized many times.

Situated on a corner lot, this expansive bungalow was professionally landscaped, and the pool encompassed the majority of the backyard. It had a diving board on one end, and white cement surrounded its kidney shape. Every morning, I climbed the staircase from downstairs, walked through the kitchen past my parents having breakfast, and mumbled, *Good morning* while proceeding onto the deck that overlooked the pool. On my way, my eye always caught the glimmer of orange juice in two glasses sitting in the sun's rays. They stood out against the stark white Dutch linen I spilled my milk on years ago—every morning until the day my father died, my mother squeezed oranges for him. Each time I walked through the sliding glass doors, she called after me, asking if I would like some breakfast. Without looking back, I politely answered, *No thank you*, knowing that her offer came with her rule of sitting at the table with them, and it was too early for that. I regretfully continued onto the deck because she made the best fried eggs on rye toast ever.

Each day, I noticed a trail of small puddles making a path from the top of the pool stairs up to a wet towel drying on the deck rail; my mother had enjoyed her early-morning swim. She often told people that she swims in the nude first thing in the morning, *No one can see me,* she would proudly exclaim as if she had accomplished the ultimate magic trick. I was embarrassed every time, wondering why anyone needed to know that she didn't wear a bathing suit in her backyard at six in the morning. At that time, living with my mother day in and out escalated my curiosity about how her mind worked. I began to realize just how much more different than alike we were. I became confused with our increased incongruity and found it almost impossible to stifle the chaos of disconnection. The discomfort of pretending to belong was overwhelming and wanting to escape was at the top of my mind, but I believed I had nowhere to go because I had no one to go to. My co-dependency on the security of our dysfunction motivated me to jump on an opportunity whereby the man of my dreams appeared. For a split moment, I believed it was synchronistic—perfect timing—but I was wrong because my most precious moment was secretly controlled at the hands of my mother. As much as I don't want to admit it, in this instance, her deception became my most cherished gift.

After one of my mother's early morning swims, she told me that she and my father were invited to their friend's birthday party. Like my parents, he and his wife were long-time members of the Dutch community, and I knew them from the many house parties they attended at my parents' house. My father had to work the day of the party, and my mother said she didn't want to go by herself, so she asked if I would go with her. She made it sound like I would be doing her a favour—I would be making her happy. Although I thought I was on the cusp of ground-breaking awareness when it came to my mother's control tactics, my familial programming overrode my intuition that day. I got sucked into believing that going to this party would be fun, and it was the right thing to do to support my mother. She won and actually had me looking forward to getting off the deck and out of my sloth-like suntanning mode.

When we arrived at her friends' home on a gorgeous July afternoon, I found myself drawn to one of three empty chairs sitting side-by-side on their deck nestled in their wooded backyard. My mother also immediately sat down, leaving one unoccupied chair beside me. Everyone attending was connected to a friend or relative there, and I was comfortably drawn into the Dutch conversation surrounding me. The woman of the house came out from the kitchen with a platter of familiar *hapjes*—appetizers: pickles wrapped in *Cerevelat* salami, Black Forest ham, smoked turkey, pastry-covered mini-sausages, and chunks of Gouda cheese with crackers. I relaxed in my chair with a napkin filled with food and wished her husband a happy birthday as he handed me a glass of white wine accompanied by a smile that was as welcoming as any I had ever received. I gently immersed myself in the bounty of *gezeligheid* and yet, there was that certain something that was just not right. That opposing force of energy I was so familiar with seemed to be present, but I could not put my finger on where it came from, so I ignored it. As usual, I found myself surrounded with the comfort of familiarity overcast with the

Escaping the Cycle of Naivety

discomfort of the unknown—something was brewing on the horizon. I didn't have clarity about what it was yet, but as moments sped by, I was pretty sure my mother had something to do with what was about to happen.

Getting ready to relieve myself of the torment of ambiguity by making an excuse to leave was interrupted by a figure unobtrusively arriving around the corner of the house towards the party. Visually, he was everything a prince in a fairy tale represents—tall, dark, and handsome...and I was intrigued. My mother immediately jumped up and hugged him. She then told him to sit in the chair beside me. There it was, and my confusion vanished, and acute clarity set in within moments of him sitting down right beside me; she was setting me up. But his calm demeanour distracted me from my disdain for my mother's interference—for the time being. Oddly, he was the hosts' son, and we had never met after all the years my parents were friends with his. Of course, neither he nor I were ever invited when they went to each other's houses, and we laughed about that. He shared that when he was young, he and his sister slept in the car in the driveway while his parents played cards in their friend's houses. It's what they did back then because they couldn't afford a babysitter.

When it was time for everyone to leave, we stood out in the driveway beside his yellow Triumph Spitfire, and he told me he was going on a trip to California with a friend for a few weeks. He wondered if he could call me upon his return. I told him that would be nice, and he got into his car and drove away. I turned to see my mother smiling over at me, and I responded with a displeased frown. I was so annoyed, having been reminded that she just tricked me again. She would consider herself the star in this situation, believing she saved me by finding my match; I knew it would end up being a story she told until the end of her time on this earth. My programmed self told me I should thank her, but I wanted to yell, *Stay out of my business; I can take care of myself!!* There were too many people around, so I just turned away.

The day I met Hank turned out to be the best day of my life, but it was also the day my mother spiralled into her version of next level self-importance. Her biggest mistake was not recognizing that he overtook her ranking in my life; when we committed our lives to each other, my loyalty immediately transferred from either one of my parents to my husband...and that drove her crazy. It took me some time to adjust to placing him before my parents because, even though I agreed with this value, I was programmed to be loyal to my mother and father, and it felt like a sin not to be. She taught me her lineage rules, modelling placing her husband before anyone else.

My middle sister was also prey to my mother's behind-the-curtain matchmaking skills, although she may not see it that way. Before deciding to take on my marital fate as her responsibility, she had long facilitated my sister's. At one point in time, my mother was the cosmetician in a downtown drugstore named Thrifty's. The store pharmacist was a larger-than-life gentleman who was married

Around The Table

and had a twenty-something-year-old son. The pharmacist and my mother got along quite well, seeing as they both shared an over-the-top zest for life. There is no question that, at her best, my mother is a fun-loving person who thrives amidst the camaraderie of others; she achieves a sense of belonging through their acceptance and reverence. There is no doubt that she found this inclusion within the kinship of co-workers.

Although I mostly fixated on my mother's traits that had an all-encompassing negative impact on me, there were many times when I noticed her passion for connection, desire to experience joy, and genuine wish to nurture and love others. Ironically, these same aspirations include everything I have ever hungered for. Sadly, her desires drove her need to control and fix the people she loved. Still to this day, I have caught her in deceptive tactics triggered by her sincerest intentions.

Somehow or other, my mother convinced her pharmacist friend that it was a good idea for his son and her daughter to get together. His parents considered him a bit of a wild card, so his father agreed it would be beneficial for his son to date my sister, seeing as she behaved to-the-book. I don't know exactly how my mother pulled it off, but she set them up in some obscure, contrived way, making it look like it all magically happened—just as it had with me. So, they began dating, and not being able to leave it at that, my mother added her quest to fix the new couple by enrolling them in a Dale Carnegie course; the icing on the cake was that she signed herself up at the same time. I found out later that the reason was part of the plan to convince them to go, telling them she was taking the course to improve herself, and they could all go together. She would pay—it would make her happy. When my mother told me this, she asked me to keep it a secret because *They don't need to know. They're both shy and need help; no point in making them feel bad.*

They were married and had two children, my niece and nephew. My relationship with my sister has been strained over the years, and I believe that tension was created by each of our perceptions of the other based on what my mother said about each of us behind our backs. Her secretive matriarchal influence continues to cause strife for many members of our family, and quite frankly, I have no idea how she manages to keep all her stories straight. Incredibly, when challenged by only the bravest and caught in a lie, she rolls another one off her tongue as easily and quickly as a rubber ball escalating down a newly-paved hill. She shares each justification as if they are forgotten pieces of the original story. Her motive is to gain the same camaraderie she can achieve authentically but chooses to slant the truth when she becomes desperate. I can't imagine the energy it takes to keep up with her tangled web, but I also know it is a finely-tuned process perfected over many years of practice. It was a response developed at a very young age. I'm guessing that, like me, all my mother ever wanted was to experience being loved, which entailed making others happy, even if it crossed the line of deceit.

It isn't easy to fathom that she could escalate any further, but my mother upped controlling her daughters, including our spouses, from the moment they

Escaping the Cycle of Naivety

entered our lives. Up to this point, I didn't notice that she also dominated my sisters. However, I realized she was way out of line when she interfered with my middle sister's romantic life and self-esteem. The difference between her and me is that I don't think it upset her, or it did, and she just didn't share her discontent with me. She seemed to go on her merry and married way without even attempting to adjust my mother's meddling sails. This sister accommodated everything my father wanted until he passed away, and she continues to do whatever my mother asks of her. She is definitely the good daughter by my mother's standards, and I commend her because it has not been an easy task. And although I find this admirable, I also empathize with her because I truly believe her loyalty is exploited by my mother, who instilled this expectation in her.

My eldest sister was a bit more like me in that she did not appreciate my mother sticking her nose in all of her business. However, I think my mother had something to do with how she met her husband. I recently heard a story that they met while she was working at the same drugstore as my mother—I'm guessing she got my sister that job. I heard that my sister was working the cash at the front of the store, and her future husband met her while going through her till to buy something. I can't be sure, but history would dictate that my mother had something to do with this setup. According to the account shared at my mother's 90th birthday celebration, when he talked to my mother later in the cosmetics department, he shared that if her daughter was anything like her mother, he had a winner. My brain did a little blip, blop, bleep, and my Spidey senses told me that they talked before that, and my mother had encouraged him to go and meet her.

After a few years of dating, they married and had three beautiful boys, each two years apart. They lived in our hometown for a few years after the birth of their first son. He was the apple of my sister's eye, cute and curious and the first grandchild for my parents. As we all did, my mother adored him. I'm guessing my mother's interfering became intolerable soon after their son came into the world because my sister and her new family moved to a city 45 minutes away shortly after that. I remember asking my sister why they were moving away, and she told me, *It's just far enough away that mom needs to call before she decides to come for a visit, and I can always say I'm busy.* She wanted to create distance without hurting my mother's feelings. They told us that my sister's husband got a transfer with work, but based on my experience, I can bet my life that he asked for the transfer to save his marriage. My mother once admitted to me that he called her domineering and controlling. She was so offended and asked me if Hank thought the same—I told her he did. Her response was exactly what I thought it would be, including a list of all the reasons she was not. My mother refused to acknowledge her demons.

When Hank returned from his summer trip to California, he called me as promised. Our first date was a car drive along the water. He picked me up in his Nissan 280 ZX, and I wondered how many cars this guy had. It turns out he had three: the Triumph, the Nissan, and an old Buick for winter driving. He was a geography teacher and loved exploring the countryside on weekends—if there was a Sunday Driving Club, he could have been the organizer. Later, he laughed any time he shared our first-date story with others, including that I talked the whole way there and back. He just listened. Hank has an abundance of attributes, but if I had to pick his best, it would be just that: he is a listener-extraordinaire, with the patience of a tiger stalking its prey—the caveat is that he always uses it for the greater good. Adding that integrity and his devotion to me into the equation, this becomes the recipe of the man who positively impacted my life forever—I can be the shittiest person, and he never fails to wait for me to recalibrate to the well-intentioned person he knows I am. He's far more forgiving than I am.

It's true, even I think this sounds like a co-dependent relationship, and being fully transparent, I believe it certainly was in the beginning. Hank was the knight in shining armour I had been seeking, and I clung to that fantasy like a freshly-chewed piece of Double-Bubble on my shoe. But moving forward, he supported me to gain the wisdom I needed to show up as an independent person, striving for my own happiness and not just my mother's. In his gentle way, he somehow convinced me that my mandate in life did not have to be fulfilling only her dreams, but rather that I could have beliefs of my own and fully commit to them while supporting her at the same time. This is how our love developed—with the vision that we would mutually support each other, as well as the goals we created together as a couple. Unfortunately, what he didn't count on, and I set aside in the recesses of my mind, hoping it would just go away, was that my mother would not adapt to my new perception about what was important to me. As a result, she became my greatest obstacle within my pursuit for autonomy and our biggest hurdle within our need to live in line with our own familial values.

Becoming our shadow in the dark, my mother has a great deal of endurance when it comes to obtaining and maintaining what she wants, and she planted herself squarely in the middle of our marriage as if we granted her our blessing to do so. This was the next level in my life-long battle to ward off my mother's control, with the difference that I had backup this time. And, as much as I believed I was worthy of having him as an ally, my greatest regret in life is that my husband was dragged into her pit of fire. The irony is that this humble human she chose as my saviour eventually became her most frustrating foe because she pushed his patience to a crumbling heap of intolerance. My mother was in for the rudest awakening the day he encouraged me to listen to my soul and make decisions that reflected what was right for us.

Long after I met Hank, my father remained the same person he always was. Up until the day he died at the age of 94, he was just as single-minded as when I was a little girl. During our courtship, my father never took the time to think about what he said but instead responded with whatever was on the tip of his tongue. Having supper alone with my parents one night, I stepped out of my comfort zone in response to my mother's query about how things were going with my

Escaping the Cycle of Naivety

new boyfriend and me. We had only been dating for two months at that time, and through my excitement for this new relationship, I let my guard down and freely shared that we went for car rides, had gone to the movies to see *Risky Business*, and enjoyed having dinner together. Then, out of the blue, my father asked me if Hank had kissed me yet. Seeing his antagonizing grin, I felt the hair on the back of my neck stand up, knowing that a question like that coming from my father would lead to an uncomfortable conversation. As an aside, I also wondered why he thought the man should make that first move. But I dismissed it because that was an added layer to clarify along with figuring out how to manoeuvre answering his pending question. I hadn't learned the fine art of taking a breath before responding to either of my parents yet—that skill came decades later—so I fell prey to providing an answer that I intuitively knew would be judged as soon as I blurted it out. Stupidly, I responded with the truth by saying, *No, he hasn't*. Naively, I thought my father would find that respectful and determine that the man I was dating was not rushing into things. I knew it was because Hank had been hurt in the past and wanted to take things slow to be sure before getting serious. But my father managed to find something wrong with him and bluntly responded with his logic that, *He must be a fag*. I looked at him in shock and shook my head while my mother immediately jumped in to say that my father didn't mean it. When I didn't respond to him, he laughed and said, *Just forget about it*.

Our 35-plus years of experiences with my family's combative exchanges around the dinner table were described by my husband as the result of my father's need to maintain authority in his home—his forever need to put others down by being right. He chose me most of the time because I motivated him by retaliating, having learned not to be submissive. This was reiterated just months before he died when I sat with my sister and parents in their living room and heard my father say that someone was a stupid asshole. He announced it with the energy of insolence that comes alongside self-importance while criticizing a viewpoint he disagrees with. And although one would think the man behind an arrogant statement like that is as confident as anyone, I noticed the same nervous shoulder tick he struggled with when carrying something just a little too far. It reminds him to let go of his ego, but he does not listen. I always believed he never would, and I had dreams of him sharing his final words, defending why he was right on his deathbed.

I continued working at the deli, listening to my mother sing along with the tapes of Dutch songs playing over and over again while she rhythmically sliced in unison with the music. She was happy. I followed her lead, embracing what I knew to be the closest thing to *gezelegheid* I had ever experienced. When things were going her way and everyone did what she wanted, everyone was at ease. However, there were those chaotic times. And the distinct contrast began to provide clarity that the *gezelegheid* she created became exactly what I found so difficult to invite into my life—the joy that comes with connection—because it was almost always erased by its adversary of suffering as a result of disconnection. *Gezelegheid* or connection are one and the same—just spoken in two different languages, with each requiring the ability to surrender the control I was compelled to hang onto to make my mother happy. My burden became the challenge of believing that any joy through connection I might be worthy of was conditional upon me experiencing it the way my mother did, accompanied by suffering. I now realize I was addicted to being connected to her kind of joy, rather than discovering and embracing my own. After so many years of trying to make her happy to the point of exhaustion, along with the layers upon layers of emotional trauma that came with that never-ending effort, I subconsciously chose to push joy out of my life because the suffering was too much to bear—it was just too difficult to experience joy her way.

After savouring our first kiss while saying goodnight at my parents' front door one night, I noted it was a mutual inclination. I never told my parents when it happened. Hank lived in an old, renovated one-room schoolhouse in the country, which I thought was super cool, and I started spending weekends there. The huge radiators rattled through the night, keeping me awake. I never complained because our time together superseded the trade-off of sleep deprivation. My mother generously gave her blessing on Fridays by sending along care packages loaded with goodies from her store: Dutch licorice, chocolate, meat, cheese—whatever my boyfriend liked, she sent. Each time, she made a point of telling Hank that all his favourites were in there. I often listened to her and thought how starved for attention she must have been when she was a child because she always made a point of sharing all the great things she did. I wondered why she couldn't just humbly do them and be quiet. Of course, we were super grateful, but it was apparent her focus was on making her future son-in-law happy. I eventually realized that she was trying so hard to gain his approval because her past dictated the need to gain the approval of all men in and outside of our family—they also had to fit her mould.

We discovered that with every present comes an expected degree of praise; *thank you* simply isn't enough. It became obvious that recognizing her as the special person is really what she lives for. And she creates these shining moments by bringing them to everyone's attention if we don't voluntarily acknowledge them. Being humble has never been part of her psyche to the degree that, if we don't express our gratitude to her within a specific amount of time of receiving her gifts, she transitions into shaming us by withholding her love.

My mother's rules around what justifies giving or receiving gratitude are expansive and develop a plethora of consequences if not followed. The problem has always been that she makes the conditions up as she goes along based on whether she gets what she wants or not, so it is challenging to keep up with her ongoing added conditions. An example is her birthday card criteria: she sends each member of her immediate family, including her grandchildren, a birthday card every year with a cheque for 50 dollars in it. Everyone is very grateful. However, if someone does not call to thank her by the day of their birthday, she refuses to call them to wish them a Happy Birthday. She has told me that she will do so when they call to thank her for their gift, *I sent them a card with 50 dollars, so when they call to thank me, I will wish them a Happy Birthday.* She recently justified this during a conversation I had with her on my daughter's birthday. It's Dutch tradition to call the parents of their children to congratulate them on their child's celebratory day, so my mother called me, *Gefeliciteerd met de verjaardag van je dochter—Congratulations on your daughter's birthday.* She proceeded to ask me if I had talked to my daughter yet that day. I told her I had and asked if she had called her, *No, I sent her a card and money, and she hasn't called to thank me yet.* That's the rule.

From the time we started dating, my mother decided she would dictate how she would incorporate herself into Hank's and my life. For some reason, she believed she should deeply embed herself into our relationship, and it became a bit uncomfortable one night when we came home to my parents' house after being out. She was in bed watching a movie, and my father was at work, so she called out to us to come to her. We walked down the hallway to her bedroom, and she told us to join her. Innocently, Hank never thought anything of it, thinking it was cute lying on top of the sheets on one side, her on the other, and me in the middle. But as I lay there, I knew that this would never happen again—I decided she was getting too familiar with him. Even though it was all very innocent, I knew that he was oblivious to my mother's ability to manipulate others. He was not yet aware of what she was capable of, and I vowed I would do my best to protect him. We had many conversations about my experiences with her, but I understood that it would take time for him to get the full scope of the chaos she could create. Having only known her for about a year, he just thought she was fun and that she cared about her daughter. I sometimes wondered if he thought I made too much out of things, but I couldn't help it because I did not fully trust her.

When I met him, he was an avid runner, having completed many marathons, and he was obsessed with nutrition. I was in awe of his commitment to optimum health and often wondered how he tolerated my horrible smoking habit at the time. But, true to his nature, he was patient, modelling the benefits of taking care of his body instead of preaching about it, and it wasn't long before I was running with him, and my craving for cigarettes disappeared forever. I quickly transitioned into a healthy lifestyle, and it became our thing. We exercised and ate well, much to my mother's dismay, whose food-pushing became obvious when we declined her snacks and sweets. She was particularly offended when Hank would not eat certain things—it was often embarrassing, and I asked her not to pressure him into eating something he didn't want. My mother does not easily take no for an answer.

He had been married and separated long before we met and was adamant he wouldn't marry again. His trepidation was real, and I honoured his decision, understanding the disappointment of what he considered a failed marriage. I knew that his main concern was hurting me should things not work out, and marriage was not necessary to me; I just wanted to be with him. So, after being together for a year, we bought our first house in a brand-new subdivision, and we chose a two-story; it was one of the first R2000 energy-efficient homes in our town. Although not perfect, that first year of living together gave me hope because it sailed by with as little drama as I have ever experienced with my mother. She managed to refrain from having too much control over me and allowed things to unfold...for the most part. I have since described this respectful side of her demeanour as my mother behaving. She gifted me with some of these moments, digging deep by not pushing the envelope too far, but they were short-lived and ultimately became overshadowed by her U-turns. It's like she cannot help herself.

One such setback occurred just after we moved into our house. Long before Hank and I met, he signed up for a five-in-four program that encouraged teachers to work for four years, get paid for five, and take that fifth year off. He had already registered for a course in England and arranged side trips to Holland, Denmark, and Sweden. He shared this with me at the beginning of our relationship, and I fully supported him still going; we could not afford for the two of us to go because we just bought the house. I was adulting and able to take care of myself, so I encouraged him to enjoy his trip. My mother shared what seemed like a compassionate concern for me when we were alone together, but I assured her that I was fine. I found out later that she told family members, including some of my aunts and my future mother-in-law, that she could not believe my husband was going on a vacation without me. The concern she shared with me about being alone was not genuine but rather a judgement about the kind of man he was for leaving me alone. She didn't think he should go without me, so she presented what he did in a bad light behind my back to others in an attempt to gain camaraderie and validate her opinion. To my face, she acted as if she cared about me, but to others, she made Hank out to be a disloyal person, something he is the exact opposite of. She didn't realize that most people she gossiped with did not want to collaborate with her false perceptions about him because they knew who he really was. This was the part of my mother's back-handed scheming that I abhorred; her hypocrisy was hurtful and lessened my trust in her every time.

When she manages to be on her best behaviour, I experience the repeated and ever-present pull towards a piece of who she is when the devil on her shoulder is shoved off by an angel—soulful bravery manages to rank over demonic fear. The mother I love, adore, and connect with from a very deep level emerges; she becomes human. I am always saddened and somewhat defeated when her adversary side returns and the vulnerability I am attracted to dissipates as she becomes merciless again.

When we moved into our first house, my mother outwardly congratulated us, but jealousy soon reared its ugly head, quickly erasing her original intention—it also diminished my worthiness of having something nice. Any time I showed her something we purchased for our new place, she made a comment like, *I always wanted one of those*, or *It must be nice*. I know that my perception of what my mother said and did became very one-sided and possibly exaggerated over time, but my trust in her was so damaged that I could not help myself back then. When I discussed this revelation with my therapist some years later, she reassured me that a mother's genuine love does not include begrudging her daughter of personal success; I learned that being envious of one's child to this degree can be the result of a victim mindset.

Meanwhile, Hank and I were building our life together, and we excitedly bought things to make our house a home and traded in the sports cars for a small truck for him and a more practical car for me. Both of my parents complimented us on our new purchases, but there was an air of condescendence when my father asked if we could afford all that. Hank was eight years my senior and had already been working as a high school teacher for quite some time when he met me. He owned homes long before I came along and had accumulated things that go along with them. He wasn't a kid who needed to be checked in on, especially by my father, and he certainly didn't need to defend his actions. This was just the beginning of their tumultuous relationship—again, there was not enough patience in the world to manage what my father eventually brought to my husband's place at the family table.

Somewhere between high school graduation and my sordid affair with the Swedish adulterer, I completed an eight-month administrative program at a private business school in town. It cost around 4,500 dollars, and my father paid for it. I had the understanding that this was in lieu of the post-secondary education he would have paid for if I had gone directly out of grade 13. He had done this for my sisters, and he never mentioned a loan to me. After we settled into the house, I stood corrected when my parents invited themselves over for coffee on a beautiful September Sunday morning. I was excited to step into the role of a first-time homeowner and proud to share this accomplishment with my parents—I think that, unknowingly, I wanted to prove I was an adult capable of taking care of myself. Unfortunately, this would be one of many future visits that ended up presenting an ulterior motive on their part.

I knew exactly what time they would be arriving because they were coming directly from mass, taking place around the corner. I made a banana loaf the night before and had the coffee ready, just having to push the button when they rang the doorbell. We cleaned the house on Saturday, and I even re-folded all my sheets because the last time my mother was there, she mentioned teaching me how to fold a fitted sheet after looking in my linen closet. I was determined my mother would have nothing to criticize. This was how conditioned I was as I constantly sought the acceptance of the person who birthed and raised me. Subconsciously, I measured everything I did by whether or not she, as well as my father, would approve of my results. And for the most part, my mother praised me for my accomplishments, but very quickly diminished their positive impact with an unexpected declaration of incompetence, deflating my dignity within moments. For instance, whenever my mother came to visit, she told me how beautiful my flower beds and pots were.

Around The Table

This was a huge compliment coming from a master gardener from Holland. Her praise fed my over-the-top desire to please her. However, every time she left our place, we found little piles of weeds that she pulled on her way in right in the middle of the walkway leading up to the step. Although this became a joke over time, it initially spoke volumes to my mother's back-handed way of telling me that, although my flower beds were pretty, they were not up to her standards in the weeding department. For years, my mother ripped the weeds out of my gardens on her way up to my door and made sure I knew she did so by leaving a pile of them for me to dispose of after she left. This told me two things: I wasn't good enough, and she was way better than me. If I didn't phone her later that day to thank her, she called to ask me if I noticed that she had pulled my weeds. I always quickly thanked her, so she wouldn't have to go on for too long.

On this particular morning, they arrived on time, and true to form, she left a heap of weeds in the usual spot. They came dressed in their Sunday best and took a seat; my father automatically chose the large cozy chair that matched the burgundy plaid sofa my mother sat on. Our house was one of the first models back in the early eighties that had both a living room and a family room on the main floor. The kitchen was adjacent to the latter. The family room had a fireplace, so we decided to sit in there to enjoy its warmth on a cool autumn morning. I served them coffee in the small Delft Blue Dutch cups and matching saucers they preferred—following etiquette, my father's set was slightly larger than my mother's because he was a man. I then gave them a small cake plate and linen napkin and walked around the coffee table with the platter of sliced banana loaf; I cut each regular slice a second time, just like my mother always did. I began the conversation by enthusiastically sharing that I had purchased the round pine House of Brougham coffee table standing before them. I was so proud because I was adamant about contributing to our household, and it cost me 500 dollars back then—that was a lot of money for someone working in retail. My mother told me how lovely it was and asked what I had to do to keep it in good repair. While I shared that we liked the rugged, worn look and would not be using product on it, I simultaneously sensed my father's energy shift, and he became quiet. His shoulders began their usual twitching, getting ready to blurt something inappropriate out. For me, his behaviour was very familiar. However, Hank was oblivious as he drank his coffee and ate his banana loaf while listening to my mother giving me advice about how to take care of my new investment. By the time we finished discussing the maintenance of our new table, I had determined that my father was triggered by me having purchased an expensive table. He immediately took the opportunity to interject with their hidden reason for coming. It became very clear that, although they may have liked our coffee table, the sharing of spending money sped up what they had planned to discuss.

My father suddenly turned to my husband and told him that he owed my father 4,500 dollars for my education. He smiled and said, *She's yours now*. Without

Escaping the Cycle of Naivety

saying anything right away, Hank calmly turned to look at me, and I knew he felt blindsided and didn't know what to do at first. While unsubstantiated, I immediately accepted guilt as if I had kept something from him. Blood rushed up into my head while a dump of shame landed in the pit of my stomach—for a moment, I retreated to my childhood and kept my mouth shut. But I managed to recalibrate and turned to my father, telling him that Hank didn't even know me when I went to that business school. I also reminded him that there was never any mention I had to pay him back, but if that was the case, I could do it with monthly payments over time. My father didn't hesitate to agree to that arrangement, adding that my payments would include interest. I looked over at my mother, sitting up stoically, sipping her coffee, *Diana, he did lend you the money.* The child in me rushed to the surface, being gaslit with a double whammy by the patriarch and matriarch of my family. Not knowing what to do, I turned back to Hank, and without saying a word, he unexcitedly stood up and walked upstairs. The story in my head immediately went to, *He is angry. He feels deceived. I should have told him about the money. I'm a bad partner.* And then I shifted, *How dare my parents do this to Hank?!* I asked my parents to go, thinking that Hank was packing to leave, punishing me due to my deception. But just as they stood up, Hank returned and reached over our new pine coffee table and handed my father a check for 5,000 dollars, *It includes interest, now get out of our house.* My father didn't argue but instead smirked, took the cheque, and then went out the front door. I watched my parents walk down the walkway and step over the weeds my mother had left behind. I reminded myself to call her later to thank her for pulling them.

Of course, Hank never left me, and life went on as usual after the 4500-dollar incident like it never happened—my father cashed the cheque. Then, Hank made a commitment to me out of the blue that I never expected. One evening after supper, I was washing the hall floor. He was reading the newspaper in the same comfy chair my father sat in while asking him to repay a debt he never made. Without putting the paper down, he asked me if I wanted to get married. I continued wiping the tile on my hands and knees and asked him why. He told me that it was good timing for tax purposes with the end of the year approaching. I smiled to myself and agreed. It was definitely not a story from a Gloria Steinem column with each of us re-enacting classic stereotypical roles, but it was what it was. We didn't put much weight into a marriage certificate or the ceremonial brouhaha of a wedding, with our motivation being powered more by tax management than romance and opulence. However, Hank can be traditional in a very endearing way. I had never told him about my father's refusal to accept my previous boyfriend's marriage proposal, so he stepped into that trap one evening after we had dinner with my parents. We were eating our dessert, and Hank asked my father for permission to marry me—noooo— and without skipping a bite, my father responded the same way he had before, adding, *But you're going to do it anyway, so go ahead.* He had a smile on his face, which made me think he was joking, but the air was void of

115

humour, and a chill ran up my spine. I looked over at my future husband, and he shrugged his shoulders, dismissing my father's disrespect. Over the years, Hank often quoted Shakespeare, *Many a true word has been spoken in jest.*

We were married on December 27, 1984, two and half years after our first car drive of hundreds. Our wedding was very different from what my mother wanted for me, and she made sure I was well-aware of her disapproval. We received a blessing in disguise because we weren't allowed to get married in the Catholic church; it required that Hank get an annulment from his first wedding—the most ridiculous rule I had ever heard of, given him and his ex-wife were already divorced. Since Hank was essentially an Atheist, I, once again, threw in the towel on religion and agreed to get married at the courthouse. We wanted to make the ceremony unique, reflecting our value of practicality. So, we initially decided to elope without inviting any family or friends other than those required as witnesses. Every one of Hank's family members fully supported us to do what was right for us. However, being told that she could not attend my wedding proved problematic for my mother, and she did not attempt to hide that from me. I understood it was difficult for her to absorb, but I was disappointed that she refused to honour our decision. And although I had many years of experience managing the consequences of my mother's selfish maneuvers, I was still fresh in the business of fully dodging them. Given that my confidence had not yet reached a competent level for effective use, I was overwhelmed with her expression of victimhood and convinced Hank to succumb to giving in a little to keep the peace. I have since learned that my concessions always lead to the eventual all or nothing downward spiral when it comes to my mother; when she pushes hard enough, I give in.

Ultimately and not surprisingly, after a great deal of self-work, I realized that I was programmed to suffer from a black or white state of mind if I was not mindful. I marvel at the prolonged release of the epiphany that could have saved me so much time agonizing over such a perfectionistic way of being. However, I have also concluded that I was meant to struggle to the nth degree in order to gain complete clarity about who I really am, rather than who I thought I should be. When it finally came to me, I wondered how I could have been so daft not to figure out that someone brought up in the strict world of right or wrong would end up being as obstinate as her predecessors.

But, as much as there were tiny underlying sparks of this insight from the day I paid attention to the whispers of a willow tree, my perception of their nudging at the age of 24 was still highly distorted by my obligation to fulfill my mother's wishes. So, Hank agreed that we should invite our immediate family: my parents, his parents, our siblings, their spouses, and two friends as witnesses—I regret allowing my mother to influence our wishes to this day.

We let everyone know it was a dress-casual occasion, but we asked them to bring indoor shoes for the photos. We made it clear to both sides of our family that we did not want a big reception and opted for a sit-down dinner in a private

Escaping the Cycle of Naivety

room in a restaurant with those who attended our wedding. We planned to drive to the airport the next day after a good night's rest to catch a flight to Barbados for our honeymoon. Everything was organized according to what we wanted while also compromising to give my mother a bit of what she wanted. But there wasn't a cap on my mother's demands in this situation, so the fine art of compromise did not work with her—what our side gave wasn't enough.

Our ceremony was anything but traditional. Hank and I woke up and got ready together that morning. I'm not an over-the-top fancy dresser, so I chose to wear a suit with a short navy pencil skirt, a matching cropped jacket, and a white-laced, high-neck blouse for a wedding touch. Hank had bought me a string of fresh-water pearls when he was in Holland, and they hung around my neck as a reminder of his love for me. He wore a tailored blue suit, crisp white shirt, and a tie and looked as handsome as ever. I was overly optimistic nothing could go wrong, having worked out every detail with Hank and given the simple approach we took to our special day—everything was planned and organized to the tee. After getting my hair done, we drove to the courthouse for our ten o'clock nuptials. Everyone in our small group of guests was waiting to start except my mother and father, who had not arrived yet. The justice of the peace told us that we had a bit of leeway with the time, so not to worry.

I had an uneasy feeling because my mother is Mrs. Punctuality, and after about ten minutes, my concern was confirmed when she flew through the door in a frenzy. All eyes turned in the direction of the heightened energy she brought with her, and her swollen eyes looked like she had been crying for hours. I looked at her feet and saw that she was wearing her winter boots. My father entered as his usual self, aloof and unscathed. She anxiously looked at me, and I rushed over to ask what had happened. Sobbing, she told me that one of my father's cousins in Holland had died. I asked who it was, and she told me he was a cousin twice removed, and I had never met him. They themselves had not connected with him for over a decade. Quickly figuring out that this man had absolutely no deep emotional ties to either one of my parents—my father didn't appear upset in the least—I responded rather heartlessly, telling her to get her shit together, *Don't ruin my wedding, Mom!!* I don't think she expected that from me, and she suddenly stood tall and looked back at me with piercing eyes, *I'm fine.* I asked her where her shoes were. She firmly told me, *I didn't bring them. You told me it wasn't a fancy wedding, so I didn't think it mattered.* This was how my mother penalized me when she didn't get her way or perceived she was in my shadow; she simply found a way to rob me of joy and misbehaved.

She already knew, but I reminded her that a photographer was going to take photos, so she would have to borrow one of my sister's shoes for the ones of Hank and me with her and my father. I told her she would be the only one in boots in the family shots. She agreed and began to describe my father's cousin's death to the others. I told her we were late and had to get on with the wedding, and she stopped talking.

Around The Table

The full family shots of our wedding included my mother wearing her shiny winter boots with her dramatic overtone reflecting off the buckles, taking attention off of me. I interpreted what she had done as a passive-aggressive way to let me know I was not getting married the right way—the way it should be done. I fucked it up by asking her to do something my way, and she would remind me every time I turned the pages of my wedding album with her boots and swollen eyes screaming back at me.

I found it difficult to forgive her unwillingness to set aside the catastrophized anguish she brought into the courthouse that day, taking the spotlight off me and onto her. There are times when I don't think my mother can help misbehaving. She's like my cockapoo, Lucy, who has a switch that flips inside her brain and can't control what happens next. With Lucy, it's food aggression; with my mother, it's jealousy. To her credit, she got what she wanted, and although I don't think it was her intention, she managed to put her shadow on my special day.

Her obsession with getting her way blinds her ability to do what is right for the greater good. The same compulsion drove her to blatantly go against our wishes of honouring not having a reception afterwards. We all had a beautiful dinner at a high-end restaurant that evening, and when my mother asked us to stop by her house to pick up our gift, we let our guard down—the web is strong. We agreed on a quick stopover because it seemed important to her. But when we arrived, there was a house full of my aunts, uncles, cousins, and my parents' friends waiting for us to celebrate with them. Shocked and caught in her devious ability to trick me, I stepped through the threshold. There was nothing I could do, knowing she could get away with it because of all the people surrounding us. She added fuel to the fire by whispering in my ear, *I told them not to bring any gifts—after all, you can't expect that when you didn't invite them to the wedding.* Bam! I wanted to slap her, but my mother always had good timing when it came to getting away with her digs. I looked up at all my relatives smiling at me, and Hank and I celebrated our marriage with them.

When I try to rationalize my mother's decisions around my wedding day, I'm sure that she genuinely wanted to do something special for us. Still, her alternate motivation was her fear of not meeting her perception of her family and friends' expectations. The story in her head may have been that there was only one acceptable way of getting married, and mine did not fit that mould. I believe she thought she was not good enough as the mother of the bride without creating the wedding that would be approved, even though that's not what we agreed upon. I can only speculate on the reason because I was not brave enough to confront her later, having been conditioned to forfeit my right to ask for an explanation. In our family, we were expected to forgive others' sins without them asking for forgiveness—just forget about it and move on.

That night, Hank was shocked to realize what my mother was capable of. We graciously accepted congratulations from her guests because we couldn't be rude and tell everyone to go home; it wasn't their fault they were oblivious to what my mother had done. Again, I had a lot of experience with my mother's breach of trust, but Hank was just being introduced to its severity, being slowly woven into her complicated web of distrust. Over the years and more than once, he gave her the benefit of the doubt, but after a while, that olive branch wore thin. I have deep compassion for my mother's motives, and back then, I wanted desperately to excuse her for stealing the show on my wedding day. However, I could not absolve someone who didn't believe she should be forgiven. So, I did what I always did and shoved the betrayal into a little corner in my mind. To this day, I struggle with the concept of turning the other cheek with those who believe they have nothing to be remorseful for. Instead, I choose to reframe the act of forgiveness into the mindset of acceptance because somehow, I can justify that with a little more ease.

I laugh at my mother's ability to find well-suited husbands for her daughters. She actually did a good job, and also had no problem mentioning her accolades at family functions. I quickly shut her down after the first few times with the same look she used when she wanted me to shut up: pursed lips, scrunched up eyes, and folded arms. My mother and I developed a way of physically communicating, void of speaking. Slowly but surely, I began responding to her with the same silent direction she used with me, adapting to her way of being when it came to getting what I wanted from her. As with my father, I constantly needed to be on guard, ready to defend anything I said or did. I am positive she felt the same way when interacting with me because eventually, I seldom gave her an inch when it came to her shenanigans.

I became more and more conscious of how she negatively affected me, and over time, I found something wrong with everything she did, even when it appeared to be loving and kind. I just didn't trust her, and we became our own worst enemies without either one of us attempting to become allies—our relationship was damaged. She was good at pretending nothing was wrong, and if we did discuss something, she acted like she didn't understand what I was upset about. I often thought I was crazy—maybe she was right. Perhaps I did make something big out of nothing as insane people do, and I began to think something was wrong with me. With my self-awareness today, I admittedly recognize my accountability for not taking her to task to discuss how she controlled and manipulated me. However, I lacked the self-awareness I needed back then, and I fully release my 20-something-year-old self for that burden of guilt.

Time moved on, and Hank and I embraced our life together. I have never been so connected to anyone. We stood by each other no matter the struggle, and most came and went supported by our perseverance and will to grow and succeed together, as well as individually. Unfortunately, my mother's effect on me continued to loom over us—it's not easy to conquer years and years of demons in a day. Without completely removing her from our lives, there was no way around the dark cloud that followed us. I continued to struggle terribly with not understanding who I was without my parents' approval, and for a while, I transferred this need for acceptance onto my husband. Like a drug, I became addicted to meeting his needs over mine for all the wrong reasons. Miraculously, he naturally made me feel like I belonged for all the right ones. I finally experienced what unconditional love was. I remember thinking, *If there is a heaven, this is as close to it as I am going to get.*

Slowly, I began yearning to be released from the co-dependent relationship I had with my mother and trying to make her happy at all costs. I recognized how she treated me affected my dysfunctional behaviour—physically, emotionally, cognitively, and spiritually: I went out of my way to do things for her, I consistently agreed with her, and I said things to her just because I thought she expected me to. All that to achieve her love, and yet, I complained about things that she did to others behind her back and judged people the way she did. Strange and uncomfortable sensations arose within me as I slowly showed up more and more like her. And yet, I continued because they served my need to please in order to achieve a sense of belonging to my birth family. This battle created a strong yearning to understand who I was without them within my beautiful new relationship with Hank.

I wanted to get to know myself from the inside out without the external forces of my parents' values and assumptions of what I represent. Hank understood my continued want for autonomy and encouraged my independence. To him, it all seemed like a natural progression of personal evolution. But I'm not sure he thought of the repercussions of what that looked like from my parents', and in particular, my mother's point of view. I don't think either one of us knew what that aftermath of defying them would entail. In fact, I know we could never have predicted the irrational thoughts it triggered in my mother. Who knew that her needs would end up being fulfilled despite the rest of her family's lack thereof? In hindsight, naivety is the ultimate nemesis of those who trust the self-absorbed, even for a moment.

VII

⋙ Escaping the Cycle of Insanity ⋘

Off and on throughout the first 60 years of my life, I walked the fine line between thinking I might be insane and succumbing to that belief. To my detriment, I considered this many times, and the consequence was that it held me back from acting on what I knew to be true. Moreover, the thought that I could be teetering on the brink of insanity dissuaded me from exposing the deception of those who alluded to its possibility.

I don't think my mother ever questioned her mind's lucidity. Instead, while experiencing the obscure reality of a hint of uncertainty, she immediately ignored its warnings and moved into warrior survival mode—dismiss and move on. I cannot condemn her for wanting to escape the havoc of the possibility of functional insanity, especially at the hands of someone else's crazy-making, because I found myself in the same situation many times. The cycle was as deliberate as the wheels on a car—once in motion, it knew no other function than to continue moving forward until I put the brakes on, avoiding any possible damage. But for the most part, the momentum overtook any reasoning that showed up as a dim shadow because my primal need to belong was so overpowering. It was like seeing my car crash in slow motion, but instead of a massive piece of metal being destroyed before my eyes, the fragility of all three of my connecting housing components—mind, heart, and soul—gradually disintegrated. The desperate continual race to seek and experience love eroded the exact thing I was trying to find and build.

Six decades of fighting for my right to trust all that I feel finally brought me to the epiphany that my mother did not intentionally break the intuitive housing within me. I now know that her race for survival was created as a natural response to inherited patriarchy carried forward from those before her. All my life, I experienced this misogynistic detachment and often wondered if it was a function of my father completely lacking the ability to receive or express emotion. I cannot imagine being married to someone as empathetically detached as he was. And whether he was responsible due to his inability to connect or not, I saw his knee-jerk reactions to his wife and children as the reason for my mother's continual misbehaving as the car she drove frantically raced towards her definition of love.

When my sister died on January 22, 1989, my mother's morality may have become unhinged, along with her car when she ran a stoplight a few days after her daughter's funeral. I believe her God was screaming at her to stop because somewhere along the way, preceding my sister's passing, she had crossed the line from being sane to insane. The connection she had been chasing for so long sent her into an unfathomable state at the expense of possibly alienating the rest of her family.

The domino effect of my mother's choices over the few days preceding my sister's passing created devastating damage for me, and I believe, others—but that is their story to tell. She fell into what she was taught while walking a lifetime tightrope of distorting reality—she had a choice to step back and do the right thing for everyone involved or jump into the demise of manipulating the truth modelled by past generations. She chose to deep dive into the most hidden personal destruction that exists—the descent into using victimhood as an excuse for deceit that I found almost impossible to forgive. It is the most dangerous kind that requires adapting one's story as it unfolds until none of the dots seem to connect anymore.

Being brought up by someone unknowingly managing that tightrope is almost impossible to understand. It becomes a struggle for everyone connected to the victim who continues to try to control them. I believe no one in my family was aware of what was going on back then or that they necessarily agree with me now. The disfunction was never acknowledged, so no one talked about it. We would never have contemplated we were subconsciously managing the madness that comes from control and manipulation passed on from so many generations before us. None of us considered the effects of centuries-long stereotypical hierarchy rulings and practices that brought daily damage upon us. That subliminal destruction was strategically implemented through patriarchal and matriarchal control under the disguise of love.

I was oblivious to how the God my mother worshipped psychologically impacted me; I believed I was not worthy of His love or anyone else positioned higher than me, which was pretty much everyone else. This was the crazy-making I fed into and believed was my destiny. Miraculously, however, I discovered that I could only deny the whisper of truth that kept nagging at me until the trauma of loss was so devastating that I had to either succumb to familiarity and accept my mother's plight or use the strength she instilled in me to uncover the secret she harboured so many years ago. The day my sister died, my mother dove so deep into the pit of duplicitous insanity that there was no hope she could climb out. Accepting her defence that she was unable to sanely reason is the only way I can reach even a degree of compassion for her.

The same woman who taught me the moral consequences of lying when I was a little girl committed to several so incomprehensible 20 years later that it forever changed the trajectory of my life. I believe she will hold onto the fraudulent story she created until the day she is reunited with her daughter in heaven—solely to preserve the very sanity she lost on the fateful day my sister crossed over. I understand, but I struggle to forgive. And not for the sake of redemption because I am not spiteful towards her. I simply have not reached a place where I can absolve her refusal to admit what she did—forgiveness remains challenging to achieve for those not accountable for their actions.

Sadly, this is the side effect of my mother's lifetime of unworthiness—the belief that her story could be twisted at every turn in order to save face during her darkest, most deceptive journey, even whilst knowing that every lie along the way could damage those closest to her. Her painful loss could have been used as inspiration to rise to the resilience her mother taught her, but her desperate anguish propelled her further into the cloud of fraudulent descent that overshadowed her relationship with me.

Christmas 1988 was filled with the eeriness surrounding my oldest sister's pending fate. She, her husband, and my nephews arrived early in the afternoon, along with my other sister and her family. Everyone was on time except for Hank and me. We didn't have children yet, but we were always late, and every time we walked through the front door of their house, I heard my mother complaining about our tardiness, echoing from moments before. But she never said anything to us, instead acting like everything was okay because she didn't want to ruin the day with an argument. I noticed that my sister was not her usual self, looking pale, and her energy was lower than usual. I initially chalked it up to a tired mother managing three young boys ages four, six, and eight during the Christmas holidays. However, when we sat down for dinner, she barely ate a bite, and when questioned, she said she might have the flu. I remember thinking how odd it was that she didn't mention feeling ill when she arrived hours before. As the peace-maker, it was like she was hoping no one would notice.

I can relate to others consciously hiding their suffering because I did the same for a very long time—I still have difficulty sharing my discomfort and asking for help. I am skilled at making life look seamlessly joyful while hiding how I really feel, just like my mother did. I learned how to imitate a functional person at a very early age while simultaneously hiding my internally-housed dysfunction. It slowly ate away at me but also became my norm—untruths welcomed by those around me became much more comfortable than the truths they chose to ignore.

I was taught to live this way, to not upset my mother or father, to not go against the grain of who they are, and to only believe what they did. Going back to sitting at that kitchen table as an innocent blonde-haired, blue-eyed child with Jesus staring down at me from above my father, I instinctively knew not to flippantly share my soul. And my matriarch lived true to her lineage by teaching me to be stoic and hide my truth while my patriarch did as his father before him, controlling me through fear—stunting my innate sensitivity. They worked as well as any fine-tuned team, honouring their predecessors, expecting their children to live as they lived, be who they were, and say what they said for no other reason but to be loyal and do what they believed was right.

I was well-trained to dismiss my initial free-flowing thoughts by replacing them with praised calculated secondary thoughts—although fake, they were safe

Around The Table

for me to voice. An unspoken and spoken understanding told me that unleashing my initial views, if they conflicted with others' opinions, was unwelcome and would result in ostracization. I did not want to create the turmoil of chaos for fear of losing their co-dependent lifeline. Over time, I knew that I did not want to be connected to parts of them, but the guilt that came with pushing those pieces—them—away was overwhelming and showing up completely as myself was too risky. So, I surrendered to maintaining a degree of themness just enough to be accepted. Until I didn't anymore…

My sister hung in that day, sitting through the Christmas dinner my mother served that included the mocha yule log she ordered from the Swiss baker in town. When I was very young with an element of joy still tugging at my sleeve, I loved the little plastic sled and reindeer that graced the top with their legs embedded in the dark brown icing—my sister's boys had the same look of wide-eyed excitement when their oma brought it out from the kitchen. History repeated itself with harmonic traditions overridden with the impending turbulence of hypocrisy. After devouring the cake, we walked downstairs to the basement rec room, where the tree was already lit. I smiled, seeing the same ornaments my sisters and me hung with my mother so many years in a row. It was a momentary memory quickly erased by a flashback, bringing my father into the scene—the same icky feeling in my stomach returned from when I was a child. I looked over and saw him assuming his usual position in the most comfortable chair in the house with an end table beside it for easy access to his drink—coffee, whisky, eggnog—essentially whatever was going depending on the celebration, time of day, day of the year, what my mother was serving, or what my father wanted. This was the same place he sat when we decorated the tree year after year, watching us choose a branch while my mother shared the story behind each ornament. As a wee girl, I was overly enthusiastic about Christmas and everything about it, but eventually, that elation was accompanied by a foreboding apprehension it would be interrupted by my father's disruptive patterning—because it always was. It over-rode my joy every time.

Snapping back to my niece's and nephews' squeals when they saw presents under the tree, my awareness was heightened that neither my father nor my mother reprimanded them for being noisy. I have heard that grandparents are more lenient with their grandchildren than with their children growing up; I considered this a blessing for both of my sisters' kids. My mother moved into her next role of the day, passing out the presents one by one and in an orderly fashion. There were rules that I have adopted with my children: if everyone got the same thing, she handed them out at the same time, and they had to be opened together. However, if the presents were different, we watched each person open their gift individually from oldest to youngest.

My sister watched intently, and, if needed, she helped each of her boys open their gifts. Once again, I noticed her subdued state and sense of being stoic; it was like she was enduring the gift-opening process while simultaneously trying not to show physical discomfort. Something was off, but I didn't ask, wanting to respect her discretion. She and her family left earlier than they usually would that Christmas, claiming she must have the flu. There are so many things I would have shared with her that day if I had known it was the last time I was going to see or speak to her.

My parents left to vacation in the Dominican Republic a few days later. This was their reward after working through a busy year and Christmas season at the store. However, they weren't gone long when my brother-in-law contacted me, saying that we needed to call my parents to bring them back home; my sister had been transported to the largest comprehensive cancer centre in Canada. This was the first we learned that she knew she had cancer while sitting around the table at my parents' house that Christmas day—she didn't tell us because she didn't want to keep my parents from going on their holiday. She kept her ill-fate from my mother because, like me, she too fulfilled her daughterly duty of making my mother happy. Unfortunately, she didn't know that her aggressive melanoma would rapidly ravage her body and kill her within weeks of celebrating her last Christmas.

Once informed, my parents called one of my mother's aunts, and she quickly arranged flights for them to come home right away. With a sense of urgency, they went directly to their daughter at the hospital as soon as they landed. They stayed by her bedside from early morning until visiting hours ended in the evening every day, only leaving her at night to sleep at my aunt's and uncle's house nearby. They drove my parents and picked them up every day for two weeks, supporting them through the agony of possibly losing their firstborn. I called my aunt's landline every other day—still no cell phones—and talked to my mother to find out how my sister was, asking when I could visit her. Every time, she told me that she was being taken care of, not to worry and that I shouldn't come; they would start chemotherapy soon, and she needed to rest. The conversation always ended with my mother telling me that she would let me know if things changed. But she never did.

Two weeks from when my parents walked off the plane and one day from my last phone call with my mother, I received the horrifying news that my sister had died at one o'clock in the morning. My mother told me there was no warning, and that everyone was surprised because my sister was supposed to start her chemo the next day. She said that a nurse came in around supper the night before and encouraged my parents to go out for dinner for a break and come back the next day. She indicated that they agreed because there was no indication that their daughter had worsened. So, they went for something to eat and then went to my aunt's, who was later awakened in the middle of the night by a phone call from the hospital with the news that my sister had passed. I found out later that she was on an IV Morphine drip throughout those two weeks, with access to pump it manually as needed for pain—in the world of cancer, that doesn't happen unless someone is in dire distress and nearing the end of their life. There may have been a treatment

Around The Table

plan sitting in a file for my sister, but I believe it was quickly set aside when her health declined.

In the days, months, and years to follow, a continuous deep nagging bubbled up within me, wondering why my parents or brother-in-law didn't call my other sister or me to let us know that she had taken such a U-turn. We had seen her just four weeks before opening presents with her children when she said she had the flu, and then she suddenly died with no indication of a significant decline! Something wasn't right, and yet, I didn't question any of it because my mother convincingly told me that her daughter's passing was sudden and unexpected; no one had any reason to believe she was close to dying. I squashed my intuition down into my subconscious, not wanting to believe that she was capable of lying to that degree and doing what I thought she had. I dismissed my intuition, substituting it with how she rationalized what happened. Outwardly, I trusted she was telling us the truth. But inwardly, I knew this story had been adapted somehow—a secret was being kept. This became a pivotal moment in our relationship without me realizing it, and although I experienced a vast and steady shift between us, I excused it with anything but what I knew deep down had happened.

From the moment we received the news that my sister was gone, a massive snowball of chaos ensued beginning with my mother telling her remaining daughters that we had to keep the store open on the days before and after the wakes and funeral. I was in shock on so many levels, given that my sister died, and my mother was adamant that we kept her deli running. We worked through such a devastating time as if nothing had happened. There were many times in the months and years to follow when my mother looked me straight in the eye and, understandably, told me that she didn't think she could live without her firstborn. Although I completely empathized with her loss, I couldn't help but feel less than as she sent her other two daughters to work the day after their sister died. Another employee ran the store while we took three days off to go to the wakes and the funeral. When I later questioned her, she told me that she couldn't process what was going on and thought she had to keep the store open to abide by her lease; she explained she was simply not in her right mind, having lost her daughter. It's not easy challenging someone's past behaviour when they admit they are on the brink of insanity.

Although I believe my sister didn't think it would happen so quickly, I am convinced that before she was admitted to the hospital, she knew she would not survive. I later heard that she was diagnosed in July and told that she would either survive or die within six months—she passed six months later, almost to the day. On October sixth, I saw her for her birthday. She was her usual exuberant self, fulfilling her Dutch-style daughterly duty of hosting her celebratory day with the entire family at her house. However, from early October to late December, she had clearly declined, not able to hide her malaise. After she passed, I heard that at some point early on, she woke up with blood on her pillow from a mole behind her ear—it was already too late with the melanoma spreading through her blood and eventually attacking her liver. It would take a miracle to survive a liver loaded with cancer.

She had all her funeral arrangements in place, right down to an open casket at a traditional Catholic ceremony, as well as the location she would be laid to rest— no cremation but a casket with her prepared blessed body buried in the ground and a tombstone honouring her short-lived life. My parents spent years placing flowers and plants at her gravesite. My mother asked me to go with her six years after her burial. At that time, I finally cried, and when I was done, I wondered what the point was. I looked over at my mother, who seemed to find comfort in being surrounded by dead people. It gave me no solace, and I refused to pray when she asked me to join her. Instead, I distracted myself by helping her clean up around the tombstone and then told her I would meet her at the car. Walking away from her, I felt like a horrible person—unsupportive and cruel to not even pretend to care more—maybe I was more like my father. Obviously, something kept me from connecting to her, but I couldn't bring myself to see it. I didn't want to purposefully uncover a piece of information I wasn't sure about and could possibly destroy her if I revealed it. Even though I knew she was guilty about something significant, I believed I should not reveal it to protect her from being hurt. Once again, I was stuck between confronting the truth and pretending it didn't exist for the sake of protecting her. Why did I protect those who misbehaved?

Sitting in the reserved family seating in the church, I flashed back to when my sister took her wedding vows. The priest interrupted my memory by saying that God would be with her to eternity, and He would walk by her side to her final resting place. I thought about the dichotomy of her wedding and her funeral, with both beginning in the house of the Lord, having the most honoured societal patriarch accompany her—first to a life filled with hopes and dreams and then to her death filled with…something else…I didn't know for sure. The difference was that one brought optimism to those sitting in the pews as she entered a new life as a wife, and the other brought despair to those same people as she retreated from them to another existence.

On that day, I truly hoped that God existed somehow, so He could provide my sister's soul with ease while leaving this Earth—the same peace that her husband, children, and sisters would have offered her in the hospital when she crossed over. I would have done anything to have told her that I loved her one more time, that I would miss her contagious laugh, and that I would be there for her children. The truth is that once she was gone, my love for her increased, and I yearned to hear her laugh that I didn't remember anymore. I also didn't see her children for a very long time. Our family fell apart within a broad divide that I believe was created by my mother; it was eventually partially repaired through the telling of stories hidden through desperate and deceptive secrets.

The priest went through his sermon, and my mind wandered to a visit I had with my sister a few years before. She spoke about her belief that she would die young, but my sister was not afraid because she was confident that she would be safe with God—that's all that mattered. I didn't share what I thought about all that; it wasn't my place to disrespect her faith. But, quietly in my head, I questioned why she was so trusting of this mystical man who had only ever scared me. Years after she died, my mother told me that her daughter told her a story while she sat at her bedside in the hospital. She shared that just after she became sick, she got up during the night to go to the bathroom and saw a bright light in the distance. They lived in the country where it was pitch black at night, and passing by the window, she saw a flickering light far back in the woods. She told my mother she believed God was calling her to join Him. At that moment, she made peace that it was her time to go.

I moved through the wakes like an obedient apostle trusting His lead. I never cried. Not one tear flowed from my eyes as I slipped into survival mode, supporting my mother, who broke down each time someone approached her. The line was massive, right out the door and around the corner of the funeral home. My sister and her husband were heavily immersed in their religious community. I remember her talking about the possibility of converting to his faith, but she refused, instead agreeing to take the boys to his church while she continued to practice Catholicism.

The kids ran by the casket as if it was part of the furniture, and my mother asked me if they should be doing that. I told her to let them be, *Their mother just died*. She did. I stood in the lineup at the funeral home, greeting people I never knew and consoling one relative after another as they struggled with their discomfort of knowing a young mother who left her children too soon. At one moment, I fainted from the exhaustion of putting strength before eating. I came to with someone shoving a donut in my face—I hate donuts. I remember taking a breather, standing in a corner in the room when my sister's father-in-law came up to me. With a coffee in his hand and a smirk reminiscent of my father on his face—I wondered if that was a guy thing— he began with, *You people have open caskets, eh?!* I knew that *you people* meant *you Catholics*. I suddenly understood the condescension my sister told me she endured for the many years he outwardly criticized her faith. He was a mason, and for many reasons, I'm not a fan. However, it was not for me to judge his preference of devotion, just as it was not his place to judge my family's. Oddly, I found myself wanting to defend Catholicism, but in this emotional arena, I chose to keep the peace by cutting him off at the knees and coolly replied, *Yes, we do*. I was shaking inside as I walked away from his patronizing vibe.

There was a reception in the church hall where relatives from both sides attended. Strangely, it was like being at a family reunion with the familiarity of having my cousins, aunts, and uncles there. My brother-in-law's extended family suddenly felt like intruders to me, wanting to be part of my sister in some special way. Of course, they deserved to be there, but after talking to his father, I unfairly lumped them all in with him. My thoughts were all over the place, from chaotic to calm, as I experienced moments of extreme sorrow brought on by the loss of my sister to comfort through the deep connection I had with my extended family. They understood because there was a history of oneness between us. The contrast between wanting to run and hide and the yearning to be enveloped in the presence of those I've known my whole life made me think that this might be what love is. But I couldn't be sure, and I was ashamed to be experiencing *gezelligheid* amidst the loss of my sister. Standing in that hall, managing the contrast of life and death, the conflict with love I experienced my whole life was emphasized. It was never consistent, with bad pieces constantly interrupting the flow of good. At the age of twenty-eight, I was already exhausted from fighting immorality with the hope that kindness could outweigh the consequence of suffering.

Everyone went back to my sister's house, and we stood scattered around, with pies, soups, stews, sandwiches, coffee, wine, and beer being served around every corner. All the makings of a party without the fun. And yet, I stood in her kitchen and heard my mother sharing her Dutch soup recipe like it was just another day. Who gave a shit about how to make soup? I stood at my sister's sink and looked out the window to the view of the woods where she had seen the light of God, calling her to go to Him. Suddenly, I envisioned her in the distance, running back to the house on a snow-covered path. Then, I snapped out of it and thought, *That's stupid; she's dead.* I tried to hear her voice, but I could only find bits of it. It was only a matter of months before I completely forgot what she sounded like. I still cannot remember her laugh. How does that even happen?

I heard my brother-in-law's father begin his schtick about Catholics with my mother in the dining room, and I knew that was going to end badly. She got away from him as fast as I had and came into the kitchen. She was nervous, alternating wringing her fingers in one hand with the other, and she started telling me how he said, *You people.* I gently took hold of her hands, pulling them apart and caressing each with my fingers, *I understand. He did that to me at the funeral home. He's probably just nervous, not knowing what to say. Just be polite and walk away mom.* She stood silent for a moment, looking at me as if she understood, but then started rambling on about it again. I couldn't wait for that day to end, and I told her I had to leave. When I found Hank sitting in a chair across the living room, he looked like he was in agony. He loved my sister and couldn't stand the thought of the boys without her. He glanced up, and our eyes locked; one nod of my head and we set out for a silent forty-five-minute drive to our house. That was the same forty-five minutes she had counted on as a buffer from my mother—I wondered if she had ever counted vegetables. That distance was part of her plan to maintain a loving, sustainable relationship with my mother. She thought she was clever and would be using it for decades.

A few weeks later, my other sister and I went back to help our brother-in-law clean out his wife's clothes from their closet and dresser. At one point, my sister went into the kitchen to get a glass of water. He was there and when she returned to me, she was completely distraught and told me we needed to leave immediately. Something happened between them that isn't my place to tell and was buried along with all the other indiscretions made during that time. I was angry with him for upsetting my sister and used it as an excuse to take something of his wife's without telling him. When they were married, my mother gave her a locket that belonged to my paternal oma. It was engraved with Oma's initials because my sister was named after my father's mother. My mother told me that my brother-in-law refused to give it back to her when she died, so I used this opportunity to steal it for my mother, forever striving to make her happy. I also took her childhood birthstone ring and encouraged my sister to pick a piece of jewellery she liked. Carrying forward my mother's family's talent to keep a secret, I told her never to tell anyone what we did, and I don't think she did. We quickly loaded the car and said goodbye. I have carried that burden of deceit ever since.

We didn't see or hear from him for over a year but not because we stole a few pieces of my sister's jewellery. What happened next definitely strained my relationship with my brother-in-law and took me 32 years to discover that it wasn't entirely his fault. I say *entirely* because, from where I stand, he chose to keep my mother's secret close to his heart to protect her. I now know he was protecting her from her deception because that is what motivates a secret.

One day out of the blue, my mother told me that her son-in-law didn't want to see us anymore and wouldn't let us see the boys again—ever. She was distraught and said she was baffled as to why. I was shocked because we had all welcomed him into our family. It didn't make sense to me why he did not want us in his and the boys' lives suddenly; I automatically wondered, *What did my mother do?* And so, I asked her, and she told me that she didn't do anything. My parents went to a lawyer to be granted visitation rights with their grandchildren. But they could not because they had no rights as grandparents, and my sister and I didn't either; if a father wants to cut off all ties, that is his choice. My parents were devastated, and I was angry with my brother-in-law. Those children were all we had left of my sister, and I couldn't believe he would keep them from us for no reason. I blamed him because I had nothing else to go on, but I knew there was more to it.

With each passing day, our hearts broke more, and I watched my mother mourn her daughter and losing her three grandsons. I empathized with her. I listened to her express the profound losses she was experiencing. I told her I understood when she told me that nothing would be the same until she was reunited with her grandsons and her daughter in heaven one day. I held her in my arms and invited her to cry a river of endless tears on my shoulder. It was the first time in a very long time that I believed we reconnected from that place not many find in the recesses of their soul. I found the closest thing to love for my mother because I could not fathom the pain she was experiencing, and I didn't know what else to do other than provide her with the compassion anyone deserves, who outlives their child. I believed that my mother was dealt the worst injustice possible with the added loss of not being able to see her grandchildren, and I did whatever I could to comfort her. However, I couldn't help noticing that neither of my parents ever expressed anger or judgment towards their son-in-law through this entire process, and I found that odd because he had taken their grandsons from them.

Then about a year later, I was told that he had suddenly changed his mind, and my parents could have access to the boys. He would drive them to my parents and set them on their front porch to ring the doorbell upon their arrival—their dad would not come in or speak to my parents. When my mother told me this, I point blank asked her, *Mom, what happened?* She was adamant she did not know but also told me not to ask him any questions that would rock the boat, *We need to be happy and not ask because it might upset him and make him take the boys away again.* I looked at her and agreed, but I continued questioning what she had done. Something was wrong, and I feared she was managing a significant detrimental mistake.

At the end of each visit, my parents drove the boys the 45 minutes back to their father and deposited them on their front porch—the same routine, coming and going. Although I understood how traumatizing it was for him to lose his wife, this just didn't jive. I could not comprehend his calculated strategy to intentionally keep his distance from us, especially my parents. He was not acting like the person I knew, and my mother actually justified his actions, which was also very out of character. She told me that everyone grieves differently, and this was how he was coping with losing his wife. I wanted to believe her, and I had no concrete reason not to, other than a reoccurring inkling deep within that told me something wasn't right. After all, my brain was conditioned to decipher everything as either right or wrong, and something about this wasn't right—so, what could be wrong, then? Unfortunately, I was also programmed to believe that to prove something is wrong, I needed evidence that it was, in fact, so. I had none other than a gut feeling, and my father taught me that just wasn't sufficient for an effective defence. So, I ignored that initial thought, that whisper from my soul, and I carried on as if my mother had told me the truth. Once again, my biggest mistake was trusting her.

More time passed—maybe months—I don't remember, and suddenly things shifted when he decided to re-enter our lives. As much as this made me happy, I blamed him for all the stress we had endured for over a year because my mother told me he didn't want us in his life, and it took a lot of emotional energy to support my mother, so I wasn't very forgiving at first. But I never said anything because her story constantly changed and spiralled in many directions, and then, she suddenly convinced me that he didn't do anything wrong; it was nothing to worry about, *He just had a difficult time adapting to being around us without his wife. We need to forget about it.* That was interesting to me because my mother is not that forgiving, and if he just needed space, why didn't he just tell us that? Why was everything kept hush, hush? His actions did not reflect emotional distress but rather acute anger—no one takes their boys out of their grandparents' lives unless they did something to piss them off.

Unfortunately, my relationship with my brother-in-law was never the same after that. My mother's tale did not convince me that he was simply uncomfortable around his dead wife's family. He never volunteered his side of the story, and I never asked. I didn't feel I should have to. So, I allowed my mother's story to prevail and ignored the uncomfortableness of knowing there was something more to it. My mind became a cornucopia of compartments capable of adapting and tucking away information to protect myself and others while simultaneously being manipulated. Even though I repeatedly heard that incessant message, *Your mother is lying*, the child in me begged to protect her just like he was to keep her happy, so my mind pinned him as the villain and her as the victim. However, very recently, upon discovering that they both kept the truth from me, a therapist asked me why I continue to protect the damaging behaviour of people in my life. Wow, that was an unexpected, loaded question! And yet I was surprisingly able to answer it, *Because, when I was a child, loyalty was the first thing I was taught as a condition of love, whether integrity was involved or not. And going against that condition to validate my own integrity, would cause ostracization from my family. I would be wrong, and they would be right; it's that simple. It would be a war I'm not trained to win—winning means conceding, allowing them to be right, even if they are blatantly wrong in my mind. The pain of disconnecting from them would destroy my co-dependency from them, which is all I know.*

My mother told me that she asked her son-in-law to go to a church counsellor with her. His specialty was bereavement, and she had been going to him and thought it would support him through his discomfort around us. I didn't believe her, knowing there was something much more he needed support with. She went on to say that this counsellor agreed to mediate their situation by meeting one-on-one about the issue: first alone with my mother and then alone with him because he said he did not want to be in these sessions with my mother. My mother said she understood, but I thought, *If this is just about feelings of discomfort, why wouldn't he meet with her?* How odd that he did not want to be with her. Again, what had she done? After their individual sessions, my mother was ecstatic, telling me that her plan worked because he agreed to be part of our family again. Just like that, my mother had fixed it; she was the heroine. Life went on as if nothing had happened, and no one talked about it again...until September 2021.

In the meantime, I became pregnant in July 1989, three months before my middle sister gave birth to her son. I was honoured to be by her side as her labour coach, even though the experience scared me to death. At one moment, she screamed, *Jesus Christ*, and the doctor told her that He wasn't there, but not to worry because he was the person she wanted delivering her baby, not Jesus. I laughed at how pre-programmed she was to call out for JC's support when she had a skilled obstetrician at the helm of her delivery—how trusting society is of someone we're not 100 percent sure even exists when facing immense suffering!

Throughout her pregnancy, she had difficulty emotionally, as she was simultaneously mourning our sister and trying to focus on being healthy for the baby she was carrying. One life was preparing to leave this world, while another was preparing to enter it. She was stoic and didn't discuss how she felt with me—we don't do that. However, I could tell she was being brave, and my heart went out to her as she hid her pain—we do that.

For 32 years since my sister's death, I experienced constant dis-ease around the mysterious series of events surrounding my brother-in-law's reaction to my mother. Still, I did not want to believe that she would contrive such a detailed story for the sake of covering up a lie—how bad could it be? And yet, the mystery connected to it made it seem heinous, almost unforgiveable, especially since no one asked forgiveness for anything. I now realize that I had an idea of what she did and placed it in one of my hidden compartments because I couldn't accept what my mother might be capable of. However, I was very sure of what I wasn't willing to forgive.

My brother-in-law remarried before our families were reunited, and my mother told everyone that his new wife was the angel who assisted in instigating our reconciliation. Apparently, she convinced her husband that the boys needed their grandparents in their lives and encouraged him to reconnect with them. My mother told us that was why he accepted her invitation to see the counsellor to resolve the disconnection between them—because his new wife convinced him it was the right thing to do. I believed my mother and was so grateful to this addition to our family for providing peace and, in particular, making my mother happy. But then I thought about her role in the secret side of all of this... And I once again reflected on why no one was talking about what had happened between my mother and her son-in-law.

I remember when they all came back to have dinner at my parents' house for the first time after the fallout, and my mother called us to the table. Each of us automatically sat at the seat we always had, and the children sat at a card table added to the end of the main table. When our new family member approached the table, the only empty chair was beside my brother-in-law, where his deceased wife always sat. It was a difficult moment we all had to accept, including the new kid on the block, who appeared as uncomfortable as the rest of us. There was silence, and no one said anything—we just watched her sit down, and then my mother suddenly began passing the meat around the table, starting with my father. I could have sworn I experienced a collaborative *whoosh* as we all exhaled together. I started talking about something to break the ice, and my father dove into his usual banter about who was right and wrong. My sister chimed in while all the guys sat back and smiled, listening to our routine while savouring my mother's home-cooked meal. I couldn't imagine what was going through my new sister-in-law's mind and wondered if her husband had prepared her.

It wasn't her fault that she landed in this insane den of thieves, and it took some time for me to adjust to replacing my sister with her sitting across from me. Every time we sat down at that table, I pushed aside how upset I was with my brother-in-law by ignoring my ever-present whispers of suspicion. I distanced myself from him and blamed him for that ugly year after my sister's death, but I never told him I did. I simply dismissed the ambiguity of what my mother said he did and what my mother was capable of. I avoided him, not being able to succumb to asking what really happened. And I protected my mother without knowing what I was protecting her from. That was a decision I could never take back. However, as a young woman still terrified of unveiling the truth and the possible consequence of being banished from the family for revealing it, I did what they did and accepted denial by pushing bravery aside. People have told me that I am hard on myself, but there is no question that I chose being a coward to keep my pain at a distance and my mother's smile on her face. Fear takes away the power of courage.

I took the win, being thrilled our family was reunited because I missed the boys and couldn't fathom not seeing them grow up into the incredibly talented, smart, and loving young men my sister was raising them to be. I knew she would have wanted us to be a part of her children's lives because she was devoted to creating strong family ties of love between her children and their relatives. Looking back, I realize this became an extension of the values she taught her boys from the time they were born. Among others, their mother instilled joy, faith, honesty, loyalty, and adventure in each of them, and she was a fierce protector—a true mama bear. She spent every minute of the day devoted to her family, from cooking and cleaning to playing and creating. She was that over-functioning mother and wife who was fulfilled without seeking external sources of happiness. Her husband and her children were everything to her.

Her eldest son was the most joyful child I ever met! His smile still melts a crowd within seconds of entering a room. I believe his mother's passing emotionally affected him in the most traumatic way. Being eight when she died, I'm sure he has distinct memories of their time together, and I know he had a deep connection with her. I have heard that he will not speak about her; there is no doubt he has suffered greatly over the years. We have grown apart because I initially did not know how to cope with his unwillingness to talk about his mom. However, a spark returned the last time we saw each other at my mother's 90th birthday party—I am hoping we can foster that further.

The second in line was six, and he is the most open to discussing his mother, wanting to know details surrounding her death and what kind of person she was. I think the more he discovers provides an added sense of connection to his mom. He is loyal, honest, adventuresome, and incredibly insightful. He speaks his truth and is not afraid to have uncomfortable conversations; we have had many.

The youngest was just a wee boy when he lost his mom. I often wonder what must have gone through his mind when he ran by her casket at the age of four. He doesn't remember much about her and is also less inclined to talk about her. It's not likely he feels as one with his mother, but like her, he uses faith to guide him through life. He is spiritual and loving, and I know that inner-peace is something he strives for and has achieved.

Over three decades of anguish passed related to the simple question, *Why was nobody called?* The ambiguity and my mother's possible role in my confusion motivated me to further excavate my life story. I journaled and wrote my story every day, determined to understand how each piece of my life fit into another; I was no longer willing to ignore those whispers. It was time to listen to my inner voice and allow it to holler the truth without the shame of believing something else happened...

Then, suddenly one day, on my daily walk while reflecting on the series of events surrounding my sister's demise, all the dots connected. I don't know why everything about what happened became very clear at that moment or why, on that particular day, I was able to focus on that persistent whisper—the one I had ignored and that tormented me for the 33 years since we laid my sister to rest—but, from one moment to the next, the truth about everything that transpired came flooding over me. It was like I was watching a movie that started from the day my mother called to tell me my sister was gone to the day my brother-in-law cut us out of his life. Every step I took along the white-paved sidewalk was a different scene that, when put together, inspired a sequence of epiphanies. With every crack I walked over, I discovered a crack in my mother's story. With every street I crossed, I navigated a part of her secret. And by the time I finished my walk and reached my house an hour later, I stood in front of the porch, staring at my blood-red door with the revelation that...she lied. I was convinced that my mother had distorted what happened to an unbelievable degree. And what was worse was that I believed she had coerced everyone into believing her story, including my brother-in-law.

I went inside, walked up to Hank, and said, *My mother lied about what happened when my sister died. She didn't tell us that she had declined during that last week in the hospital because she didn't want us there. She didn't call us to come to the hospital because she wanted to say goodbye to her without us being there. She never told anyone, and she deprived my sister of seeing her husband and kids one more time.* He looked at me and replied, *I thought that all along.* Once again, I had no proof, but I was wiser and much more confident than the frightened girl who never got to say goodbye to her sister so many years ago. Something inside me never believed my mother when she told me no one knew her daughter was going to die within days. And I wanted validation—not to prove she was wrong because, at the age of 61, I was well beyond that—but to honour those dear to my sister who never got to see her one last time to say goodbye: her husband, her children, her sisters, and her friends. I wanted them to know that any perpetual inkling they may have had about what happened was real and that my mother should never have kept us from saying goodbye to her. My mother claims she was out of her mind, but in my mind, she was sane enough to put herself aside and do the right thing.

I needed to clarify what had tormented me since the day my mother shared those words that kept repeating in my head, *She just died from one day to the next.* They haunted me because they just didn't make any sense. I knew that finding out what really happened would acknowledge that my sister should never have been robbed of her right to have her loved ones supporting her in her final hours. It would also validate that we should not have been stripped of our right to be with her. So, I grabbed my last bit of hope that there might be a God—the one my sister so devoutly believed in—and I recited my last prayer. I asked Him to tell her that she deserved to be surrounded by her family during her final moments. I begged Him to tell her that she was loved and told him I would prove it by discovering what really happened and sharing it to honour her truth.

I called my sister's middle son, and we briefly discussed his mother's death and the events surrounding it and afterwards. I mentioned my concerns about my mother's story, and he confirmed that there were holes in it that needed clarification, so I asked if we could get together to tell each other what we knew to be true... and false. He was more than willing. So, on a beautiful fall day, we met for lunch on a patio, and he greeted me with his gorgeous smile, *Hi Auntie!!* We ordered food, and I had a glass of wine to steady my nerves; I was worried about triggering him with uncomfortable memories. When I reassured him that my intention was not to upset him, he said the most profound thing any thirty-something man has ever said to me, *You cannot upset me, Auntie; only I can allow what you say to upset me.* Wow!

So, I went on, *What do you know about what happened during the events surrounding your mom's death? Why did your father not want to see us afterwards?* He shared that when he was old enough, he wanted to clarify the circumstances around his mother's death and the events that followed. He decided to gather everyone's feelings and recollections to have a full account of his mother's death. He clearly and confidently shared what he was told by each of them. My mother told him the same version she told me—plain and simple, *She just died* from one day to the next with no signs of decline. She indicated there was no need to call the family because she was not told her daughter was close to passing. She said that she and my father had not seen a doctor in the two weeks they sat by their daughter's bedside for twelve hours a day. *She just died.* She also told her grandson that his father was emotionally distraught after his wife's death and did not feel comfortable being in contact with our family.

My nephew then told me his father's account... my brother-in-law had not received any indication from the doctor or my mother that his wife had declined over the few days before she passed away. But he received a phone call from the doctor afterwards when he asked, *Didn't your mother-in-law tell you what was happening?* The doctor then indicated that he had been telling my mother that things were getting worse. My sister obviously made a U-turn after her husband left the hospital a few days before when he was told to go home to spend time with his boys for the weekend. I'm sure he would have come back had he known that her status had changed. So, the question is whether or not he believed my mother intentionally didn't call him. And then, did he believe her plea of insanity when he asked her why she didn't call him?

Everything was set in motion as per my sister's plans: the wakes, the funeral service, the burial, the reception. And then, once his wife was laid to rest and everyone went home, my brother-in-law continued to move through his grieving process. Given that the doctor questioned why my mother didn't contact him, my conclusion is that she withheld his wife's status from him, which was what motivated him to end contact with my mother. Rightfully so, I think he was angry and had to process what she had done—I know I would have if I had known. When he finally agreed to meet with my mother's counsellor at the church a year later, she convinced him that she had stepped over the line into insanity and could not process what the doctor was telling her.

Unfortunately, far too many incongruent sides to this story don't make any sense. For example, my mother told me she never once spoke to a doctor the whole time she was there. And yet, the doctor told my sister's husband that he consulted with my mother several times to let her know her daughter's status. The doctor also asked my mother to give my sister's husband an update during the days leading up to her death, so why didn't she? If she was so distraught that she couldn't think clearly, was my father also on the brink of insanity?

I have been told that my brother-in-law accepted that my mother did not know his wife would die the day she did. After hearing a few sides of this story, I don't dispute it either because my mother would never have gone out for dinner and left her alone. However, she did know that her daughter was very close to dying because the doctor told her she had declined significantly. For me, it's really not about that night but rather about the days leading up to it. I understand my brother-in-law's intention to justify my mother's lack of communication with him and turn the other cheek—the trade-off being the boys having their oma and opa in their lives. However, I still question her state of overwhelm and her declaration that she didn't know what to do when the doctor looked her in the eyes and told her to call her son-in-law.

This was all kept a secret, and secrets are created to hide deception. I don't know if my other sister knew what really happened, but I was certainly never told—for over 30 years. And even then, it was my intuition that motivated me to unravel the bits that intuitively never made sense. And somehow, my brother-in-law felt the need to protect my mother by not volunteering what he knew to the rest of the family—as far as I know. Unfortunately, I will not likely find out because our family is very good at keeping secrets from those who don't tolerate them.

What I do know is that I shared my discovery with several of my aunts, and they too had no idea why my mother kept us away from my sister during the final days leading to her demise. There are so many secrets spread around my family that I cannot fathom anyone being sure of what is true and what is not. Perhaps,

I should have asked my brother-in-law since I knew something wasn't right, but it didn't occur to me because my mother had me convinced that everything was out of her control. I realize now just how out of touch I was because my mother always has everything under her control, no matter where she is on the spectrum of insanity.

I value all aspects of truth—speaking, being, and responding to the world within it. Any challenge that arises from it always stems from the discomfort people experience in reaction to it, including me. But that usually occurs due to my unwillingness to face it. I had to gain clarity about what made sense about why my mother, whether consciously or not, didn't call anyone those days my sister died. The only other person she let in on her plan was my father, and the fact that he went along with her speaks volumes of how loyal they were to each other. Even during her daughter's death, I believe my mother was motivated to be the special one, and my father didn't stop her...because he chose not to. He followed her lead as she convinced him that they were more privileged than anyone else to be by her side at the end of her life. And in the process, they robbed their daughter's husband, children, and sisters of the same gift of closure. Neither my mother nor my father dared to do the right thing for everyone.

If there is a God, He supported my sister that fateful day when he decided to send the nurse into my sister's room to convince my parents to go out for dinner that night. His plan changed everything because my sister was alone when she died. Just as my sister moved far enough away from my mother before she got sick to create the space she needed to live in peace, God provided her with the space she needed in the hospital to die in peace. Briefly, I thought maybe He does work in mysterious ways. My sister died in the tranquillity of God's devotion, while my mother lived on having to manage the torment of what she did.

I used to believe that those who die young have completed the good deeds they came here to do, while those who live a long life suffer from the guilt of their bad choices until they die. But, although I'm sure she was tormented inside, my mother outwardly moved on with ease. Her alibi inflicted suffering upon everyone around her because she could not bring herself to stand in her truth. I can never fully relate to the agony she went through when she lost her child—I am well aware that is the worst thing a parent can endure. However, once I uncovered the hidden details of her story, the compassion she initially squeezed out of me because she could not see her grandchildren waned significantly. I could not comprehend the lengths she underwent to lessen her guilt by justifying the agony she created for the loved ones who supported her. She strategically convinced her son-in-law that she was the only victim, and we all bowed down to dutifully rescue her. I will admit that I did not think I could ever forgive someone who refused to acknowledge an apparent fatal lapse of integrity, whether sane or not.

My 91-year-old mother is sharp—intelligent, on the ball, and for the most part, sane. So, when we met for lunch on my 61st birthday, I made one final

Escaping the Cycle of Insanity

attempt to provide an opportunity for her to fess up to the decisions she made when she sold her soul to the devil. But she did not, standing firm that she was unaware her daughter had taken a turn—no doctor spoke to her during the entire two weeks my parents were there. The problem with hanging onto a lie for decades is that it just gets more and more embellished. Putting myself in her shoes, I get it; a lot of shame is manifested when too much time has evolved to unleash a secret, without accepting blame for it.

I have wrestled with this dilemma since the day I stood staring at my front door, suddenly hit by a lightning bolt of clarity that she tricked everyone for her benefit. Since then, I have concluded that this happens when one takes that fatal leap off the edge of the ambiguous line between being sane and insane. My mother leaned into the dark shadow of intense emotional trauma, deciding that only she and my father would be privy to my sister's last few days on this Earth. Within this rationalization, insanity becomes the justification for her decision-making and inspiration for the possibility of my forgiveness—how can I expect acts of lightness from someone who finds herself nestled in darkness?

The real sadness lies in how long my mother has managed this tightrope between integrity and corruption. How many times during my lifetime has she taken that tempting step into deception to emotionally survive? If insanity is the culprit within the negative impact she had on me, do I have the right to judge her? Is insanity an excuse or simply a reason? Pressuring someone to forgive another is often used as a weapon of shame, and I have learned to fight it off to maintain my own sanity.

My family's dynamic changed forever on January 21, 1989—not because my mother knew her daughter was going to die that day and didn't tell us, but because she knew she had worsened before that day and didn't tell us. As a result, she took away the opportunity for us to choose to see her one last time. Everyone can justify it any way they like, but my mother indirectly decided who would be privy to bidding my sister farewell. Was this done with the awareness of its consequences? Was she oblivious to the damage that occurred? Was she insane when she made this choice? The latter creates the world's expectation for me to forgive her somewhat plausible. Suddenly, there's an excuse for her immorality—evidence backing up why she wasn't wrong because she couldn't help herself.

Sadly, I could not let her off the hook that easily because I continued to be badgered with the thought that one must be incredibly savvy to be able to manipulate their loved ones to that degree. I don't believe I was the only one haunted by internal whispers, questioning her actions. But sane does not necessarily go alongside smart, and insane and naïve do not necessarily go hand-in-hand either. To complicate things even further, I believe my mother is capable of choosing sanity over insanity and vice versa when convenient. She can also add the elements of either awareness or naivety to the level of crazy-making she happens to lean into—and whichever is to her advantage at the time. This is how she cons others

Around The Table

to believe whatever she says. I cannot think of anything more detrimental than performing acts that can potentially emotionally destroy another human being with the intent to cover up your guilt. A written-off car gets thrown in a dump while my emotionally-damaged persona walked around for years within embedded trauma that eventually crept into the lives of those around me, impacting them in the most detrimental ways. My mother often made me think I was wavering between sanity and insanity. So, to this day, I still wrestle with the question my therapist asked me, *Why do you continue to protect the bad behaviour of others?* And all I can come up with is, *My conscious wrestles with the possibility of insanity—theirs, mine, or both—and I cannot risk the consequences of what comes with the uncertainty if I am wrong.*

VIII

Escaping the Cycle of Delusion

There I am, once again, sitting at the retro 60s yellow Formica kitchen table. However, I'm not tucked in tight, and I'm content being alone with a tin of assorted buttons sitting in front of me this time. I'm not allowed, but I get up on my knees to see inside the tin from high above it. I then immerse my hand deep in and push the hundreds of shapes around. Hearing them click together while watching the rainbow of colours flow through my fingers, I visualize the delusion of a mini tidal wave. The buttons bang up against each other and the metal sides of the tin, and my imagination goes wild as I contemplate what to do with them next.

I'm four years old, and it's the first year I'm alone at home with my mother during the day. If my father was home, he already had his breakfast and was in bed after coming home from the midnight shift. In September 1964, one of my sisters began grade one, and the other moved up to grade three. I would start kindergarten the next year. So, for now, my mother and I spent a lot of time together…just the two of us.

It was glorious being at home with my mother, even though she wasn't a play-on-the-floor-with-the-kids kind of mom. I get it; I never was with mine either, being more of a creative inspiration for them. I also didn't have a lot of fancy trendy toys, but my mother had combined ingenuity and imagination and used them to entertain me. She knew I loved art and was drawn to colourful knick-knacks and such, so she found a way to entertain me when my sisters were at school, and she busied herself with housewife duties. Just like her mother and her grandmother before her, she had a scheduled daily routine filled with chores: dusting, vacuuming, laundry, ironing, cleaning, and of course, cooking. A different chore was fulfilled at a specific time each day, with a lunch break incorporated into the schedule. It was early, around 11 o'clock, and we ate together at the ambiguous kitchen table, except it was different when it was just my mother and me: I wasn't afraid. When no one else was home, I got to sit in my oldest sister's spot beside my mother with my back to the cross. As a result, I wasn't plagued by God's many expectations but pleasantly distracted by our uninterrupted chatting—I never spilled my milk when my mother and I ate lunch together.

She was done her chores by three in the afternoon, just in time to watch The Guiding Light before my father got up at four. This meant that all her work needed to be done before she sat down in front of the TV. She used that time to recalibrate before taking on her next duty—suppertime. She was very organized, having her potatoes and vegetables cleaned and sitting in cold water in pots on the counter long before she had to turn the stove on. My mother took her roles as wife and mother seriously and wanted to excel at both based on her predecessors' standards. Subconsciously, her success was measured by how well she achieved the expectations of her matriarchal role models. I didn't think she did a good or bad job; I just thought this was what mothers did while fathers slept and worked. And I was right. However, I also wasn't aware that part of her job was keeping her children busy while maintaining her matriarchal self-worth through expected duties. One of the ways my mother achieved this was by distracting me with the various buttons she stored in a *speculaas* cookie tin sent over by her mother years before.

Speculaas is a traditional Dutch cookie usually baked in a rectangular shape resembling a windmill. They were hard, and unless I dunked them into tea, I didn't like the taste of the combination of spices in them. However, I connected to what they represented—generations of the familial afternoon tea tradition. I ate them because they were a conduit to connection, and I loved that they were sent to us by my maternal grandmother from all the way across the ocean. And I especially liked the tins they came in and that my mother collected buttons in them once all the cookies were gone. The buttons in our speculaas tins were different colours, shapes, and sizes, and I was mesmerized by what this trilogy created. I also wondered where they came from, whose shirt, pants, coat, or skirt they had fallen off, never to be put back on. And why? Why had they not been sewn back onto where they came from? Perhaps they fell off unnoticed and were found in the corner they rolled into without the finder knowing their origin. With nowhere else to go, they landed safely in the button tin in case they were needed later. To my recollection, no one ever bothered to find out where they came from. I never saw my mother bring the button tin out of hiding to find a match for a missing one. I only remember her bringing it out and placing it on the kitchen table when she had to dust or vacuum. I thought they were collected for me.

Over the years, I became a collector of things of no practical use—like the buttons. For example, I could never throw away an elastic band. They came in various lengths from the grocery store holding together bunches of fruits and vegetables and other household items. As an extension of my peas and carrots counting days, I could not bring myself to throw one in the garbage—just in case it might be needed later. I saved every elastic I came across for decades and sorted them: red, blue, beige, small, medium, large, thin, and thick. And yet, I barely found a use for one on any given day. I packed them in a box every time we moved from a house we sold. Each time I picked up the tin they were stored in, I opened it to evaluate whether I should throw them out or not, and like my fragile dishes, I always ended up wrapping the tin with hundreds of elastics in brown packing paper as if it was just as valuable. Collecting elastics like buttons became one of many ways I controlled my environment, and it wasn't until I turned 60 that I could decisively free that obsessive-compulsive mindset. It took decades of inner-work and being opened to discovering just how much the circumstances surrounding my sister's death impacted my response to the world, and particularly, my mother.

Months after discovering her secret, I began naturally releasing many controlling behaviours I clung onto for years. I didn't need them anymore because I realized they were used to compensate for my perceived insanity. However, I wasn't crazy. And having clarity about what really happened allowed me to let my life unfold as it was meant to instead of controlling everything around me to justify the deception that I always knew existed but couldn't prove. I wondered if this was why my mother manipulated the unfolding of my sister's death; did she need to control the ending of her daughter's story to cope with something that happened to her when she was younger? I suddenly remembered my aunt hinting years ago about something that had happened in the attic of my mother's childhood home—the youngest three's bedroom—and my mother's adamant refusal to admit anything transpired. Apparently, when questioned, she immediately ended the conversation, saying nothing adverse ever happened, *Just forget about it.*

The life I lived as a child was guided by my mother protecting the life she had dreamed of and created using the self-awareness she had. This included protecting the poor behaviour of those who came before and alongside her, including me. None of us could manage discomfort, but more importantly, anything that did not fit the mould of a perceived perfect family. She had an incredible skill for taking anything that didn't fit into the constructs of that ideal world and adapting it. All my mother ever wanted was to be a participant in what she saw as a loving family that included a doting and loving husband and children, along with all the little experiences that would make them happy. She never complained about her stereotypical role as a housewife, and she actually excelled within it. My mother kept a clean house, adhering to the organized daily schedule she created, and she cooked a beautiful dinner every night. She was the epitome of a 1950s housewife. My mother would have been honoured to play June Cleaver if she had been asked.

But, even if she had been given that opportunity, she would have rejected it because she had her family to take care of. She would never place an acting career before running her household and striving to fulfill being the wife and mother that was expected of her. Among other things, this included having a tin of buttons on hand—just in case. I fully understand why my mother held onto this tin of buttons and kept adding to it. Even though she never did, there was the original possibility of needing one to sew onto one of my father's shirts. But besides that, the collection was traditionally passed down from all the matriarchs before her. So, just as I connect to the old Dutch traditions my mother passed on to me, she also clung to her mother's and Oma's. I'm sure that having the button tin handy reminded her of her mother sitting in her chair by the fire, replacing buttons that had fallen off any one of her 14 children's clothing. Back then, the buttons would have been used for the purpose they were made, being far too valuable to play with; clothing was repaired and seldom replaced.

I saw the buttons as a remarkable assortment of the most fascinating pieces of uselessness I could touch, examine, and organize while determining where they belonged within the piles I assembled on the shiny, polished kitchen table. They were an effective distraction from focusing on being quiet when my father was sleeping and keeping out of my mother's way when she was doing the laundry. I sorted them first by colour: reds, blues, yellows, and greens. And then, I extended that theme into variations of those colours: light and dark. But I couldn't stop at the vibrant array of colours because such a vast selection of shapes also came into play. From there, my attention went to the extraordinary collection of shiny buttons that looked like they came from an ancient time and place. I associated their prestige and unmistakable grandeur to God, who was platinum, Jesus, who was gold, my father, who was silver, and my mother, who was bronze—in that order. They were each unique in their own way and exuded an element of humanness that I connected to a level of power within the hierarchy of the buttons. They were impossible not to honour; in my world, it would have been wrong to ignore their status.

I methodically placed each bronze button in a line from large to small along the edge of the table where my father sat at suppertime. On top of that row and in order, I did the same with the silver buttons, then the gold, and the platinum was at the top—my mother, my father, Jesus, then God. Suddenly, I realized I had defaulted by sitting in my usual spot during my button-sorting, and, without thinking, I took a moment to glance up to where Jesus was. Something in me said I should trust this man who watched over me every day, yet I experienced a great dichotomy in what I had been taught and the distrust I intuitively felt. Unfortunately, I was far too young to determine what any of this meant, but later as an adult, I shared this with a friend; he smiled at me and said, *Diana, my father used to quote an Arab proverb: Trust in God but tie up your camel.*

That would have encompassed what I empathically experienced back then. Looking up at Jesus even for that brief moment, I noticed how His outer shell matched the gold colour in the buttons I had assigned to the second-from-the-top row. I also saw the blood dripping from His hands, and I was uncomfortable, absorbing his physical pain and emotional misery. I managed to shift my gaze away from Him and continued to arrange the shiny buttons to block my discomfort, to tie up my camel—*one button, two buttons, three buttons, four buttons...* I noticed that He didn't seem to have as much influence over me without my father sitting beneath Him.

Red was the next row of importance because it is my favourite colour, using the same shade, shape, and size criteria. I continued this patterning with the remaining buttons until I had numerous rows, ranking in importance from top to bottom. They all had an assigned position within the upside-down pyramid—the bottom row was definitely the shortest with the most uncomplimentary colours and ugliest attributes. When I think about what I was doing back then, it is obvious how hierarchy was already permanently tattooed on my innocent mind within the first four years of my life.

The following year, my mother began working for Avon when I went to grade one because all three of her children were in school during the day. On weekends, she let me go through her Avon kit, which included a massive number of tiny white lipstick samples. The colours were endless and reminded me of the Crayola box of crayons I got for Christmas the year before. I didn't like how Avon arranged the lipsticks by the numbers on the bottom of the tubes rather than colours because that made no sense; they were all mixed up, having the reds with the purples and the pinks with the oranges—that seemed wrong. So, I took them all out and methodically put them back arranged by their colour and shade from dark to light—that seemed right. When I was finished, my mother always told me, *Make sure to put the lipsticks back in order of their numbers*. I was uncomfortable using the numbers to organize them, but I did my best to please my mother. I only knew my numbers so high, so my mother added the ones that I couldn't.

When I was pregnant with my son, I was drawn to seeking old-fashioned toys for him. I wanted him to have the sensory experiences I did with texture, shapes, and colours, so I bought an abacus to inspire counting and old-fashioned wooden cars and puzzles that would stimulate his brain's left and right sides. I am sure the things my mother gave me to play with influenced my need to provide my child with the same positive experiences I had. The difference was that I vowed I would do everything in my power to eliminate the need for him to control his environment and protect himself from dysfunction.

I called Hank at work mid-January in 1990 to share that the first time we tried to conceive worked! We were going to have a baby. He was working out of town at the time, standing in the children's section of the store he co-owned with two business partners. He happened to be folding a Patagonia fleece jacket, sized 18 months, which he promptly purchased and brought home as Simon's first piece of clothing. We were a little shocked by the news because when I went off my birth control after being on them for over ten years, my doctor told me that it usually takes women at least six months to a year to get pregnant. We did the job the first weekend Hank came home after we decided we wanted to expand our family.

Hank wasn't sure about having children. He had been a high school teacher for seven years before becoming a business owner, and he hadn't always experienced the positive side of kids. I appreciated his honesty, telling me that coming home to children would be difficult after being with a couple hundred students all day long. However, when my sister passed away, he recognized a heightened value of family, and he was no longer teaching, so he asked if I was ready. I was 29 at the time, and he was 37. There was nothing I wanted more than to have a child with him. So, on April 13, 1990, 16 months after my sister was buried, our son arrived and changed everything about our world.

When my mother heard that I was pregnant, she was very excited, *My baby is having a baby!* I was so conditioned to react to anything she said that I became annoyed hearing those words; not because I wanted to take any happiness away from her because I believed that was my duty, but I hated the implication that I was somehow more special than my sister, with me being the baby of the family. It was just us two siblings now, and the dynamics had shifted; she was first in line now, and I'm guessing that created added pressure for her to step up as the eldest sibling. I believe that her perception of her role as the eldest child subconsciously changed when she was suddenly bumped up. Over the years, she assumed the added weight of responsibility, wearing it like a badge of honour. As a loyal daughter, my sister took on her expected parental caregiving role just as my cousin had. She was also the eldest in her family and stoically and gracefully cared for her mother, my aunt.

If anyone should not feel less-than, it is my sister, given that she devoted over three decades of her life to being the most devoted daughter there is. She would never say no to either one of my parents. On the contrary, she always asked them what they wanted within a situation and then followed through fulfilling their wishes—I don't believe it mattered if she agreed with their decision. My parents lived together well into their 90s in their apartment, and after my father died, my mother continued staying there; the only reason she can is that my sister supports her to do so. She does her groceries, runs her errands, takes her to her doctor's appointments, and faithfully visits her every Tuesday morning for coffee on her own and on Sunday mornings with her husband. My sister is the perfect example of what an overall good Dutch daughter is, and she is a model eldest daughter, having flawlessly stepped into the caregiver role when required.

On the other hand, I have never been comfortable with the criteria my parents, and in particular, my mother, believes a good daughter is. In fact, my entire being is triggered when those expectations arise: committing to visiting her on a specific day every week, phoning her every day to check in, sitting around the table with my father all those years when he complained about the horrible people in the world, or succumbing to how my parents wanted me to think and be. The way my mother managed the last days of my sister's life gave me clarity about how I didn't want to be, and, more specifically, how I did want to show up as a mom.

When I held Simon in my arms for the first time, my soul spoke to me in never before heard vibrational volumes; they passed through me at warped speed. There was no way I could ignore the message that enveloped me, and I paid very close attention because the mama instinct in me became fierce. I wanted to be the best version of myself I could for my child. Giving birth suddenly bestowed a responsibility that I wanted to fulfill. And, just as Hank only allowed my mother and father to adversely affect us to a certain degree, that tolerance lessened significantly when it came to the day his first child was born. He quickly ended the madness when his integrity was compromised beyond what he could morally allow. This came naturally to Hank, but I had to learn to trust this level of intuition and the whispers that sent warnings of personal emotional harm. Back then, I had yet to discover the level of confidence my husband possessed. As a result, I faltered significantly for many years, having one foot sucked in the abyss of conformity and the other desperately attempting to step fully into my uniqueness—to somehow find the courage to discover what being fully empowered entailed.

It wasn't an easy delivery. I was induced on my due date because my last ultrasound showed that Simon was failing to thrive. I taught an aerobics class on the morning of April 12th, and then went to the hospital, where they gave me a bed and a pill and told me to relax. The contractions started slowly, and I thought I was a rock star until I reached the 16th hour of labour and wondered what the fuck I had gotten myself into. Then, I remembered that story my mother told me about never feeling a contraction, and it was easier for her to give birth than to go to the dentist, *You will be just like me!!* I was glad she wasn't in the room for me to disappoint her.

I was sure they would tell me to start pushing each time I was measured for dilation, and I found strength by holding onto that hope. The doctor who was there from the start told me she had to do an internal to check the baby because I wasn't progressing. She placed my bed on an incline with my head at the bottom, and I didn't think much of it until she shoved her hand up me just as I moved through one of them. I have been told I have a high pain threshold, but the expectation of enduring that level was inhumane. At that moment, I believed she should have known better because she happened to be eight months pregnant while inflicting the most excruciating pain I've ever experienced while probing my cervix. So, I yelled at her, *Just wait until you have to do this!!* She looked up between my knees and smiled, and when she and my contraction finished, I was overwhelmed with shame and apologized to her. She didn't look overly forgiving, but I think my perception was slanted with childhood guilt creeping up, telling me that I had placed another notch of sin on the bedpost. When recounting the story later, I realized that the good doctor was simply focused on saving my baby and not worried about a delusional woman's reactions during labour.

Moments later, Hank and I were told that I was only two centimetres dilated, and Simon's heart rate could not be detected. The same doctor inserted a heart monitor into my baby's head, and my mind raced back to my mother's story about my grandmother having one of her babies at the age of 30 and how ill he was, dying at the age of five. Just like my sister during labour, I found myself succumbing to seeking God's help with unreasonable thoughts circulating through my head, *Oh my God, was my son's fate manifested through this familial tale?* It's incredible how I justified the possibility of His power during my moment of weakness while simultaneously cursing my mother for sharing that fable.

Around The Table

I was quickly distracted when a new shift of doctors and nurses walked into the room. At this point, I was somewhat comforted by the idea that I had tied up my camel by doing everything right during my pregnancy, so maybe I could trust God to send me an angel during my time of need. I later referred to her as Angel Mary, remembering how she walked into the room with the most calming aura; every medical person there could have taken a sensitivity lesson from her. She quietly and slowly told me that the baby was in distress and convinced me that this didn't need to be that hard. Not once did she tell me what to do but instead gave me several options. One was an epidural to allow my body to relax and my cervix to dilate quickly. The other was to continue through natural labour, but the consequences could be dire for my baby. I was exhausted and overwhelmed, and I noticed that my husband was not in the room to discuss what to do. The new shift doctor had not met Hank yet, and I asked him where my husband was. He was well over six feet tall and loomed over me from the end of the bed; he asked me what my husband looked like. I described him as tall, dark hair, handsome. He smiled and told me he believed he was sitting on the floor in the hall crying—I immediately told Angel Mary to order up the epidural.

It was such a relief to make that decision, only to be devastated moments later when I was told that someone came in through the emergency department with a brain aneurism. Angel Mary told me the anesthetist had to go there first as if it was obvious. *What?!* Hank was now back at my bedside, and he noticed me shifting towards anger, and then suddenly, his hand slipped gently into mine with the reassurance of his fingers tenderly squeezing mine. He helped me breathe through the next sequence of contractions, and before I knew it, the anesthetist rushed through the door and placed the epidural in my spine—another surge of relief enveloped me. I noticed how quickly I transitioned back to myself again, but it made me wonder who I really was. Was I the bitchy woman who had no problem degrading an obstetrician who was eight months pregnant? And was the resentment I felt towards the anesthetist who tried to save another human's life something I needed to evaluate moving forward? Maybe I was insane when it came to moments of desperation. Suddenly, I was terrified of becoming a mother and inflicting this delusional family legacy upon my child. I took note that this was something I needed to work on.

Once the epidural took effect, it didn't take long for Simon to enter the world. At 1:20 in the morning, we joked about it being Friday the 13th with the saving grace that it was Good Friday that year and Angel Mary had saved our son— subtly, God had crept back into my life. And I succumbed to praying to Him when Simon was rushed over to a table and worked on him for what seemed an eternity but was likely only minutes. Incredibly, just like in the movies, both Hank and I were blessed with a third wave of relief when a long sharp scream echoed through the sterile room and made everyone smile. Hank cried, watching me hold him momentarily, and then, a nurse took him from me and told us that Simon had to go

Escaping the Cycle of Delusion

into an incubator; he was 27 inches long and only six pounds, seven ounces. We were told that his ideal weight should have been around ten pounds, but when I released my placenta, it was completely shrivelled up, indicating that Simon had not been receiving the nutrients he needed. That was why he had not grown in the last couple of weeks in gestation. The doctor mentioned that this often happens when there is a blow to the abdomen, and I was suddenly filled with immense guilt, remembering tripping off a street curb downtown and landing on my belly. I never said anything to the doctor who delivered him, worrying that this was my fault. I wanted to tell him but defaulted to protecting myself from possibly having done something wrong. Another secret in the family history book.

I learned that my confession wasn't necessary because the real culprit was likely the external cephalic version I had around my 37th week of pregnancy to turn the fetus from a breech to a head-down position. Guilt diminished, a new surge of anger presented, and then, a fourth and final wave of relief that all was okay for now—*just forget about it*. In the end, it didn't matter because Hank and I welcomed the most precious gift a couple can receive, and even though he needed the support of an incubator for two weeks, we took home a healthy baby boy.

I was taken to a recovery ward with other new moms right after his birth, and Hank and I were able to hold Simon for a while before going back into the incubator. I was emotionally and physically depleted as I watched Hank hold his son out in front of him with his long body resting on one arm and his little head cupped in one of his hands. Their faces were so close together that their noses almost touched while Hank told him stories, and Simon cooed back in return—Hank had entered an entirely different world and was one with his son. This is one of the most memorable father-son moments I have as I listened to Hank end his conversation, telling Simon how much he loved him over and over again—right from the start, he instinctively wanted his child to know he was loved. To this day, *I love you* rolls off my husband's tongue when they leave after a visit or end a phone call with him.

As much as I resisted taking my eyes off of this intimate moment of connection, I finally asked Hank to pass Simon off to the nurse because I was desperate for sleep. He laughed, said goodnight to his son for the first time and went home to get some well-deserved rest. He shared the news with our families when they woke in the morning. The next day, my in-laws arrived at the hospital bright and early, and Hank's dad was the first grandparent to hold his grandson. He was beaming with pride while his wife watched and praised me for doing such a great job. Then Hank took Simon and handed him to his mother. This was a special moment for her, and I had a deep knowing she would be an incredibly impactful influence in my son's life. Scanning the room, I sensed my paternal grandmother's presence within a whisper that bubbled up from inside me and told me, *Geniet daar van—Savour it all*. I reflected that this had to be what developed from the seed she instilled in me so long ago, the miraculous combination of joy and love.

And then, without any warning, Oma's presence began to retreat when my

Around The Table

mother burst through the door with an influx of opposing energy. I have yet to shake the vivid image of her smile quickly shifting to that infamous pursed-lipped expression when she saw my mother-in-law holding her grandson. Many times, I have witnessed the unconscious systematic process she moves through when triggered by significant events that aren't unfolding the way she wants them to. I understand what she goes through because I was handed down the same self-serving mentality that tells me I deserve what I want, and everyone else be damned. I continue to consciously manage it to this day; I don't think it will ever go away because it was embedded far deeper in me than the seed of love my Oma planted.

However, I try to shift to the manifestation that knowing better allows me to do better. I want to believe that my mother always wanted to do the right thing, but it seemed that no matter what kind of meaningful event our family was immersed in, she sought self-importance within it. Like a villain in a fairy tale, something took over whereby she succumbed to being drawn back into the childhood attention-seeking ingrained in her —not a caring, connected presence, but a jealous, detached one. Was this her fault? No. I don't think my mother could do better because, although more genuine parts showed through, her need to be better than anyone else over-ruled making decisions based on a different kind of love she held imprisoned in her heart. Without releasing her attachment to unconditional love, she could not step back and allow someone else their moment in the light; her patterned brain quickly found why she deserved to shine instead of them.

So, her mind raced towards a perception that she should have been the first to hold Simon when her eyes landed on him resting in my mother-in-law's arms; he was her daughter's son. Somehow, the fact that the baby came out of her daughter's womb decreased Hank's mother's status a notch. It didn't take long for my mother to justify her reasoning, and her jealousy took over.

Suddenly, a matriarchal shuffle occurred, accommodating my mother's uncomfortable energy. My oma's presence faded away completely, and my mother-in-law silently handed Simon over to my mother and retreated to a chair in the corner. She and I locked eyes, and we smiled; she nodded her head as if to say, *It's going to be alright*, and I knew it would be because my grandmother had graciously made space for Hank's mother to humbly fill her role in my child's life. My mother sat proudly holding her grandson, and she appeared more triumphant than grateful to everyone surrounding her.

In my vulnerable state, I surrendered to my conditioning to be at peace and maneuvered around my mother's antics. I reframed what had just happened as her doting on my firstborn. But I could only sustain that for so long because the looming dichotomy of harmony and discord between my son's grandmothers was the red flag that I eventually learned to be mindful of for the rest of my life. My mother's obvious jealousy over my mother-in-law became obsessive. It motivated her to use passive-aggressive tactics to win my children over, rather than being the

Escaping the Cycle of Delusion

loving person I knew she could tap into. But she couldn't help herself; from the moment she was deprived of being the first to hold my son, she competed with my mother-in-law, her rival. Years went by, and I repeatedly witnessed my mother's response to her own perception within the grand scheme of my life. And even though I knew it wouldn't make a difference, I prayed to her God, asking Him to support her to find a more humble and gracious way of being. But He did not answer my call.

Every now and then, my mother's love broke out of its shell, and she surprised me with an act of kindness. Over time, I did not trust it, knowing there would be a catch. However, when my parents arrived at the hospital early the next day, I embraced the beautiful traditional Dutch Easter breakfast they brought for me. And although I was grateful, I felt the expected pull towards the Catholic faith again and the expected push from my mother to conform to her religious traditions and beliefs. I began questioning whether or not my child needed the opportunity to choose religion or not. I asked Hank if he would go to church with Simon and me every Sunday—his response was an unwavering, *No.* In hindsight, I have no idea why I thought he would consider such a thing. And more to the point, I now recognize that I was being drawn into the expectations I thought my mother had of me once again—the same cyclical, generational patterning that validated my worthiness within the familial role. As a new mother, I jumped into the trap that it was my obligation to implement religious coherence on my son. Because if I didn't, I did not belong to this family. And if I did not belong, neither did my son. It was one thing for me to choose to be an outcast, but entirely different for me to inflict Simon with the same. Is this thought process insane? Probably. And yet, being on that ledge was my reality, so it seemed to make sense. Once Simon completed his five-month ordeal with colic, I started going to the Sunday nine o'clock sermon with a bottle in tow. I did this for two years and finally let the façade of religion go again while further embracing my faith in the universe.

My mother still had the store, so she was limited in how much time she could offer to support me through motherhood, but I understood and was grateful for any help she provided. Without me complaining, she often overdid her rant about being too busy to help me because she had the store. I understood, but to her dismay, she watched my mother-in-law step in to give me breaks from Simon's colic. She was a significant influence in my life because, as much as she didn't want to create conflict with my mother, she would not deprive herself of the gift of spending time with her grandson; within this devotion, she modelled the confidence that pure love provides. I gratefully accepted her help because I was so sleep-deprived that there were nights when I went to lift Simon out of his crib only to find my hands wet from the water in the toilet; I didn't even know where I was. She came almost every morning and pushed Simon in his stroller up and down the waterfront while screaming at the top of his lungs. This gave me time to have a nap after being up most of the night with him. As a result, this little duo created quite a bond that extended beyond his early years through being a teenager and an adult. He still has fond memories of his oma picking him up and driving him to the golf course because Hank and I were working. She always had a sandwich and a drink for him and often slipped him a twenty-dollar bill. Now, in her 90s, she was recently told that her *Simon-Looch* will become a father at the age of 32. My mother-in-law showed me how a matriarch can be an unconditionally-loving influence in a grandchild's life.

 Colic usually subsides when a baby reaches the three-month mark. I counted the weeks and days leading up to that potentially life-changing day, only to discover that Simon was in the small percentile of babies inflicted for up to five months. He cried all the time: in the morning, in the afternoon, before supper, after supper, and all through the night. On top of his constant screaming, I could barely get him to grab onto my bleeding nipples, finding myself turning my chair towards the wall and pushing my foot off of it in pain until he finally latched on. I held my breath throughout the process and wondered how anyone could describe this torture as a bonding experience.

 We tried everything to relieve him from his agony, from setting him in his baby seat on top of the running dryer to driving around in the car with him for hours. Nothing worked, so my GP referred me to a pediatrician at the hospital to see if she could do anything. She was an anomaly, presenting as a human being before a doctor. And if I only ever received her genuine words of empathy that day, I would have been grateful enough. However, this person stepped up to support me beyond any medical professional I have encountered, and although her initial words were not comforting, *There is really nothing medically we can do for Simon's colic*, I was astounded with what she said next. She told me to bring him into the hospital every day at one o'clock in the afternoon. She would need two 15-minute appointment spaces for him, and I could drop him off, leave, and come back at one-thirty. I was silent for a moment, not understanding, so I asked her, *What are you going to do to him while I'm gone?* She smiled and replied, *Well, the nurses will take turns walking with him while we make our rounds, dear. You can take the half-hour to go for a walk and get some fresh air. And we will just love him.* I asked her if she was allowed to do this, and she said, *We don't always ask what we can do here; sometimes, we just do what is right.* She couldn't eliminate Simon's colic, but because she could give me a bit of ease going through it, she did.

 During her initial exam, she discovered that Simon was not gaining as much weight as he should—*failure to thrive* was written in his chart. As his mother, I was mortified because I was unable to provide him with enough milk. I remember hearing my mother's voice in my ear, *I breastfed all three of you, not a problem. You will be like me.* I was told that he needed formula, and since my sister happened to be coming over for coffee that day, she told me not to worry—she had my back. She stopped at the drugstore on the way to my place and bought everything needed to implement the formula transition. And when she arrived, I watched in awe as she immediately and methodically made up six eight-ounce bottles and handed me one to feed him. Sitting down on the sofa, I was past regretting that I had to change from breast to bottle-feeding; I just wanted him to get the nourishment he required to be healthy. My sister and I watched as he enthusiastically sucked that first bottle dry, and then we laughed when he proceeded to throw the majority of it up with a burp. The best part was when he smiled right after.

Simon finally stopped screaming after eight weeks of me taking advantage of my doctor's team's generosity. Both Hank and I opened our eyes to daylight for the first time in five months after finally sleeping through the night. I remember staring at the ceiling smiling, only to then panic because I didn't hear my baby crying; I thought for sure he must be dead. Jumping out of bed, I ran to his crib to find him cooing at the mobile I bought him when I was pregnant; this was the first time he noticed it. Suddenly, his room seemed brighter, and the sapphire-blue cushions on his glider chair Hank bought me seemed much more welcoming—I had only ever used it in an attempt to stop his crying. Lifting him out of his crib, I wrapped a blanket around him and enveloped him in my arms. He gently sunk into me, and we fit together like a mother and baby are supposed to. Hank stood in the doorway, relieved that we could move forward from the chaos of colic.

Two months before I gave birth, Hank left the retail world, having been taken advantage of by one of his business partners who drove their company into bankruptcy. We moved back to our hometown to start over, and we were excited to share our son with our extended family, believing it would enhance both his and their lives. Hank became a partner in an insurance firm, taking a risk by borrowing a million dollars to buy a book of business while simultaneously fulfilling his value of taking care of his family. My heart ached for him, having to abandon the passion he had been pursuing. It made me think about my father and his sacrifice, doing the same back in 1952 when he immigrated with his family to Canada and again in 1972 upon returning from our brief move to Holland.

It was now the early 90s, and my awareness about the importance of equality between men and women was amplified. And even though Hank and I weren't competing with each other, it was evident that I always landed in temporary lower-paying jobs while he excelled building a higher-income long-term career. He developed his business from the ground up, working 10 to 12-hour days while I found part-time, home-based businesses to dabble in for extra income. Of course, I wanted to be the mom who did it all with a full-time career while equally contributing to my family. Still, I wrestled greatly with also wanting one of us to be with Simon most of the time, so we found ourselves in stereotypical societal roles—I realized that I landed where my mother had in this realm.

I felt guilty not being able to make an income anywhere near Hank's or that allowed him to be home with his son more of the time. However, I'm not sure we could have done anything differently because our family values conflicted with what feminism promoted; how could we give our child the time we believed he needed and deserved if we both had demanding careers? At the time, I felt less-than, convinced I was not fulfilling society's expectations to be and do everything: wife, mom, a successful career woman. However, the beautiful trade-off was enjoying precious time with my boy, going on hikes, playdates with other moms in the neighbourhood, and having long chats while doing crafts together—just the two of us. If I could go back in time, I would have forfeited any job and money to have spent more time with both of my children.

I've never really fully fed into the idealism of the feminist movement. To be fully transparent, it's the notion of fairness that seems unattainable to me—is it actually possible to achieve equality between sexes without detrimental trade-offs? Yes, I believe women and men should have the same opportunities, but only because I believe human beings should—without considering sexual orientation or gender. In saying that, I am not convinced that both partners in a relationship, whether straight, gay, non-binary, transgender and the list goes on, can be totally fulfilled, or achieve financial success without sacrificing a relationship value of balance. In my experience, it ended up being unimportant to gain the same income, position, or accolades as my husband simply to prove I could within being considered the inferior sex. If equality was indeed my goal, I would have achieved it only on the merit of being a human being, not because I had the least important ranking based on having a vagina.

Admittedly, it took me a long time to gain this clarity, and I raced around for years, trying to deem myself worthy based on my bosses' acceptance of my work. I always chose jobs with authoritative men at the helm of the ship who treated women as beings beneath them, rather than the few, fair men who treated women as equals; they were hard to find. Some therapy supported me to understand that I was strangely drawn to them because they were like my father, and I was surprisingly comfortable with the uncomfortable way they treated me. One such person was the director of a daycare I accepted a position at after graduating from college when Simon was two. I became an early childhood educator with a childcare centre in our home. This allowed me to be with Simon while earning an income. I did that for a while, but the money didn't justify the number of hours I spent caring for other people's children, so I sought a position at the city's university daycare. I made a top salary there compared to private centres because it was city-funded, and Simon went to a smaller, quaint daycare just up the road.

I loved my life with our little family of three, and Simon was the sweetest, easiest child to be with. It seemed like he was eternally grateful to have survived the agony of colic, and all he wanted was to be a carefree little boy. He played contently with his toys in our living room, sitting on the floor with his legs swung out to either side. And when he got tired of that, he toddled over to the big window and yelled at the people going by. One of our neighbours was a man named Earl, and every time Simon saw him, he called out, *Earl the Squirrel!!* And when he saw our neighbour, Arnold, across the street, he yelled, *Nold!!* He was also fascinated with

Escaping the Cycle of Delusion

trucks and often stood at that same window, repeating the word *truck* after one drove by. On weekends, Hank sometimes took him to a construction company's parking lot to sit in their loaders, bulldozers, and dump trucks. When they got home, Simon would pull out his *Truck Book* and show his dad each page while naming all the trucks. That book became so torn and tattered that I bought him a new one, but he never opened it, preferring the one he already had.

My favourite times with Simon were when we went for long walks in a popular conservation area that bordered Lake Ontario. We frequented this haven a couple of times a week, walking and talking while checking out the ducks, chipmunks, trees, and plants. He was so pleasant to be with and always eager to please. By the time he reached his second year, I anticipated the terrible twos everyone talked about, but they never came. I looked forward to walking through his bedroom door every morning after being awakened by him chanting my name, *Moooommmmyyyyy, Moooommmmyyyy*. He sang it in a tender tone that made my heart melt. Everyone told me, *Just wait until he gets older; boys are so difficult to manage!!* But he never was. Simon was a wise, gentle soul from the time he was born.

He spent a lot of time with his paternal grandparents because they set aside a few days a week for him to go to their house instead of going to daycare. These were precious times because they dedicated every moment to him. His opa was the most generous, kind man I have ever met. And although he made some parenting mistakes with his own children, he definitely made up for it with his grandchildren. I do believe he loved them more than he loved his own life. Simon was fortunate to have been a part of his opa's life before he became quite ill. While they spent countless hours in his workshop in the basement, his oma worked away in the kitchen making snacks and intermittently delivered them to the boys. She often went downstairs with this ulterior motive because her husband was not the safest when it came to tools and such. He sat Simon on top of the workbench and let him hammer nails into a piece of wood for hours; he often ended up with a few self-inflicted injuries. Whenever his wife asked him why he had a band-aid on various parts of his body or where the blood on the floor came from, he quickly came up with a fib to account for his clumsiness. Although this scared me a bit, I think it's good that Hank and I didn't know half of what happened down there. We feel fortunate that no one was seriously injured.

Opa captured his grandson on an old-school video, chattering and working away with his tools. We have since put these memories on DVDs and spent endless hours listening to and watching these two interact; they are magical moments never to be forgotten. This grandfather and grandson had a natural bond inspired by deep love—and sometimes influenced by an abundance of candy—that only comes once in a lifetime. The ability to submerge oneself into the present moment with a loved one while letting the rest of the world go by unnoticed is a gift that only my oma ever gave me. I am so grateful that my father-in-law chose to provide this to my son. He showed me what unconditional love for a child is and gave Simon an abundance of it to experience.

Both of Hank's parents loved and welcomed me into their lives when he and I began living together. I know there was some trepidation on his mother's part, knowing I was eight years younger. She was also worried because Hank had been through one divorce already, which greatly affected her. She was only ever concerned about his happiness, but I knew I had to nip that in the bud when she told me he didn't like clutter on top of the fridge. She tried telling me what Hank preferred a few times, including moving a statue from one corner of a side table to another and telling me that Hank would like it there. I finally decided to have a conversation with her, and after letting her know that I only had Hank's happiness in mind, I asked her not to worry about our relationship. She immediately retreated, never to interfere again. I wondered why having a conversation with my mother couldn't be that easy.

Meanwhile, it had been a few years since my sister's passing, and my mother continued to grieve. My father never spoke of his daughter's death, and understandably, that frustrated my mother. This was when she sought bereavement support from one of the counsellors at the church and ultimately convinced her son-in-law to do the same. Everyone's relationship seemed strained, so I sought solace in spending time with my son and continued to desperately try to connect with my side of the family, to find some sort of commonality and create the familial bond I wanted for my child.

I remember picnics with my parents at the same conservation area where Simon and I frequented. We visited my mother's deli and had Sunday morning coffee at their house after church. Simon enjoyed being greeted by his oma when we went into the store. She always gave him Dutch licorice and a variety of the same traditional food I was brought up with, but only after making a point of asking my permission. At first, I found this respectful, until I realized that our time with my parents was often strained with my mother's apparent need to please me. I believe asking my permission had nothing to do with honouring my parenting style and everything to do with seeking attention through being accepted as the better oma. Again, I found that our roles slowly reversed; she needed acceptance and went out of her way to ask me what she could or could not do with Simon. She wanted a rule book to have the confidence to interact with him. I could relate because I grew with hers—the familial cycle continued.

The difference was that, in her quest to do the right thing, my mother convinced me that her way was right by defaulting to her habit of creating similarities between us, *You're strict like me; You have a schedule like I did; Your house is clean and organized like mine.* She even went so far as to add, *Your sister isn't a confident mother like you are; She lets her kids stay up late; She doesn't clean regularly.* Although she made it sound complimentary, her passive-aggressive affirmations always left me wondering how my sister would feel being put down behind her back. And yet, I went along with them because I, too, was seeking the same sense of belonging that my mother sought from me. I understand her intention to acquire comradery in order to feel accepted, but she, perhaps unknowingly and simultaneously, created distance between my sister and me to achieve this gain.

Over time, my mother managed to sneak me into her expected programming of scheduled activities; she had a way of creating these expectations without even asking if I agreed with them. My old pattern somehow crept back into my psyche without me seeing it coming. From one day to the next, I was at her beck and call, back to adding making her happy while juggling a family and career. In the meantime, her passion for the deli waned substantially within her grieving process, and it didn't take my mother long to decide that she needed to put it up for sale and retire. It was sold to a Scotsman and a Frenchman, and my sister continued working there as a manager, but when the business eventually folded, she went to work in a grocery store deli. Because my mother no longer worked and had time on her hands, she wanted to play a more significant role in my life. Her need to control me expanded into dominating my husband and child, and her competition with my mother-in-law spiralled out of control.

She became obsessed with special occasions and how she believed they should be celebrated. Birthdays were her number one preoccupation, and she had very specific guidelines for us to follow. It is a Dutch tradition for the person of honour to host the gathering; to this day, this still baffles me, given that the birthday person does all the work, and their guests arrive and relax. The celebration must take place on the exact date of their birth, with no exceptions. The host—birthday person of honour—provides and serves the food, including and in this order, coffee and cake, lunch, then drinks and *hapjes*—snacks. The presents are opened after the cake and coffee, and the entire celebration begins at around 11 in the morning and ends around two or three. These are the rules.

I tried so hard to accommodate my mother's desperate need to control every birthday each of my family members ever had, but at one point, my life became so busy that I could not make our birthdays about her anymore. We were a full-on busy household that included two working parents and a child participating in various activities. Hank and I also had close friends with kids, and we spent time with them as families and travelled with them as couples. We often went away for weekends, leaving Simon with his paternal grandparents because they couldn't wait to have him with no strings attached. It's true that my parents didn't have those initial opportunities because they were busy with the store when we first had Simon—that couldn't be helped. As a result, he established an intimate relationship with Hank's parents that I was unwilling to compromise just because my parents suddenly became available. They would have to start from scratch and do their own work to create that magic. Simon was only two, and they still had lots of time to create a connection with him. Sadly, they were often attached to conditions that decreased the authenticity of their bond.

Around The Table

    We tried really hard to continue to welcome our extended families into our nucleus. But their status based on familial ranking became secondary influences because we were now the heads of our family, and we took the lead role of responsibility and great pride in loving and guiding our children through life in our way. We used our newly clarified values that served us well rather than those of our forefathers and mothers that did not. That didn't always go over well with my mother, and she fought me tooth and nail when we chose a different path from hers. When she thought she was right, there was no stopping her, which worked in her favour most of my life. However, when I became a parent and it came to my family's mental and emotional health, something inside me sparked retaliation when she crossed a line.

    One day, she pushed me so far over that line that I reached a breaking point, and I suddenly decided to fight back. She nudged me far enough over that I decided I would prove her wrong if it killed me. I was not a delusional little kid sitting at a table distracted by a tin of buttons anymore but rather an adult. It was time to stop the madness of her manipulation before I ultimately succumbed to her way of being. There was no trade-off big enough to keep me from fighting for my family and what we believed was right for us. I was ready to forfeit my wish to belong to someone who didn't fit who I was.

    At the age of 33, the birth of my second child changed my perception of absolutely everyone and everything. I brought a daughter into a world dictated by generations of hierarchal authority. So, when I held her in my arms for the first time, I vowed she would not live a life dictated by the same familial matriarchy and patriarchy suppression I experienced. From that day forward, I knew I had to escape this inherited legacy for both my daughter's and my son's sake. It was time to cut my mother's damaging influences off at her knees, and it felt like an audacious move on my part. However, even though I had glimmers of courage when I made that decision the day Olivia entered the world, it sadly took another six years for me to follow through.

IX

~ Escaping the Cycle of Regret ~

Growing up, my sisters and I interacted in the most distant of ways. I had feelings for them but, simultaneously, experienced an indifference towards them. As kids, the two of them were far closer than I was to either of them, but I didn't notice a tight sisterhood between them either. One might think I would have developed a heightened bond with the one who was less than two years older. However, other than a photo in my baby book reminding me that she and I had a tea party one day, I don't recall a reciprocal connection with her. As the years rolled by, she and I never really saw eye to eye. This caused tension, as well as an emotional distance between us. Even now, if I voice an opposing opinion to hers, she is immediately triggered to defend her viewpoint rather than simply share it. In turn, this prompts a similar reaction in me. And then, I contemplate, *Why is it so important that we agree?* I have asked this question many times because we have generally defaulted to discussing the weather, our health, or things we agree with—undisputed facts void of emotion.

Her consistent protection of her beliefs reiterates that she was programmed the same way I was, constantly needing to prove we were right—not what we believed was right but that we were right, and everyone else was wrong. To this day, I think my sister's defence mechanism kicks in as an auto-response to her commitment to our parents' beliefs. When I experience her fight or flight energy, it is because we have landed on the landmine of a disagreement in values. I am immediately brought back to sitting around the table, being encouraged to share my voice, yet struggling to honour my truth. I wonder why I bother, knowing it will be challenged and disagreed upon. For a long time, I held onto the hope that maybe one day, my father might validate my point of view or even bits of the concrete facts I shared. However, I came to understand that this would only occur if I agreed with him, so it never did—respect was never part of the equation.

My sister inherited the same condition I did that creates automatic agreement. I understand how she constantly strategizes how to consistently defend and honour my parents, even when she disagrees with them because I did the same. I was exhausted, with almost every conversation becoming a battle of wills. If I am fully transparent, I am equally accountable for reactivity when challenged to be right, which instantly raises my defences. Decades of conditioning are hard to shift within an instant, even when I desperately wish our responses were different—it's always too late, as we throw out our reactions like uncontrolled vomit from our mouths.

Around The Table

With my other sister being four years older than me, a meaningful relationship was beyond my scope of reasoning when I was very young. I don't remember ever arguing with her, but we didn't have in-depth conversations either. My ability to share my innermost anything with anyone was stunted until I was much older. Even then, I struggled immensely. It wasn't until I approached my mid-twenties, and she became a mom that we began to connect on a deeper level—I loved being an aunt, and spending time with her boys became a conduit for connection between her and me. And then, of course, *she just died*.

The sibling dynamics in my family would have been the opposite had our parents genuinely nurtured individuality and freedom of thought. They encouraged us to have a voice, knowing it was the right thing to do, but more often than not, it was shut down and tossed aside as quickly as it was shared. I never heard my parents express their emotions unless within hurt or anger. So, as a child, I learned how to respond to my sisters using dysfunctional interactions as examples of communication; that's how we thought we were supposed to talk to each other.

I was privy to many of their arguments, which usually involved my father criticizing my mother. As with me, he used name-calling as weaponry to win. My mother was intimidated by the power of his personal attacks, and he could diminish her to tears with one short spiteful phrase spoken with the heated tone of his voice. He repeatedly used the same few damaging utterances he used with me, *Hou je mond dicht*—Shut your mouth, along with, *Je ben gek*—You are crazy. The spiteful words were harmful enough, but the added volume, inflection, and intensity behind his voice impacted me the most. Whether he directed his venom at me or my mother, he scared me, and although she tried to hide it from me, I saw that he scared her too. I know she was significantly impacted because I lived through the same emotional damage he created every time he fired one of those insults at one of us, and it was irreparable for both. Once discharged, the bullet of perceived hate went into full flight, never to be retrieved. Each subsequent shot created the burden of layered emotional trauma that ate away at me…and her.

After the ammunition ceased fire, she responded in tears, and I watched him suddenly end the war by ignoring her emotional outburst and leaving the room. This was where he faltered, not having compassion in his wheelhouse. But he managed this shortcoming by simply walking away—the same way he swam away when he was done with me in the lake. She, in turn, dried her tears and began preparing dinner. Unobtrusively, I slid to my room to process and recalibrate what I had seen and heard: hostility, control, pain, anguish, detachment—trauma. I repeated his mantra under my breath, *Just forget about it, just forget about it, just forget about it*—*eleven peas, eleven carrots, twelve peas, twelve carrots…* He taught me to fight to win no matter how harmful the attack and to end the battle when uncomfortable emotions presented—control was the ultimate indicator of a win. And my mother taught me that it was okay to argue as long as I succumbed to stepping back when my opponent gained control—it wasn't considered a win, but it was indeed a smart decision when it came to the need to emotionally survive. I did this most of my life until I couldn't anymore because I discovered that my opinions mattered, even if others didn't agree with them. My emotions were worthy of validation, even if others didn't feel them. And I mattered, even if I believed others didn't think I did.

From a very young age, my sisters and I argued all the time, so often that my mother frequently told the story about the appointment she made with our family doctor to discuss our constant nattering. She was pleasantly surprised that he told her to let us argue without interjecting. He gave her permission to let us fight and said it would all work out. But it never did. We resorted to what we had experienced and knew best—fight to be right, and the winner, well…wins. What we felt or believed were never considered important because winning the debate was the prize. When recounting this story, my mother thought our doctor was a genius because his advice justified how she learned how to communicate, growing up in her family of 16. It also excused how my father treated her every time they argued—he won fair and square because she wasn't cutthroat enough. And even though she suffered through the process, it was her norm, so she accepted it. As the years went by, we never stopped arguing around the table every night until someone either succeeded or backed off. I still see my father sitting there with his infamous grin, revelling at whether he created victory or defeat—so much power void of compassion.

All my life, I wondered why my siblings and I couldn't get along. I enviously compared us to many of my friends who I watched engaging in meaningful relationships with their sisters and brothers, and I couldn't figure out why I didn't have that. I remember our conversations, *You know what it's like when your sister feels this or that?* I always emphatically said, *Yes, of course!!* But I didn't mean it. I had no clue what they were talking about because I had never experienced the kind of camaraderie, connection, or loyalty they had with their siblings. However, I couldn't admit that to them because my friends shared their familial conviction as if it was a given that I experienced the same—that because I have sisters, I should naturally experience the same allegiance they had with their siblings. Uh, no, I did not.

In 1985, the year after Hank and I married, I met a woman who became my best friend. Besides Hank, she changed my perception of sibling love by providing me with buckets and buckets of the acceptance I had been searching for since I was a little girl. I have never laughed as much as I have with this feisty little bit of a thing. Her nickname was Smurf, and she managed an aerobics studio where I applied for an instructor's position. I was hired, and Smurf fine-tuned my teaching skills. I worked there for four years, and out of all the jobs I've had, it was where I got paid the least but had the most fun—because of her! She was hands down the most popular instructor in the place, and when she came out of one of her classes, she always said she felt like she had been hit by a truck. She was known for her sweaty crotch—the result of putting everything she had into her classes and never disappointing her participants.

Around The Table

She and I often bought lunch from a restaurant across the street, and within an hour of eating their meatball soup, we were farting uncontrollably. When we needed to let one go during a class, we wandered around the room and relieved ourselves far away from our spot at the front. We believed no one ever knew it was us, but they did.

At that time, there was a sewer system linking all the basements on that street. The owner of the place, who also became a dear friend of mine, sold aerobic wear, and we went down to the basement to grab inventory when we needed to restock the shelves. I knew there were rats down there that came out of hiding once in a while, and every time I descended the creaky steps, I held my breath, hoping this would not be the day they decided to make an appearance. Unfortunately, there were a few times when we met face-to-face.

The first time was when I reached for a sweatshirt, and a mama rat came parading out with her babies; she sauntered in front of me, moving from one wall to the other. I think she was preparing me for the next time by keeping her distance. That came when I headed down to get some shoes one day, and Smurf called me from the kitchen at the top of the stairs. She wanted me to bring a few other things up, so I stopped on the second step to make a list. Just as I turned to look up at her, I felt something heavy on my foot, and her eyes grew incredibly wide, *Don't move!!* I didn't want to admit it, but I knew that Mrs. Rat was resting on my foot, and I thought I was going to shit my pants.

She put her pointer finger up in the air, telling me to wait, and she slowly walked backwards. Wait?! I couldn't look down, and when she returned, she had a hammer in her hand. *Holy shit*, I whispered, *What the fuck are you going to do?* But she had a way of making every ridiculous idea she came up with make sense, *Just stand very still; I'm going to throw the hammer and hit it on the head.* I don't know why, but I said, *Okay* and stared at her in terror. At that moment, I wondered what would happen if she either managed to hit the rat or didn't. So, I stood there as still as a mouse and watched her lift the hammer up and over her shoulder in slow motion and then flung it towards my foot!! I'd like to say that she hit it, but she missed it by a mile, and the rat went flying up the stairs past her and hid behind the furnace in the kitchen. I was shaking so hard, but Smurf ignored me and continued to hunt and ran past me down the stairs to retrieve the hammer and then back up again to take another swing at the rat. She never did get it but instead called a pest control company to set traps for the rats.

Just as she and I are soul sisters, Hank and her husband became soul brothers. They are the gifts of friendship that every person wishes they were blessed with. For years, we went away together for Thanksgiving long weekends and spent many Saturday nights cooking dinners for each other. We went on so many adventures, including a trip to Hawaii, and my heart remains full of the memories we created without so much as one argument between the four of us. Although we live far apart, they remain our people to this day.

Escaping the Cycle of Regret

It's not that I didn't care about my sisters, but we didn't have what Smurf and I had or what my other friends described they had with their siblings, and I wanted that. It took me a long time to discover that not only was my relationship with my sisters different from what I had with her, but I was very different from my sisters. Just as my mother was conditioned to experience her siblings within the duality of love and hate, she subconsciously and systematically prepared her children to do the same. Behind our backs, she twisted our perceptions about each other's reality and then secretly complained about each of us to the other when we weren't around; this was all in the name of achieving connection with who she was with at the time. Perhaps unintentionally, she used us for emotional support and continued this backhanded ploy throughout our adult lives. It gradually escalated as we got older, and she did it in a way that made us feel strong when praising us to our face but weak when we found out she criticized us to our opposing sister. Her middle daughter and I were the most impacted by her strategy, given that it increased after her eldest *just died*. The mission was to gain camaraderie with one daughter over the other, depending on who she needed on her side at the time. This was the same system she and her sisters inherited through their lineage, which wasn't surprising given the size of their family and the dynamics that went with that. By default, my sisters and I were gifted the brunt of this emotionally manipulative game. We slowly and subliminally inherited the family legacy of deceptively gossiping behind each other's backs.

When alone with my mother, I was praised as the favourite, strong, competent daughter, who was most like the resilient side of my mother—like the strong side of her sisters. And yet, I was the selfish one when she shared how she felt about me to my sister. Then, when she was alone with my mother, she was acknowledged as the extraordinary, supportive, compassionate daughter, who was most like the dutiful side of my mother—like the loyal side of her sisters. Yet, when my mother talked to me about my sister, she pointed out her weaknesses and incompetencies. When I didn't do enough for my mother, she complained about me to my sister, and when my sister didn't do what she wanted, she was sure to let me know. My job was to reinforce her sense of matriarchal control, and my sister's responsibility was to boost her sense of matriarchal entitlement.

The problem was that neither could be accomplished through the endless cycle of attempting to. And even though she talked about us behind our backs, as long as we continued to fulfill our roles of making her happy, I know she loved us, even though this was the only way she knew how to express it—by shining a light on each of us to lift us up and then dimming it by pulling us down. Unknowingly, my mother gradually pitted the remaining two daughters she had against each other. Instead of fostering a meaningful sibling relationship, she deprived us of what I saw my friends share with theirs.

Not surprisingly, I struggled when Hank and I discussed having a second child in 1992. Besides simply wanting another baby, we appreciated the advantages of having a sibling for Simon, and logically, we believed it should be a natural progression. However, given my experience having sisters who barely related to one another, I wasn't overly sold on the idea. Hank has a sister, but their relationship was tarnished with a dark shadow of jealousy that may have been warranted on her part. She always thought that their mother loved her son more, and my sister-in-law outwardly shared that with me many times. As much as I wanted to side with Hank's mother, there were times when I understood where her daughter might be coming from because her mother had a special bond with her son; it was perhaps the kind of exaggerated connection that sometimes develops between a first-born and a parent. Although I never favoured one of my children over the other, there were times when I observed and even understood her perception of being the *ongedeelde kind—the divided child* or the one who receives less attention and affection. I could relate because I craved more attention than my sisters had, and I believe I got more than they did. Just as my life-long perceptions have chased after me and damaged my familial relationships, so have those of my sister-in-law. Even though they still contact each other, significant disconnect and divisiveness are prevalent between her, Hank, and me.

I observed that when empowerment is created through inner-strength and autonomy, there are those who choose to feed into the belief that they are unworthy of achieving it. It is emotionally abusive to attempt taking away someone's confidence to compensate for one's lack thereof. My mother taught me to be resilient, but she could never fully commit to a degree of strength that empowered her integrity for the sake of herself and those around her. Many want to be strong but often succumb to weakness by blaming others for their self-professed victimhood. They deem themselves unworthy, blaming everyone else but themselves. Just as I have, many people in my life have accused others of their circumstances, and their lack of accountability halted their personal evolution—been there, done that many times. I empathize with them because I understand what it's like to be a victim in response to others' inflicted venom and not know how to respond to it for fear of losing them. This is the co-dependency roller coaster, and I was on it far too long. It took me decades to discover just how close to the line of insanity people get when projecting their insecurities onto others—it's self-survival of the fittest victims. And there is no shame in that because this is a consequence of emotional abuse without a visible bruise.

These sibling interactions weighed heavily on Hank and me as we considered having another child because we did not want to transfer these dysfunctional patterns onto our children. We were concerned that if we had another baby, our children might not establish the life-long familial connection I had yearned for all my life and that Hank wished he had with his sister. We could not be sure, but we threw caution to the wind and took the plunge. Deep down, we knew we could do better than what was passed down to us. And we did.

However, after trying for over a year, we gave up and decided to be grateful for just one child. Then one day, I took a day off from the daycare to have an x-ray taken of my left thumb. It had been causing problems by constantly dislocating, so I decided to have it checked. As a precautionary measure, I was asked to have a pregnancy test before going for the x-ray due to the potentially harmful effects of radiation on a fetus. However, I forgot to check with my GP for the results before heading to the hospital. I had no signs of being pregnant but hadn't gone back on the pill yet. The x-ray department receptionist asked me for my pregnancy results, and I asked her to please phone my GP for them—still no cell phones. Moments later, she called me over to the desk, *You're not having an x-ray today.*

My first ultrasound indicated a girl, and from that day forward, I had a deep knowing that every person this baby touched in her lifetime would be changed in some way for the better. I received a different sort of whisper that she was being brought into the world to show everyone a different way. She would be determined but not selfish, kind, and compassionate towards others and herself, strong but also vulnerable. She would empower others while never, ever allowing anyone to control her. Unbeknownst to me, my daughter would inspire me to finally be who I truly was. She would draw the authenticity out of my bones and motivate me to be the woman I was meant to be from the day my mother pushed me out without suffering one labour pain. I knew I had to be the matriarch she deserved, and I stepped up to the challenge—but not without a few missteps along the way. Bad habits are hard to break.

This pregnancy was not as easy as Simon's, and I fought nausea every day. The only thing that helped was greasy food, so I started going to a local breakfast place every morning, eating far more than any person should. I gained 60 pounds in total and continued working at the daycare, where I eventually jumped into a patriarchal trap that questioned my integrity. I was around seven months pregnant when I started noticing that my curriculum supplies were dwindling, with supply orders always coming in short. When I put in reports of things needing to be repaired or replaced, they were ignored and neglected. Then one day, I went to the kitchen to get the children's lunches and noticed there was no milk. The next day, there was no bread. I went to the daycare director the following morning when I saw that snack portions were cut in half. Bringing my concerns to his attention, I asked him what was going on—was the daycare in financial trouble? He sloughed me off, making me feel like I was making a big deal out of nothing. But when I persisted, he told me, *Let it go, Diana.* At that moment, I heard my father's stern tone in the elevation of his voice. This man wasn't just asking me not to worry about the situation but insisted on abruptly ending the conversation. In his own words, he told me to, *Just forget about it.* I stood there wanting to say something else, to be determined, strong, and the empowered woman the little girl growing inside me needed me to be. But I froze in fear. Embedded trauma does that.

The director told me to leave and not to bring it up again. He was firm and threatening, and that old icky feeling in my stomach was as intense as when I was

Around The Table

a little girl sitting at the table across from my father. For a moment, I became a victim, thinking how unlucky I was to have landed a job with an authoritative male as my leader. My fear elevated further, and instead of using it to determine what to do next, I turned towards his office door to flee with my tail between my legs. But just as I did, I felt her roll over with my hand on my stomach. Woah, what triggered that? Was she trying to tell me something? I'm not sure if I believe in that stuff, but she did catch my attention, and my interpretation was that she was calling me to task! Suddenly, I was in a situation whereby I knew what the right thing was to do, and I needed to quickly process my fear to respond in a way that represented who I wanted to be—for her. In just a few brief moments, I was clear about what my trepidation represented and what it was asking me to do; I was suddenly that little girl, reacting to someone sitting in front of her for years at a kitchen table, who seemed to relish in squashing her emotions, thoughts, inspirations, and beliefs. It was just spilled milk for God's sake, and it was time to stop feeding into his power.

Thinking about how much and how long I was controlled made me want to fight for the freedom of all the little girls who sat at kitchen tables, terrified of what would happen if they spilled their milk, shared their emotions, were too sensitive, had an opinion, or spoke up for others. So, I became very calm and slowly turned around to face this man—an extension of the patriarch who toyed with me my whole life. I felt the daycare director channelling my father, but my unborn daughter summoned me to deprive this man and my father of their misogynistic power. I was clear that I didn't need to forget about anything because I could stop their control by speaking my truth.

Looking him square in the eyes, I firmly said, *I'm going to the board of directors*. I then walked out the door and finished my shift. Although I felt empowered, the repercussions of that statement were ten-fold when I received a phone call the following morning from the assistant director, informing me not to come in that day because I was under investigation. I had no clue what she was talking about and asked her to explain. She told me she couldn't because it was confidential, and child and family services were involved. I was not to come back to work until requested to do so.

I woke up early that day and went downstairs to the kitchen to prepare for the day. We lived in a large two-story that we bought when we gave up hope of having another child, and once we discovered we were pregnant, we decided we would sell after her arrival. We knew we couldn't afford it anymore with a second baby on the way, and giving it up was beyond worth it. The 3000 square-foot tutor rested on a street corner with massive pine trees and expansive flower gardens. There was a sizeable two-tiered deck off the kitchen where we often sat in the summer months with our morning coffee and breakfast. However, this was January, just after celebrating Christmas, so Simon and I were having a leisurely morning, sitting at the kitchen table before leaving to drop him off at his daycare. I was on the late shift, and I didn't have to go in until ten, so we took our time. Hank was already off to work, and I savoured these slower mornings because I was struggling with my sciatica; gaining so much weight during pregnancy served its purpose in alleviating nausea but caused back pain due to a lack of physical alignment. Hank and I had recently discussed the possibility of me going on early maternity leave, but I chose to stick it out as long as I could, wanting that time with the baby after she was born.

Simon and I were chatting when the landline rang, and I slowly got up, compensating for that nagging pinched nerve. I managed to get there on time but had difficulty processing the information I was given. I tried desperately to remember anything I could have done that would have prompted a complaint associated with any of the children at the daycare. I knew for sure that I would never intentionally harm anyone, let alone a child; after everything I had been through, I was a fierce protector of all humans, young and old.

I called Hank, and he immediately contacted legal counsel. The long, arduous process began when our lawyer discovered I was being investigated for child sexual assault. It turns out that the director used a conversation he had with one of the parents and manipulated it into an accusation to get rid of me before I could report him to the daycare's board of directors for his possible fraudulent behaviour; he was later charged and fired from his position. Ironically, compassion stirred within me for a moment because I thought about how desperate this man must be that he would attempt to end my career in order to cover up his deceptive behaviour. However, I could not allow his lack of integrity to influence my abundance thereof, and I relied on my truth to move through the horror of what he inflicted upon me. My reality was all I had, and for once in my life, I wholeheartedly trusted it despite someone trying to dismiss it.

I waited for a week or more for someone to contact me after receiving the initial phone call to stay home. No one talked to me until a police officer knocked on my door one day out of the blue and requested a visit to discuss what was going on. We sat on the sofa in my beautiful sunken family room, which meant absolutely nothing to me anymore, and she asked me if I knew why I was being investigated. I told her that I did not but would be grateful if she could tell me, so I knew what I was dealing with. She told me there was an incident on the last day I worked, which happened to be the same day I confronted the director. She told me that a parent accused me of inappropriately touching her daughter while wiping her bum after a bowel movement. The police officer asked me to describe what happened at the end of my shift that day. I told her that the only thing I had in my defence was my perception of what happened, and she gently said that's all she wanted to hear...

At the end of that day, I was the only teacher in charge of signing out the last five or six children, ranging from three to five years old. The daycare closed at six in the evening, and at about five-forty, one of the older children asked to go to the bathroom. Because I was the only teacher left in the building, we all went into the washroom together. It was a large room with a washer, dryer, laundry tub, and cubbies along the wall. There were several toilet stalls, and the little girl who asked to go to the washroom went into one. I asked the other children to sit on the old wooden bench that spanned the length of the end wall to wait for their friend to finish going to the toilet. The bench had been painted bright blue at one point, but most of it had rubbed off after years of this very situation—I watched as one of the pre-schoolers picked some of the remaining paint off the wood and flicked it in the air.

The girl in the stall was in there for a while, so I asked if I could help her, and she agreed. She unlocked the door, and I opened it a crack and noticed she was quite soiled, so I got some warm, wet washcloths for her to clean herself. We encouraged the children to be independent, but in the end, she needed some help, so we got the job done together. By the time we finished, the children's parents began arriving to pick them up, including the mother of the one I had helped in the washroom. Her daughter was happy to see her, and I shared what had happened and how we handled it. She took the plastic grocery bag with her daughter's rinsed, soiled clothes. Neither the child nor the mother seemed concerned at that time. In fact, the mother thanked me for helping her daughter.

I told the officer that was my story, and I had nothing else. I didn't tell her about my conversation with the director because I hadn't yet connected the dots that he would concoct an accusation against me in order to shut me up for his deception. I wanted to be absolved solely based on what happened that day in the washroom; my defence had to be my story exactly as it occurred.

As we sat side-by-side on my sofa, there was a moment of silence. Then, she explained that the mother was chatting in the hallway with the director the following morning, and she told him how the last-shift teacher helped her daughter with a toilet issue the day before. She said that everything was okay until later in the evening, when the incident triggered memories of the daughter's known past sexual abuse. The mother said she was initially concerned, but she and her daughter talked it through, and she was fine. However, the director took advantage of the situation and convinced the mother that I should be investigated for possibly inappropriately touching her child—just in case.

I looked at the officer and reiterated that I only helped the girl by following protocol, and I had no witnesses other than the other children they would never question. Sitting beside her, I could tell that she was reflecting as she looked at me in all my seven-month pregnancy glory. She told me that was all she needed, and she dismissed the allegations. I don't think she realizes what a gift her decision was; she was the first person of authority in my life to listen to my truth and trust it. This went against everything my father had taught me, given there was no proof.

However, I experienced a double-edged sword because using my voice got me in this mess in the first place when I took the director to task about his unethical behaviour. In desperation, he had retaliated and crossed that same line towards insanity I had witnessed so many times in my life—I was well aware of where that could lead. And even though I was absolved of something that should never have been reported in the first place, my career and reputation in the daycare industry were ruined—I could never return to that daycare or any other in the town I lived. No one else would hire me due to the possibility I had sexually abused a child; I understood that risk. In the end, he achieved what he set out to do, and misogyny reined.

So, I took my maternity leave early without any additional compensation and focused on the arrival of my little girl, who arrived on March 24, 1994. Olivia came into the world with the passion and drive that still motivates her today, and yet she had a lovely softness about her that she continues to carry with her. Her birth was not difficult, just really fucking fast!! Having had the marathon labour with Simon, I never expected her to come out like a speeding bullet. I had been proactive and hired a labour coach, who didn't make it on time because her drive to the hospital was longer than the delivery. We were fortunate that our doctor arrived for the final push, but it was very close.

I woke up from mild contractions that morning at around four. They were just strong enough to let me know I was in labour, so I went back to sleep and stirred each time one gently approached and then dissipated with ease. I wondered if my mother had told the truth, and there might be a possibility I would give birth without experiencing pain. At around six, Simon began calling me with his usual mommy sing-song, and I went in to let him know it was alright to get up. He was turning four in three weeks, but he maintained the routine of waiting for me to go into his room every morning. We did our usual cuddling in the same gliding rocking chair I soothed him to sleep in after getting through his cholic. We then went into Hank, and I leaned into his ear, *You're going to be a daddy again.* He got up right away, but I told him not to worry because the contractions were far apart and manageable. He got ready, and as he left to take Simon to daycare after breakfast, I told him I would call him at work when it was time.

Based on Simon's lengthy birth, I made an error in judgment because I escalated into the transition stage of labour an hour later without warning. Boom!! I knew this meant I was at least seven centimetres dilated, and my girl was well into descent mode; she was quickly moving down the birth canal. I found myself hanging over the railing of the sunken family room, staring at the sofa where the police officer validated my story. *Just forget about that, Diana.* I desperately panted to manage the excruciating contractions that were so close together I didn't think I could walk over to the phone to make two critical calls. However, I was not prepared for a home delivery, so between contractions, I pushed myself to get to the phone, called my labour coach, and shared my status. She told me to immediately call Hank.

His secretary answered, and I asked her to tell Hank that the baby was coming. She said he was on a call but would let him know as soon as he got off. I

Around The Table

urgently told her, *No, the baby is coming now; cut him off the call and tell him to come home right away.* She did, and because his office was around the corner, he arrived within minutes. He was not thinking straight when he got there and decided that he needed to change out of his suit before we left. I was back to hanging over the railing and yelling at him to hurry up. He ran upstairs faster than I'd ever seen him move. After a few moments, I called out that we had to go, *Right now!!* He came down in a casual shirt and his dress pants, not having time to put on his jeans. He loaded me into the back seat of the car, where I laid down panting non-stop as he pulled out of our driveway.

Speeding along the waterfront past the factory where my father worked years ago, I experienced the most prolonged, excruciating contraction ever—this would not be a pain-free birth. Next, I released my first push and crazily envisioned a little girl jumping off her daddy's shoulders into the water. She screamed with glee at the same time I screamed bloody murder—pain—little girl—joy—discomfort. This was too much to process through labour in the back seat of a car, so I pushed it aside and looked up at Hank's terrified eyes in the rear-view mirror, *Hurry up and get me to the hospital!!* I really didn't think we were going to make it but managed to hold back three pushes, and as I stood panicking in the hospital parking lot, I told Hank to tell the doctor that I wanted the epidural right away, *Yes, dear.* He put me in a wheelchair and rolled me into the hospital lobby and onto the elevator. It stopped at a floor along the way, and a man entered and went to push a floor button before our destination. I looked at him, pursed my lips, and firmly said, *Please don't.* I saw my mother's face staring at him at that moment. He immediately stepped back.

The next thing I knew, I was standing at the nursing station, signing admission papers, and I informed the nurse that I needed to push. She was as cool as could be, telling me it would only be another moment, so I began pulling my pants down in desperation. She got the message and quickly took me to a room where I lay on a bed, asking if I could push. Another nurse told me that I likely needed to have a bowel movement. Seriously?! She was adamant I take a trip to the washroom, which proved to be quite an ordeal while in active labour. But okay, I did what she told me to do. Once on the toilet, she stood in front of me and told me to go ahead, so I allowed my body to do what it had to—no bowel movement, but my little girl's head began to crown. I found myself back at the dinner table with my father, proving I was right. The nurse visibly panicked, realizing she was wrong and immediately moved me back to the bed, where I pushed as hard as I could as soon as my ass hit the sheet. Hank stood at the bottom of the bed, wanting to be the first to see his little girl, and she shot out like a cannonball with her afterbirth landing all over her father's dress pants. The doctor caught her in mid-air.

Unlike my mother, I did experience pain through this process, but the speed at which my daughter introduced herself just after eleven in the morning that day certainly distracted me from it. She was a healthy seven pounds, eleven ounces. And

Escaping the Cycle of Regret

when the doctor placed her on my chest, I sensed the most magical whisper with a powerful message telling me that someone extraordinary had been brought into my life. This little girl came in guns a-blazing, and from the first day of her life, I had faith that she was destined to make a difference in others' lives. Furthermore, I had a deep knowing that both of my children would grow into the kind individuals that they did. I was sure of this because it was all we ever expected from them—to be guided by loving-kindness no matter what they might be dealt, having faith it would support them through both good and bad.

As with Simon, my daughter had difficulty latching on to me. I tried everything I knew determined that *failure to thrive* would not appear on her medical chart. However, much to my dismay, I found that my fortitude got me into a bit of a life-threatening pickle when I woke up one day riddled with fever and inflammation coursing through my left breast and around to my back. Overnight, I was battling mastitis, an infection of the breast tissue caused by a lack of milk flow or a clogged milk duct.

Simon had an appointment with a specialist regarding reoccurring ear infections that afternoon, and we waited six months to see this doctor, so I was not about to cancel it. Instead, I took some Tylenol and went on with my day. However, by the time we needed to leave for the hospital, I was in bad shape—almost delusional from the fever. And yet, I managed to pack up the baby, get Simon in the car, and head downtown. I'm not sure how I got through that appointment and absorbed all the information I was given. But I did, and I got my children home without collapsing and having an accident while driving. Looking back, I am grateful for the perseverance I inherited from my mother because I was able to hang on until I walked through the door and got each of my kids to safety, one on each sofa. I told Simon to have a nap on one, and I placed pillows all around Olivia on the other. I then got up to go to the kitchen but passed out on the way, and Hank found me on the family room floor when he got home from work.

Our doctor lived close by, and we knew each other well because her son went to the daycare where I had taught. After shaking me awake, Hank called her, and she assessed me at our house and then drove me to the hospital. Hank took Simon to his mother's and then met us there afterwards. The infection was septic, and I was admitted along with Olivia so she could continue breastfeeding. Every time she latched on to me, the pain was severe, and I was appalled to see drops of red liquid dripping from the corner of her mouth when I looked down at her. My nipples were so chapped that my daughter was drinking my blood. Hank sat beside my bed, watching me cry as I tried to feed our baby; I was beyond exhausted and unable to put into words what I wanted to do. Inside, I was screaming, *Please get her off of me and give her formula,* but on the outside, I put on a brave face and did what I thought everyone around me expected me to do—persevere and suffer.

An orderly interrupted the feeding when he arrived with a large stainless-steel machine that the nurse said she would attach to my nipples to get the milk flowing.

Around The Table

It looked like one of the milking machines my uncle on the farm bought years ago when they transitioned from manual to automated milking. I had become a cow. Perhaps I would become a chicken next, and they would twirl my neck around to put me out of my misery.

Soon after, I became hopeful when a woman from the La Leche League knocked on the door. She smiled when she pulled up a chair on the opposite side of the bed where Hank sat. Initially, she was kind, reassuring me that everything was going to be alright, and we were going to work together to support Olivia to latch on properly. I was grateful but told her that I had inverted nipples and had the same issue with my firstborn; I wasn't sure this would work. I knew I was in trouble when she immediately dismissed me by turning to Hank. Her soft voice became a few octaves louder, and she inserted an authoritative tone while proceeding to give him instructions. I tensed up and started to shiver, which, in turn, prompted Olivia to detach from her feeding. I wiped her red lips dry and watched Hank take control. He had reached his limit.

As the nurse stood by, the La Leche League woman told Hank to go to the local grocery store and buy a head of cabbage. She then advised him to take the cabbage home, boil it until tender, and then bring it back to the hospital to apply it to my breasts to draw out the infection. Hank listened, allowing her to finish as she shared her detailed instructions; once again, I marvelled at how composed he could be under duress, but I also felt it coming. I looked up into the nurse's eyes, knowing she also realized his patience was waning. And sure enough, once the breastfeeding guru finished her speech, Hank politely replied, *Thank you for your advice.* He then turned to me and asked if I wanted to do all that. I told him I did not. He then turned to the nurse and said, *We need to put Olivia on formula right now.* He waved his arm around the room encompassing the lady in Birkenstocks and the milking machine, and he reiterated our decision, *We are done with all this now.* The nurse looked at me and smiled as if asking if I agreed, and I nodded and smiled in return; she turned around to get the formula. Relieved, I thanked the La Leche League lady, and she packed up her bag and left. She was the only one not smiling. The milking machine was taken out of my room an hour later.

I can always trust Hank to do the right thing and step up when needed. Over the years, he did so when it came to my parents' interference, as well as within situations when I was confused and controlled by outside forces. He always encouraged me to trust my gut. As parents, we reiterated this philosophy when our children faced uncomfortable situations and difficult people. However, I often struggled with my own advice. Childhood insecurities continued to haunt me, so I surrounded myself with my dearest friends through the ease of a cup of coffee. Around this time, I recognized just how empowering meaningful conversations could be, naturally translated into support and deep connection. I had one such friend who shared my passion for community support. She was a constant source of comfort because she also led a simple, genuine life guided by human advocacy. She often called and told me to put down my dust cloth and do something I enjoyed, *The same amount of dust*

Escaping the Cycle of Regret

will be there next week. As much as I agreed with her, I was still subconsciously feeding into what I thought my mother expected of me in terms of being a good wife and parent.

We understood each other on a deeper level because we had both experienced childhood trauma. While mine included what some therapists categorize as small-t emotional trauma, hers was definitely big-T physical trauma. We often chatted about the impact the people in our past had on us and that neither the small nor the big trauma was worse or easier to manage than the other—trauma is trauma. But to me, hers always seemed much worse because she suffered extensively from PTSD associated with past abuse, and although I tried, I could not save her.

I will never forgive myself for not trying harder because she unexpectedly knocked on my door one day wanting to talk, and I told her I was too busy to get together. I was too busy dusting my house. Two days later, in November 1994, she died of an overdose, leaving behind her husband and two young children. Her passing was a different circumstance than my sister's, but the result was the same, being guilt-ridden with not having the final conversation I was meant to have with each of them. I know I could have done better to ease their suffering had I stepped up and been there for them.

This remarkable woman's passing provided an awakening that, even though I believed my mother had a hand in depriving me of saying goodbye to my sister, I was just as accountable for ignoring the persistent whisper that begged me to get in my car and visit her. The same was true in my friend's case, with my soul telling me to put down the dust cloth. But I didn't and chose to watch her walk down my porch steps towards her car—alone. In both cases, my choices ultimately took away any opportunity I had to make a difference in their final moments. Once again, I was reminded that I could do better if only I dared to be my truth and push away others' expectations.

Four months later, in March 1995, a group of my friends moved through the sudden devastating death of one of our girlfriends. She was a beautiful, free-spirited, hippy girl who got married in bare feet on the top of a hill. Care-free and full of joy, I still wish I could allow myself the freedom of her laissez-faire approach to life. As a group of five, we had some incredible times, taking turns gathering at each other's houses once a month for pizza nights with our babies. One night, this friend mentioned the sad state of her breasts due to breastfeeding. We all agreed that we were not impressed with the tubular, skinny length our breasts had become. But, after a few drinks, she suggested that we line up on the floor on our hands and knees with our tops removed to compare our breasts as they hung free. Her suggestion was not a surprise, but what happened next was. The front door opened right into the living room, so when our other friend's husband came home early, he found himself standing in front of our exposed breasts lined up in a row. With his eyes and mouth wide open, he immediately turned around and went back outside, shutting the door behind him.

Around The Table

This was our hippie girl. She craved the openness of living in nature far from the city with her husband and 18-month-old daughter. Had she lived longer, I know she would have wanted to grow her own food and do everything she could to be more sustainable and protect the environment. But unfortunately, she never had the chance after crashing into a tree a short distance from her house. She was driving home from work one night and fell asleep at the wheel; her house was visible from the accident site. She was gone in the blink of an eye.

She was known as the best server in downtown, not just because she was organized, timely, and could easily balance a stack of dishes, but she also possessed something that made people feel special in her presence. She was kind and generous, and her smile was contagious. When someone sat at one of her tables, it was like she had invited them into her dining room at home. Everyone was treated with dignity, respect, and kindness. That was her legacy—being a human advocate of the most considerate kind.

Her best friend was part of our group, and she organized a farewell from us. We met at her gravesite one afternoon, and this time, instead of sitting around her table, we stood around her tombstone with a Margarita in hand. Her bestie made a toast, and we all took a sip and poured the remaining contents of our glasses into the ground that was her forever blanket. We laughed and cried over one last toast and conversation with our friend—it's exactly what she would have done for us.

In September 2014, we lost the friend who made the Margaritas 19 years before. She found relief from the struggles of her life through death. She left behind her two boys, and I received the news the following morning, two days before Hank and I were to move across the country to British Columbia. Our flights were booked, and the moving truck was already in transit. I remember sitting on the side of my bed in shock, my whole body shaking and my mind trying to process that she was gone. I found myself stuck, making another difficult decision to leave before saying goodbye because her funeral was scheduled a few days after our departure was.

Her sister is also a very dear friend of mine, so I went to see her right away. I don't think I have ever witnessed the degree of grief she displayed that day. Holding her was like absorbing years of accumulated sisterly love through the tears of unbearable pain. These two were as close as any siblings could be, and I did not initially know what to do with the emotion emanating from her. So, I did what I learned to do and tapped into my courage as I compartmentalized all my misery; I tucked it away so I could push through to support her. My strength was all I had.

When I envision this so-called heaven so many believe in, I am witness to my sister and three friends sitting around a table, asking our children to spend time with each other by putting down their dust cloths, walking in their bare feet, and slowing down to have a conversation while sharing their accumulated awakenings. The wisdom passed down from my long-departed soul sisters provides our children with the confidence that they can do even better than we did.

X

❦ Escaping the Cycle of Manipulation ❦

With the birth of each of my children, my mother's compulsive behaviour reached a new level of absurdity. Her perfectionism was obtrusive as she focused on creating what she perceived a family should look like from the exterior. She moved well past passive-aggressive behaviour into blatant intense performances to achieve her goal. I was astounded at the lengths she took with each dramatization to try to get her way.

A year after Olivia was born, we moved out of the large tutor home where I was tortured by the vision of my friend standing before me each time I opened the front door—my guilt lingered and tormented me until I managed to tuck it away in the same space the rest of my shame occupied. I never felt comfortable surrounded by the luxury of expansive space this house provided. The hallway at the top of the stairs on the second floor was so large that it could have been a room on its own. At one point, I envisioned my children playing a grand piano in this massive foyer. However, I became anxious with the distance it created between our room and the children's; I was never sure if I would hear them cry out in the night. Then there was the guilt I experienced living in what my parents and sister would have described as opulent because I was raised to judge others who had more than what we had, and I now had more than they did. The fear of being criticized by my family transitioned into being ashamed of what Hank and I had achieved.

I don't think I mentioned any of this to Hank, and then thankfully, he told me we couldn't afford it anymore since I no longer worked at the daycare and Olivia arrived. So, we moved to the other side of the township to a brand-new subdivision and began a fresh start in a smaller, more affordable home. It was here that Hank, me, and our children formed close friendships with many of our neighbours.

We loved our home on this crescent. We genuinely became part of a close-knit community and established life-long relationships. Everyone knew their neighbours, and we would do anything to support each other. Hank and I hosted and were invited to dinners by other couples on our street. The families collaborated to provide our kids with experiences to remember forever, including neighbourhood barbeques, picnics, Canada Day fireworks, camping trips, and a skating rink in the park that the fathers built and maintained. When the moms were on maternity leave, we had weekly coffee groups and kids' play dates. For the most part, I embraced being a stereotypical mom, cooking, baking, cleaning, and organizing birthdays and special events. However, there were other times when I loathed how it reflected the patriarchal familial structure I was brought up in, so I did everything in my power to be guided by my unique matriarchal style.

Simon began senior kindergarten at the local Catholic school, and Olivia was under two, so she stayed home with me. Since I was no longer working full-time, I accepted an opportunity to sell registered education savings plans after being recruited by a mom and close friend in the neighbourhood. Hank and I worked out a system whereby I called potential clients during the day, we had supper together when he got home from work, and then I went to the appointments I had booked for that night. He cleaned up after dinner, spent the evening with the kids, and got them bathed and ready for bed. We committed to supporting each other throughout our marriage in both our personal and professional endeavours. Hank always had faith I could achieve anything I set my mind to. Because of his encouragement and my determination, I achieved top provincial sales records and earned a few trips, including a Caribbean cruise that my manager and I went on. There is no doubt that my confidence increased due to my career achievements based solely on what others deemed as such. I began to experience a shift in my self-worth, equating it to success in the corporate world's eye.

Unfortunately, I had to put my career on hold because the surgery for that pesky thumb joint could not wait any longer. Olivia was now 18-months-old, and every time I changed her diaper, my thumb popped out of its joint. I had to stop and push it back in, and the pain was beyond tolerable. What I didn't know at the age of 32 is this would be one of many surgeries throughout my lifetime, with an undiagnosed disease looming in the background.

With Hank working ten-hour days building his business and our financial security, I was pretty much on my own during the day after the surgery. My mother thought he should have taken time off to take care of me, but she didn't realize it was her who motivated me to tell him not to worry; I was a good wife and mother and could take care of myself. In fact, I insisted he go to work every day—that's what my father would have done. I remember looking back at when she suffered a gallbladder attack. I took care of her because my dad went to work that morning, leaving her lying in bed in pain. I wondered if her judgement towards Hank reflected her disappointment in her husband's lack of caring for her when she needed him. Back then, she had a 14-year-old eager to do whatever she needed to be well. But when I had my surgery, I had a six-year-old son in kindergarten and a toddler at home, and my mother never once came to help me or cook a meal for my family. Instead, she popped over for coffee and complimented me on how strong I was—*just like her*, she said. I survived without her help.

We became a busy family, and as much as we worked hard, we enjoyed spending quality time with our children, friends, and family. I hang onto the memories that my parents displayed gestures of love to us, inviting my family over for meals and

Escaping the Cycle of Manipulation

offering to meet my children at the school bus when we couldn't make it in time to pick them up. I believed these acts of kindness represented an expression of love for us until they didn't anymore. The meal invitations were initially sporadic but true to my mother's M.O., they became scheduled expectations after we accepted numerous times on what became specific days of the week. I recognized that it didn't take my mother long to coerce me into having standing dates, either with her alone or with my father. She was exceptionally good at establishing ongoing weekly activities without me agreeing or even realizing what was happening—she somehow lured me into doing what she wanted and when. If I suddenly deviated from her plan, she let me know how disappointed she was, making sure to mention how many times my sister came to visit every week.

A couple of Sunday morning coffees or Wednesday dinners transitioned into a weekly assumption. Hank continued to work long hours, building up his practice as a partner in an insurance firm. With my blessing, he dedicated Wednesdays after work and early Sunday mornings to golf, so he could not always make my mother's programmed invitations. I wondered why my mother chose those days and times to invite us as a family when she knew he was busy and would disappoint her by not coming. He was quickly scrutinized for not spending enough time with me and my family, and things escalated from there. Many times, while sitting with my parents over coffee and cake, my mother smoothly integrated critical comments, questioning his whereabouts during the conversation. Over time, her negative opinions about my husband became an annoying scratch under my skin that wouldn't disappear. It got to the point whereby I found myself defending Hank about something I was not upset about to begin with, and I realized she had lured me into the camaraderie of judgement.

She made Sunday dinner a ritual that included our entire extended family. We sat around the table as we had when I was a child devouring her delicious meals, including that infamous roast chicken dinner. I savoured the positive aspects of sitting around the family table with three generations gathered together and experienced the connection and conversation of a mixture of adults and children. However, ultimately, there was always that anticipatory element of my father starting a debate—one that involved at least two or more of us and always included me. He got my goat every time because I was still conditioned to argue and defend against anything he presented. I cannot count how often Hank suggested I not feed into my father's antics, but I couldn't help myself; I was forever that well-trained dog, trying to please her owner by being tricked into his self-righteous abyss. My father genuinely took pleasure in continuously baiting my need for approval because it simultaneously fed his ego as he watched me falter every time.

Eventually, Hank, the kids, and I spent the minimal amount of time with my parents that we felt was required to appease my mother. It sounded horrible to fathom scheming like that in my tortured mind, but we believed it was necessary to maintain our autonomy and sanity as a family unit. So often, being with both or

Around The Table

alone with either my mother or father gave me a sense of not belonging. When my extended family was together, I often looked around the room and wondered why I was the only one inflicted with the consequence of their continual crazy-making; everyone else seemed to go along with the flow of behaviour that fed into what I considered irrational discussions. As I listened and scanned each face, my eyes would finally lock onto Hank's. He routinely tolerated his time there merely to support me through my need to endure a familial duty of emotional suffering. I questioned why I invited such misery into my life...and his. And yet, I continued going back...

I know my mother complained to her sisters about how little time I spent with her because they told me. She thought their loyalty extended to keeping secrets about me, but it didn't. Hank and I had friends, careers, and busy lives, so trying to accommodate what my mother believed we should do became impossible enough that we came up with a more elaborate plan by setting clear boundaries around how much time we spent with my parents and when. We also made a pact that we would leave a gathering before I got caught up in the vortex of right and wrong. We began organizing our lives as we chose rather than scheduling things to meet their approval. Even though we still considered them within our decisions, this became problematic for my mother because she was an all-or-nothing kind of gal. I'm not sure why we doubted she would eventually act out because her past reactions to our implemented deal-breakers were an indication that she was about to shock us into her drama—full throttle.

My mother called one day to ask if she and my father could come over for a cup of coffee. I was pleased that she chose to pick up the phone rather than show up unannounced. However, I foolishly let my guard down, believing this was a positive step forward due to the boundaries we had put in place. They sat down and got settled in with their coffees. Then, my mother turned to Hank and me sitting on the sofa and announced that they had just bought the house across the street from us. My father sat with a grin on his face while we sat in silence, absorbing the impact of her words. It felt like an earthquake had suddenly struck, and we were completely unprepared for its jolt. I also realized that our lack of verbal response would be interpreted as precisely that. So, instead of allowing them to process our genuine disappointment, I hypocritically compensated for it by acting like I was thrilled by her news. Hank sat there in complete silence as my mother explained how they could help us with the kids and how much fun we would all have.

This was not a good day. And after they moved in, that unforgettable day turned into weeks and then months, and living on this street was never the same. All of our friends got to know my parents, and most loved them because both my mother and father were very skilled at presenting themselves differently from outside and inside the front door. Although each side had positive elements, the inside included additional fragments that caused a lot of damage to those who were invited into that inner circle. To this day, the confusion I experience when people

Escaping the Cycle of Manipulation

tell me how lovely my mother is or how kind my father is, eats away at the part of me who knows their inside-the-door persona. I want to scream and tell them there is another side to them that you don't see or hear when you cross that threshold. But, of course, I don't because this is our family's best-kept secret. Everyone in my family knows it exists, but we keep it hidden because we all know the shame involved in admitting such duality.

I have shared this confidence with several intimate friends. Some responded with something like, *I would never have thought that about your mother; she's so lovely.* Or, *Your father is so kind and gentle!!* Of course, these statements of surprise triggered an immediate nagging imposter syndrome in the back of my mind, and I was embarrassed that I had such evil thoughts about my parents; the sense of insanity arose again. But then, and more often than not, there have been those who bravely revealed their truth to me, *My parents are the same!* and they shared their detailed familial secrets with me with such immense relief because, like me, they kept them compartmentalized for a very long time. I have not only experienced freedom by sharing my voice but also by inviting others to share theirs. I believe it is my responsibility as a human being to tell my stories to others—friends, relatives, strangers—especially the painful experiences, so they are inspired to share theirs. I discovered that the common thread is not that everyone has experienced emotional trauma, but that everyone who emotionally suffers has experienced trauma.

While my mother lived happily across the street, Hank and I suffered from the strain their close proximity put on our family. She watched all our comings and goings and didn't shy away from sharing what she saw, including when we went out with our friends or had company. My mother often asked me where Hank was, why he went to work early one day and late the next, why our bathroom light was on at three in the morning, and she stopped in without warning all the time. She continued to find flaws in my husband and made sure I knew she didn't approve by pointing out how she believed his actions negatively impacted me. The husband that she chose for me became her nemesis because he didn't turn out to be the conformist she counted on.

Hank was scheduled to go on an annual golf trip with his friends when I got the call for the laser eye surgery that I was on a waiting list for. They had a cancellation, and the doctor advised that I not be alone the first night should the children need something. So, I went to my mother and asked if she would sleep at my house that night. I made the mistake of faltering with the assumption that she would support me since she initially told me that was one of the benefits of living across the street from me. Instead, she told me that Hank should cancel his planned trip, given I was now having the surgery at the same time. I explained that it was not a major operation and just a precautionary measure that someone was with me that one night, but she insisted on not staying over, telling me to either cancel my surgery or tell Hank to stay home. I looked at her and asked, *Mom, why are you doing this?* And she told me, *Because your husband should do the right thing and be home with you.*

Around The Table

My mother really believed she had the right to weigh in on what my husband should or should not do, and she was adamant that she would teach him and me a lesson. Ironically, she actually thought I would heed her advice and make Hank cancel his trip, or I would cancel my surgery because, in her mind, someone needed to make a compromise. Much to her dismay, I chose to go through with my surgery. I didn't tell Hank what my mother said until after he arrived back home because my mother could make even the most confident person second-guess themself. Instead, I went to the person I should have asked in the first place, and my mother-in-law generously spent the night without batting an eye. She ended up not needing to do a thing. However, she gave me peace of mind through the first night of my recovery and even encouraged me to sleep in. She also insisted on making her famous egg pancakes for the kids and got them ready and off to school. After she left, I went downstairs to get something out of the fridge to eat and found a pot of homemade chicken soup in the fridge. Nothing was said, with continual unconditional acts of kindness provided for years on end.

At the same time, my mother became more and more easy-going with her daily comings and goings. I would no sooner get in the door, and there she was behind me, *Yoo, hoo!!* I wanted to ask her to call before coming by, but I was too influenced by my never-ending need not to disappoint her. She was so happy, and her assuming way of presenting herself made it very difficult for me to reject her forced presence in my life. Without any warning, she would suddenly just appear as if she was supposed to be there. I began questioning myself, thinking I was a horrible person for not wanting her there, and I tried to convince myself that I did. Thirty-four years after spilling milk, I still struggled with what was right and what was wrong.

Then, my mother offered to take the kids when they got off the bus every day so I wouldn't need to use after-school care. I wanted to say no because it felt like another trap, but I agreed because it was such a nice gesture, and the convenience was just too tempting to resist. I wrestled with wanting my children to have a relationship with my parents, knowing that critical trade-offs came along with spending more time with them than they already did. I just didn't weigh this all out very well. I was torn because I was very clear that I didn't want my kids influenced by the emotional roller coaster my parents took me on as a child, knowing the consequences would be life-altering for them. However, some of the same fun things my mother did with me when I was growing up were greatly appreciated: playing board games, reading books, and going for walks. She always had an after-school snack ready for them when they came through the door, and when I arrived to pick them up, she always had the teapot and *speekulaas* ready. Unfortunately, there were times when I had to tell her that we couldn't stay because I had to get supper going and drive one or both of the kids to karate, basketball, or soccer. She always met me with those pursed lips, *Okay then.* My mother liked the controlled continuity that her daily expectations created, and when I broke that flow, she made sure that I understood her disappointment with a few words, tone, or gesture.

I recognize how hard my mother tried to please my children and me; the sad part was that seeking that acceptance was her primary motivation, and she always tried way too hard. She became preoccupied with being recognized for her efforts to the point that she made sure to list all the great things she did with her grandchildren as soon as I walked through the door, including what she fed them, what time they napped, and how amazing my father was with them. Just as she quietly left piles of weeds on my sidewalk years before, she now added the details of describing each weed that made up that pile. She practically begged for gratitude, and I found myself endlessly accommodating her addiction to it. As a result, I became a fraud through the simple virtue of repeatedly thanking her before she had the chance to ask.

I also noticed that my mother only did things that seemed to suit her, and over time, I realized that the things she refused to do for me were influenced by what my father was not willing to do. In January 1998, Ontario suffered a devastating ice storm. Hank had to work 24/7 for months to keep up with the insurance claims streaming in from his clients. People lost hydro for weeks and months and accumulated thousands of dollars in damage to their homes. Even worse, farmers ended up with massive financial debt through lost income due to the death of their livestock and the destruction of their land. We were fortunate because we were only without electricity for a little over a week compared to others. However, after sleeping in front of our gas fireplace in the family room for a few days during the coldest month of the year, we needed to find somewhere else to stay because we didn't know how long it would last. We were cold and had no means to cook, so take-out was getting expensive. My parents had oddly not lost power across the street because they lived on a different grid that was not affected. And yet, we were not invited to sleep at my parents' place or offered any food. Sitting in the dark with candles, we looked across the street and saw my parents in their living room reading the newspaper after supper. Neither Hank nor I discussed how odd it was that they didn't come over to check on us—not once. After the storm subsided, we reflected back and realized just how normalized we had become to their lack of natural nurturing. I mean, who doesn't offer to take their grandchildren out of the cold when their house has no heat?

We held out each day during the storm, thinking we would have electricity any time. Hank's parents had been asking us to stay with them, but they lived further away, so when we finally decided to leave our house, I went across the street to my parents. Even though I heard my mother's voice telling me that she would help me when they moved in, I should have paid attention when something inside me told me not to go to her. And yet another little hopeful voice said to me that my parents would surely help us in our hour of need. I listened to it and asked them if we could stay there until the power was restored. My mother looked at my dad and then back at me. She asked if we had to bring our dog with us, and then it all

Around The Table

made sense. My father didn't like dogs, so we weren't welcome if Sparky-Boy was part of the entourage. Staring at my mother, I let a few moments go by as I allowed what she said to soak in. Then, ignoring my mother, I took a breath and asked my father what he was worried about. He told me that the dog would poop and pee in the backyard and ruin his gardens. It was winter, below zero, and the gardens were covered in ice, so I knew this was just an excuse. My father didn't want to be inconvenienced by a dog in his house, so I stood up, not bothering to continue the conversation. Instead, I went back across the street and asked Hank to call his mother and father.

We packed everyone up, including Sparky and our fish, and drove over the bridge to my in-laws. When we walked through the front door, both of my kids didn't hesitate to run and hug their oma and opa, and we were so relieved to have a warm place to stay with family who only cared about our well-being and not some pee in the snow or the inconvenience of having a dog in their house. And as much as the ice storm was a terrible catastrophe for so many, my in-laws used it as a time to connect and get closer to their grandchildren—mission accomplished.

The more time our children spent with my parents, the more evident my father's self-centeredness became. He rarely got up from his chair to greet them, expecting them to go to him. He sat there as the king of his castle being served by my mother, and she ran around in circles to keep him happy. When he spoke, I was embarrassed as he wore his bigotry like a badge. When I picked the kids up after work, he incorporated people's skin colour, differences, cultural inadequacies, and derogatory, racist references into our conversations. My children were uncomfortable around him because, just as he did me, he poked at my kids to try to get them going. I realized that if he did this when I was there, he must be doing it when alone with them as well. So, I repeatedly asked him not to pester my children or be discriminatory in front of them but rather share kindness and highlight how we are all the same. He just looked at me with that condescending grin, and my mother, wanting to please me, automatically reiterated my request to him and then turned to me and said, *He doesn't mean it*. My father just never got it, and he never changed.

In 1999, after a few years of juggling scheduling appointments during the day, working at night, and managing a house and family alongside Hank, we agreed it was time for me to get a day job. I initially tried making money by tapping into my creative side, but I needed a regular-paying job to help support both children's interests in various sports and activities while Hank continued to build his book of business. So, after a few years of stencilling kitchens and bathrooms and wall-painting, Hank encouraged me to apply as an administrative assistant at the financial side of the company he worked with. I pretended that my experience selling RESPs attributed to me getting the job, but I knew that being married to one of the firm's partners was what influenced me to get hired. In fact, I'm pretty sure my boss was told he had no choice but to hire me. It was exactly everything

Escaping the Cycle of Manipulation

I hated, sitting at a desk doing paperwork all day long. But this was similar to the sacrifice that Hank made when Simon was born, and we agreed that the trade-off was providing our children with opportunities that cost more than we could afford with me being a part-time painter.

It turned out that the job was much more complicated than I thought, and it was way over my head. The financial consultant I worked for was not accommodating at all, and he intentionally made my life hell by not willingly taking the time to train me. Instead, he did his best to get rid of me by using berating tactics and condescendingly pointing out my errors without attempting to teach me the right way to do things. His assistant took the time to support me, but she had her own job and couldn't dedicate the time required to get me up to snuff. He did his best to make me feel stupid, and it was very apparent to me that he didn't like being put in a position of giving Hank's wife a chance; he wanted me to fail so he could justify firing me.

At the time, I didn't know why I subjected myself to this emotional abuse, but I do now. It was part of my programming, having been brought up by someone who saw women as less than men. I was so anxious, going to work every day, knowing that I would be put down and treated like I didn't belong there. I believe that the stress I endured trying to make this job work manifested illness within me. Every day, I came home and told my husband what a great day I had and pretended everything was okay. I wanted him to be proud of me—a relevant person in the same world he worked in—and see me as someone other than who I really was.

Then, one night while we were making love, Hank uncovered my ill-health in the form of a lump in my breast. He was worried, but I dismissed him, saying it was probably nothing. I went back to my toxic workplace the next day, and when he asked me to call my doctor to have it checked, I told him I would. However, when I came home that day, he asked me when my appointment was, and I told him I had forgotten to call her. He was clearly upset, telling me he was sure he felt a lump and to please make an appointment. That night before closing my eyes, I looked over at him sleeping and thought about the urgency with which he begged me to have the lump checked. I searched for this foreign thing by running my fingers over that breast, and I suddenly found myself back to the time I lay in my bed as a young girl soothing myself to sleep. The shame from so long ago when my mother startled me out of my self-nurturing state had come back to haunt me. I was ignoring this lump growing inside of me because I subconsciously believed it had manifested from the sin of teenage promiscuity. I thought I was doomed to suffer through life, particularly at the hands of the authoritative figures who continued to present themselves to me. Initially unaware, I was willing to ignore this lump and possibly sacrifice my life to hide my shame.

There was no doubt in my mind I was fucked up and needed help, but for the time being, I had to deal with the task at hand. I came to my senses only because Hank persisted, and I had no logical reason not to. I was embarrassed to share my insane reasoning with him, so I moved towards sanity and made an appointment with my GP when I got to work the next day. She wanted to see me immediately, and I had a mammogram that afternoon and was scheduled to see a surgeon a few days later. My lumpectomy was booked for the following week, and I was sure I had cancer and would die.

In a moment of weakness one evening, I went across the street to tell my mother about my plight in hopes she would console me. I was clearly in some sort of delusional state, believing she would retrieve the strength she used to support her eldest daughter when she was diagnosed with cancer. I thought she would do the same when I gave her the news that I was having a lumpectomy. Instead, the first words out of her mouth were, *I can't go through this again.* She disregarded my situation and became the victim, so I told her I understood and went home to prepare for my operation.

I chose to take my surgeon's advice and had the lumpectomy without anesthesia or sedation. He had a nurse stand by my shoulder the entire time, topping up my freezing when I felt a bit of static. The beauty of not being put out was that Hank and I went out for breakfast at our favourite spot after the surgery; we each devoured a plate of Dutch pancakes with strawberries and whipped cream. I find that relief is best savoured with good comfort food.

That lump turned out to be old milk hiding in my nipple for five years since my disastrous mastitis experience. In my case, just like milk that sits past its due date in the fridge, it began to get hard and go bad. The surgeon told me that the biopsy indicated the lump was benign but was well on its way to becoming cancerous—milk, whether spilled or stuck in my nipple, had definitely become my nemesis. When I told my parents I was cancer-free and explained the situation, my mother breathed a sigh of relief and told me she could never have relived my sister's death. I sat across from her and told her, *No, you couldn't, Mom, because you would have been living mine for the first time.* I wasn't very compassionate at all.

One day, after returning to work after recovering from my surgery, my boss's wife came in, arriving just as he was arrogantly criticizing my work on something he never taught me how to do in the first place. Her empathy washed over me as she watched on. And, when they went into his office, she shut the door and loudly told him to give me a chance. I didn't need to listen to his response because the toxic energy of his cowardly whisper seeped under the door towards me—I was let go the next day. When we met next at the firm's Christmas party that year, he approached me and tried to make small chat, *Merry Christmas, Diana.* I smiled and replied, *Merry Christmas* and walked away. This was not my first workplace misogynistic experience, and it wasn't my last.

I moved on to a job at Investors Group where I worked as a part-time assistant for a consultant for a while. She expected things to be done right, and I appreciated that because *right* was my middle name. The difference between her and the last person I worked for was that she was kind and patient, and even though I'm a

Escaping the Cycle of Manipulation

creative right-side-of-the-brain kind of gal, I am also one in a rare breed, who can, simultaneously, use my logical left side. She recognized that and worked on activating it by making the monotony of filling out financial forms systematic, which fed my OCD. She never made me feel redundant or stupid but rather valuable and intelligent.

Unfortunately, she didn't have enough work for me, so after just six months, when another consultant offered me a full-time position, I accepted because Hank and I wanted to get ahead financially. I became the assistant to a fascinating character, and yet, he was one of the most sexist, conniving, manipulative, and sometimes heartless individuals—to others. However, he surprisingly respected me and treated me like gold. I loathed so many things about him, but he took the time to teach me everything I needed to know to be a great assistant. I was never devalued or taken for granted, and I laughed every day I went to work. Until September 11, 2001, when I sat down in front of my computer at 8:55 in the morning and looked at my screen at what I thought was the movie, Apocalypse Now. I saw one clip of a plane flying into the North Tower of the World Trade Centre, and then just after 9:00, another flew into the South Tower. Later that morning, a third crashed into the Pentagon. Looking up at the expression on the other assistants' faces who were watching the same thing, I realized this was not a movie trailer but a real-life catastrophe.

My boss called me into his office, and he didn't crack one joke that day. After the tragedy of this world disaster and almost three thousand lives lost that day, the financial world came tumbling down. The drastic and quick plunge did not support the sustainability of my job with this consultant, and I was let go soon afterwards. As much as this terrorist attack was one of the most devastatingly violent events I have ever known, the end of my time at Investors Group was a blessing in disguise. I existed in a world that didn't represent any part of who I was from my inside-out; my agonized soul was chained to a desk and a nine to five job. The day the stock market tanked in September 2001, I walked out those corporate doors and began my long emotional healing.

Then, while having a coffee at my parents' house one day, I made a spur-of-the-moment bold move and asked my mother why she chose to move across the street from us without discussing it first. Without blinking an eye, she coldly said, *Well, Hank's relatives live beside each other, so we thought you would like it?* It was an odd response, but there it was. They never really moved close to us out of love or to support us but instead due to her jealousy of the bond that Hank's family shared. She used the example of his uncle, who had generously purchased three lots and built homes on them, one for him and his wife, one for his son, and one for his daughter. Eventually, they all moved to different areas of town and the country, but my mother used their situation as a reason to buy the house across the street to be close to us. She knew that we would not like them living so close, so that's why she didn't tell us before buying. But she justified her secret because she got what she wanted. I believe she actually thought I would respond by telling her that it made total sense, but instead, I kept my mouth shut, thinking, *We are like the characters on Everyone Loves Raymond, except none of this is funny.*

I don't know why I thought anything I said to my mother would ever make her think twice about how she treated or reacted to me. I certainly didn't have the right to expect her to be different from who she was—who she had become due to her past trauma. I guess I hoped both my parents would one day consider setting their egos aside for the sake of becoming more intimately connected to my family and their grandchildren in particular. But without me blatantly telling them that although I loved them, I didn't like them, they continued putting themselves first. No matter how much I tried, they always defaulted to their manipulative ways. As a result, both Hank and I became very worried that our children would be influenced by my parents the same way I had been, and I could not live with myself knowing that I could have stopped that kind of emotional destruction. Hank was very aware of how they adversely affected me, and we were sick and tired of my mother's meddling. So, we decided to move back to the neighbourhood where we had lived before.

In the back of my mind, I heard my sister tell me to maintain distance between my parents the way she did when she and my brother-in-law moved away, and I knew she was right. So, one evening over dinner, we told them we decided to move because we wanted a larger home closer to a particular school where the kids could walk. And although all this was true, we kept out the part about not wanting them around our children as often. I was a coward, still bound to not entirely speak my truth for fear of being shut down. And because I didn't, they also didn't challenge me, but I think they knew because there was elevated tension between us from that moment on.

We moved in 2002 when Simon was 12 and Olivia was 8. Both kids were heavily involved in competitive sports that involved many hours travelling to out-of-town tournaments, which we thoroughly enjoyed. Spending time with all the parents on the teams, we formed additional close friendships in this new community. Our children's teammates became their friends, and we all socialized for many years together. To this day, I maintain deeply meaningful relationships with them, as well as those from our old neighbourhood. My children consider this house, the school they transferred to, and this particular community their childhood home.

Hank and I continued working hard to create the family life we wanted for our children. We instilled the ethics and morals we valued and also encouraged them to be curious about what was important to them as individuals. However, I know that I didn't always make choices in line with what I really believed because I hadn't reached the wisdom I needed to confidently show up within my authenticity. My past still tortured me, and my inner critic often became overpowering, steering me in the wrong direction towards patterns modelled by my parents and my mother in particular. I didn't know then that I needed to listen to my inner voice because sometimes it was right and compassionate instead of wrong and critical. I needed to allow the space for her to tell me what was on her mind instead of shutting her out; that took a few more years to get to. I am now sure that, just like my mother, I did the best I could, given the tightrope of insanity I walked towards her while she continued to walk towards me on hers.

Unfortunately, both her and my unpredictable behaviour, coupled with her obsession with birthdays having to be celebrated *on the day*, presented the perfect shit storm for us to cross our dysfunctional lines one too many times. For the most part, Hank and I accommodated my mother's wishes when it came to gathering on the day of each of our family member's birthdays. If it landed on a weekday, we squeezed in a visit after work in the evening, followed by the expected traditional weekend celebration. One year, however, we ran into a snag when we decided to rent a cottage from one of Hank's friends, and the only time he had available was the week of my mother's birthday on July 26th. We thought long and hard about whether we should take it because we knew she would make a fuss about us missing her annual outdoor party, which included much more than just coffee, cake, and lunch. She hosted a huge barbeque in her backyard every year, with everyone arriving just after lunch and staying well after supper and dessert. I did enjoy these gatherings because it was a time to relax and reconnect with my extended family. But my holiday time with Hank and the kids was a higher priority, so we chose to book the cottage. We explained the situation to my mother, but she did not understand that I chose my husband and children over her birthday. It didn't fit into her chain-of-command rules. However, I stood firm and apologized, telling her we would celebrate her birthday upon our return.

After that first year at the cottage, it naturally grew into our family's most magical annual vacation destination. It was nothing fancy, but it did have indoor plumbing and electricity, which we liked because we wanted a rugged cottage vibe. It had a screened-in porch that we ate breakfast in, and once the kids went to bed, Hank and I sat there for hours, relaxing and chatting with a glass of wine. This was where I first began dreaming of writing my memoir. Hank was the only one I shared this with, and he encouraged me to do it. So, every year, I brought a notebook and pen but never wrote a word. In hindsight, I am glad that I could never peel myself away from spending time with my family. I also realize that I could never have written the ending because it hadn't been lived yet—that took another 20 years to get to.

Olivia, in particular, loved being by the water, and we spent a lot of time doing crafts on the dock, painting rocks, and exploring the shoreline, while our new dog, Jake, searched for frogs. Then, one day, she found a piece of driftwood that she told me looked like the shape of a fish, so we got out the paints and began adding eyes, a mouth, fins, and a tail. It became a beautiful piece of art filled with every colour in our palette. To this day, it hangs proudly in our garage.

Around The Table

Hank took the kids out fishing every day, and I cleaned any catch big enough to cook for dinner. Sitting on the dock, looking out into the distance, I smiled, listening to their muffled conversation and laughter. I reflected on how lucky I was to find such a patient man and father for my children. I knew that people often find partners similar to their parents, but Hank was the exact opposite of my father. I thought back to the day my father forgot the key to the cottage we were renting and how he blew up at my mother. Every time that memory came up, shivers ran down my spine as I envisioned the fear in her eyes—I had to close mine to shake off the scene and the sound of the irritation in his voice. I never wanted my children to experience the fear I did when I was a little girl.

Hank was also the one who mainly took the kids swimming because, 30 years later, I was still traumatized by the leeches at the cottage where my father scared the shit out of me. I hadn't been in a lake since my mother poured that box of salt on my legs. So, when my children begged me to get in the lake and threw pool noodles at me, I had to compartmentalize the sensation of my feet sinking into the mud with those critters nibbling on me so long ago. I took a deep breath each time I placed one foot after the other on the slimy dock steps going into the water, and I agreed to do so once or twice a summer…for them.

I find it unimportant to face a phobia if I don't see the value in the outcome. For example, I tried to overcome my fear of a lake's bottom year after year, but the emotional trauma linked to those leeches didn't go away simply because I bravely jumped off a dock, and it never will. It's not about the leeches that tried to suck the life out of me when I was little but the people who tried to do the same for years after. In addition to being afraid of what lies on the bottom of the lake floor, I am terrified of heights and have been for as long as I can remember. I believe my fear of climbing comes from projecting my emotional pain onto the physical pain I may experience should I happen to fall. If I avoid the physical discomfort that may occur from falling on concrete, I don't have to face the emotional pain residing in my soul that needs to be worked through. When I believe I am insane, this all sounds ridiculous. However, when I am leaning towards sanity, I find my brain incredibly brilliant, coming up with such schemes, all for the sake of protecting me from reliving past trauma.

So many people have told me, *You need to face your fear and just get into the water!* Or, *Just climb the ladder right to the top a few times, and you will be fine!* Uh, no, the little girl at the table says, *I don't want to, and you can't make me.* And my 60-year-old-self agrees with her, *I'm perfectly fine without swimming in a lake or climbing ridiculous heights that make me feel like I'm going to vomit.* However, as much as I believe I can continue avoiding the fear that evolved from the trauma I relive every day, I also know that confronting and forgiving those responsible—including me—will dissipate that very fear into a speck of nothing. Neither the confronting nor the forgiving comes naturally or even seems necessary anymore because I'm still not convinced it's not all in my head—something I contrived as a sensitive wee child who was crazy all along.

Escaping the Cycle of Manipulation

Over the years, I have come to realize that it's okay to let my children know that fear itself is not something else to be fearful of but rather something to acknowledge and move through without necessarily conquering it like a superhero. Sometimes embracing fear and accepting its experience motivates me to do the right thing for everyone involved. When I was a child, fear turned into trauma because there was never an invitation to work through it. I have learned to embrace my fears, and I encouraged my children to do the same. Like the summer Hank took Simon and his friend out in the boat after breakfast one day. They were quite a distance away from the cottage, but I saw them fishing from the screened-in porch where I was sipping my second coffee. Suddenly, I heard a blood-curdling scream and instantly recognized it as my son's. I ran out of the cottage to the dock and saw the boat speeding towards me. Once docked, Hank helped Simon out of the boat as he continued to scream. I noticed that Simon had one prong of a three-pronged fishhook stuck in his shoulder. Hank had cut the line from the pole, but the hook was embedded deeply into his skin. It turns out that when Simon had swung the line back, getting ready to cast out, it hit his friend's hat and bounced forward with the one prong catching Simon's shoulder. The problem was not so much that it was caught in his skin but that it had a barb on the end of it, so it was impossible to take it out by simply reversing the way it went in. He had to go to the hospital.

The worst part for me was listening to Simon suffering as he could not control himself. I kept trying to console him, asking him to take deep breaths with me, but he was completely hysterical. He didn't hear a thing I was saying as his mind catastrophized, telling him that the situation was far worse than it was. So, I instinctively held his head on either side with my hands, brought my face in close to his, and looked him straight in the eyes to get his attention. Then, albeit calmly and slowly, I said something firmly that I never thought I would: You - need - to - shut - up - now. And he did. He immediately stopped crying and became completely subdued. I think he may have been shocked that I said what I did, and when I told him to go with his father, he calmly turned and walked toward where the car was parked.

Once he, his friend, and Hank drove away to go to the hospital, I sat in the sunroom and played a game of cards with Olivia. I questioned if I had scarred my son the way my father did when he told me to shut up when I was little. I was terrified I had become my father. But when they returned later that evening, Simon seemed unscathed and thrilled that he made the fishhook wall of fame at the hospital. Apparently, this kind of thing happens all the time, and I wondered how many parents told their children to shut up when they didn't know what else to do. So, when I tucked him into bed that night, I did what my father never had and apologized to him for saying what I did. He looked at me and told me, *It's alright, mommy, I wasn't scared anymore after you told me to shut up.* These words from my child's mouth validated what I already knew: it's seldom what is said, but rather how it is said and what follows that creates the perception of intent.

Around The Table

Simon continued to fish with his dad every summer, and one year, he caught a five-pound bass. Hank made such a big deal about it that our son thought his catch would have been prize-worthy had he been competing in a fishing derby. So, we found a taxidermist in the area and had the fish mounted. It still hangs in our garage alongside Olivia's painted rainbow fish. These are the reminders of fond distant memories that Hank and I created for our son and daughter, knowing how influential those childhood years were regarding how they, as adults, would perceive the world and people who passed through their lives. It was never about how many things we could give them, but rather about the experiences we provided them and how we modelled responding to life and those around us. We never once told our children that their life would be perfect. Instead, we instilled the philosophy that if they were kind and did their best, that would set the foundation for what they received. They were worthy and belonged simply because they existed.

The message of perfection versus imperfection was reiterated in 2004 when a significant experience broke the camel's back—that same camel I was warned to tie up while simultaneously trusting God. We had been living in our new home for several years, and the first day of school was on a Tuesday, September 5th that year. That meant I was turning 44 the Sunday before. In the mind of a Dutch woman who values generations of celebratory traditions, this would be considered the perfect day to celebrate a birthday. It had a double bonus of landing on the weekend and on a Sunday, the day of the Lord, coffee, and cake. I knew that my mother had already considered this the perfect day to celebrate her daughter's birthday.

The problem was that I had reached my capacity, working full-time, trying desperately to keep up with my kids' activities, and running our household. Furthermore, although I knew how important celebrating each of our family members on their specific date of birth was to my mother, I just couldn't imagine fitting it in that year. I had managed to accommodate her tradition for twelve years since Simon was born, but it was always a struggle, and labour day weekend had become a tradition for us to prepare for the upcoming school year. So, Hank and I decided to celebrate my birthday the following weekend to give us all ease. It made sense to us, but I knew my mother wouldn't love the idea, and yet, I naively hoped she would understand. Unfortunately, when I let her know, she did not accept it… not at all. I remember being unsurprised and yet stunned at the number of times she phoned me over and over again in an attempt to change my mind. This was definitely an escalation due to my inflexibility to do things her way. Yet, even more astonishing was how her repetitive reaction made me even more determined to stand my ground.

The phone rang:

Hello.

Diana, you cannot have your birthday party next weekend; your birthday is this weekend.

Please understand, Mom. I need time to get the kids ready for the first day of school, and I feel too stressed to fit my birthday in as well.

But it's your birthday, and it's on a Sunday.

No, Mom, not this year; I can't do it.

But you have to.

No, I don't, and I am not.

I hung up, amazed at how she persevered. The phone rang moments later:

Hello.

Don't hang up on me! We must get together with the family for your birthday—our whole family. I have a gift for you, and I want to give it to you on your birthday.

No, mom. You need to respect my decision and leave me alone this weekend.

I hung up—many times.

This wasn't the first time my mother invested heavily in being right. However, I noticed that this was the first time I was not equally consumed with being right but rather confidently determined to do what was right for my family. Something shifted that day, and instead of diving headfirst into the deep end of the tumultuous waves of insanity, I stood upright in the shallow end where I could walk safely, unafraid to possibly be somewhat sane. And as a result, when the phone continued to ring, I picked it up each time and promptly hung it up again without speaking to her. It rang at least ten times before she stopped. I was furious because I knew my mother was using my birthday as a conduit to create her perception of the perfect little family setting. Yet, I was calm because, for once, I didn't feel responsible for making her happy within this scenario.

She was equally furious but quiet for a few days, which was a little scary—the calm before another storm. I knew she would fight with all she had to avoid defeat, and I remember telling Hank about this encounter, advising him to prepare for her subsequent vengeance of willpower. He laughed when I predicted her unwelcome presence at our house on my actual birthday that Sunday, and he was amused that

Around The Table

I knew her that well. Anticipating her arrival, I prewarned Hank and the kids not to answer the door that morning. This was the kind of trade-off I had to manage as a parent because I didn't want my children to think that I was playing a game with my mother just for the sake of winning an argument; in my mind, that would make me the same as her. And yet, I was because I had to stop the madness of her incessant control over deciding what was best for my family. I reframed it as a lesson in boundaries, seeing as they might need to use it on me someday, given my track record of following in my mother's footsteps. She was all or nothing, and her determination is truly mind-boggling. I inherited that from her, and it showed, seeing as I had to cut her off at the knees to make my point. I recognized that I also tend to be all in or all out.

Our doorbell rang at 10:15 in the morning, the exact time that my parents would have arrived after the first scheduled Sunday morning mass had I invited them for my birthday that day. I was putting clothes away in Olivia's room at the front of the house and looked out the window at my mother's car parked in our driveway. I immediately noticed that infuriating, icky feeling bubbling up inside of me. She rang the doorbell a second time. Moving away from the window, I ignored her and distracted myself by matching socks and tightly rolling them in little bundles the way my mother taught me when I was little. The doorbell rang again, and my mind wandered to my linen closet and what a mess it was—she would be appalled. And if I ever gave her access to it, she would start folding every sheet and towel properly—her way. The doorbell rang a fourth time, and I heard her attempted convincing voice, *I know you're in there. I have your present.* I faltered for a moment, feeling bad for her standing on the front porch with a gift for me, and I almost abandoned my post. But, instead, I became distracted as I turned towards the bedroom door and was drawn to the crucifix above it. Ugh! When we moved in, my mother helped me unpack and left Jesus sitting on the dresser as a cue to hang him up. So, I did.

Hank suddenly appeared in the doorway just as I shook that off, *She's gone,* he told me. I was shaking, *Thank God!* Why do I keep saying that? He smiled, *You okay?* I inhaled, *Yup.* I exhaled and wondered, *Now what?* It was fine that I followed through, but what kind of shit storm would we have to move through after that judgment call? As if not believing Hank, I looked out the bedroom window to ensure she was, in fact, gone; the last thing I needed after going through the agony of the last fifteen minutes was to have it back-fire with her still standing on the porch. I saw the back of her car drive away, and again, guilt washed over me. An overwhelming confusion surfaced around how that was possible after everything I had gone through with her. The pertinent question of *why I protect those who behave poorly* was not yet entirely within my scope of decisiveness.

On my way out of my daughter's room, I quickly grabbed her desk chair, stood on it, and reached up to remove the crucifix above her door. Days later, I

Escaping the Cycle of Manipulation

removed all the crosses in the house, and in December, I left the manger in the storage bin in the garage and set up a table for the Buddha that I recently bought. It represented all that was loving and kind. This was the closest to the meaning of a spiritual leader I had ever resonated with, and I never put my manger out again.

That fateful day when I turned 44, I walked down the hall and opened the front door to a large glass vase with gorgeous fresh cut gladiolas radiating out of it. I knew things were going to be different between my mother and me from then on. I knew this because the guilt I experienced before taking down Jesus had dissipated entirely. And the flowers made me sad when I saw them because I realized that my mother had ruined my birthday, and I believed that was a choice she made.

What also became clear was that even though she still came to my house on my birthday, I had the power to respond to my mother in a way that was right for me. I won. And I don't mean I won like a boxer takes down their opponent in the ring because even though she went down, she didn't stay there. What I mean is that I won by establishing what was acceptable for me, and I followed through. The dilemma surfaced within doing the right thing because, as much as I believed I should fight for my family's rights, I saw myself fighting the way that she did—simply to win. So, when I replayed what I had done, I saw myself being equally manipulative—I was a hypocrite and suddenly very aware that I had innocently been an imposter most of my life by shear virtue of not having the courage to communicate my beliefs, feelings, or thoughts.

As a result, I began taking the time to determine what my part was in this game of right or wrong, and what I discovered was that I was a wishy-washy mouse who never clarified my wants and needs because I was fearful of being cast aside by my family. I also recognized that my mother took advantage of my self-doubt whether intentionally or not. She was the adult who allowed me to take the same path she had and actually guided me towards it, encouraging me to walk it with her. As the matriarch of my family and once achieving this clarity, I decided to end the cycle of insanity by not following in her footsteps.

However, having the guts to defend me and win for once was a lot to digest. It was still too early for me to consider going to the next level just to further my personal gain because I had yet to reach that degree of worthiness. This had to be about my children, so I moved into mama warrior mode because I knew without a doubt that when innocent children are involved, the onus must fall on the adult to make the choice that is in their best interest. It had taken me 44 years to even consider speaking my mind, but I needed to step out of my childhood and into adulting to protect my children. That was my job as their mother. So, I made another bold decision and wrote my mother a letter to set my boundaries. Although we had moved across the bridge, it was still within drop-in distance and not as far away as my sister would have advised. So, I went to war for my children at this stage of the game and made a decision that supported their emotional survival.

Doing this for my children created a natural source of motivation; I don't

Around The Table

think I would have sat down and put pen to paper if it were not for protecting my son and daughter. And in the end, within the cathartic process of writing pages and pages, I summarized my ultimatum, *Either stop controlling us, or you will not be allowed to be with my children.* I brought the letter to her house, and I asked her to read and sign it in front of my father. Surprisingly, she did, and my father smiled at me. Ironically, I did not feel victorious but somewhat suspicious of his brief camaraderie. Every September third after that reeked of the anticipation of my mother's next manipulative scheme. I lay awake many nights contemplating what her next move would be.

XI

~ Escaping the Cycle of Betrayal ~

That letter jumpstarted years of therapy as I attempted to figure out why I was so compelled to prove I was not only different from my family but also more integral. I experienced panic attacks surrounding the thought of spending time with them and made many excuses not to. I bold-faced lied about why I could not attend a birthday celebration or visit my parents. Layers upon layers of deep reflection and self-work finally brought me to a place of knowing that I am not who they are, I do not want what they want, and I don't have to behave or love the way they do. My personal integrity was challenged each time I was with them—not because of our differences but because I couldn't convince myself it was okay that we were different. Every time I attempted to present myself with some sort of semblance of whom I thought I was around them, I believed I was committing a mortal sin by choosing to be unique. Sure, there were moments when we connected, and I believed they loved me, and I, them. But the fact that I didn't think they accepted me kept haunting me—I'm sure they thought I didn't accept them, and to a degree, they were right.

I was especially tortured by the sensations of betrayal that arose when they kept things from me. Days, months, and years went by, and suddenly I found out about an incident that everyone else knew had happened, but I didn't. There was always an excuse that made what they did sound reasonable but made me sound crazy. There is no doubt that hypocritical moments surfaced when I disingenuously succumbed to agreeing with what they said or went along with what they did because they had strength in numbers; I was not as confident as I appeared. Nevertheless, I went along with the flow of their reality because I desperately wanted to be a part of them, my family, and I thought being like them was the only way. And in the end, that was true.

Continuing on my quest to embrace my unique belief system, I had an epiphany that there was no need for me to fight to be right anymore. And that required committing to living fully in line with my values and no one else's. During one session with a life coach, I was jolted into the awareness that being authentic means giving up the need to be right and the fear of being wrong. Wow! Suddenly, I realized that my ingrained fear of being wrong didn't have to be my forever struggle because it was a choice. Since I was a child, the story I had been telling myself was that I had to prove my worthiness of being loved by agreeing with what others said was right. There was very little chance that after close to half a century of conditioning, I would be able to make that inner voice piss off completely because it had profound roots. But somewhere in the recesses of my mind, there was a spark of resilience; it was the persistent gift of strength my mother had instilled in me. And although I was grateful, I suffered emotional traumatic consequences by using that fortitude to survive her self-righteousness instead of using it to make space for mine.

An epiphanic moment presented on my 45th birthday in 2014. It was significant because no one outside of my immediate family talked about my birthday leading up to it. During a conversation months before, I mentioned to Fran that I didn't like big birthday parties and preferred to have family dinners instead. I had established the kind of *gezeligheid* I craved around the table with my children, which I leaned towards when celebrating special events. Neither she nor my parents mentioned my birthday when it rolled around, and it coincidentally landed on the same weekend that my brother and sister-in-law were hosting a big family reunion. Many of my aunts, uncles, and cousins were attending, so Hank and I were excited to go and connect with everyone.

Sadly, it was one of the last times we saw one of my cousins because he was terminally ill with cancer and passed away a month later. When we arrived, Hank went through the carport to get to the backyard, and he found my cousin tucked under a tent canopy on the other side. He went right over and sat down beside him for a visit. I had gone another route walking through the front door to get to the back deck off the kitchen. I saw my mother right away with her back to me, and she was chatting with one of my aunts, who was facing me. As I approached my mother from behind to say hello, I saw her point to Hank, and she annoyingly said, *You see, he ignores me completely!* My aunt's eyes went wide, and I said, *Oh hi, Mom.* She almost jumped out of her skin and immediately swung around in shock at being caught trying to defame my husband in order to make herself more important than someone who was dying. I walked away.

I mingled with my relatives, and then suddenly, my sister-in-law came out of the kitchen with a cake and candles, and everyone joined in when she began singing what I thought was the Happy Birthday song for me. I was quickly corrected when it turned out to be an anniversary cake for another cousin, who was celebrating a milestone anniversary as a nun. Luckily no one saw my shame for being so presumptuous assuming my extended family would gift me such a surprise. Obviously, my sister had told my mother my celebratory preference, and she used that as an excuse to punish me for the boundaries I set the year before by withholding any celebration at all. I didn't say anything, and we left after a few hours. Hank and the kids surprised me with three days at a resort the following weekend. It was the best, spending time with the three people who meant the most to me.

The ability to advocate what is right and just for myself and others eventually transpired from the ebb and flow of being someone other than who I truly was.

Escaping the Cycle of Betrayal

I was born having to fight for that unique little girl who was intuitively sensitive, moral, instinctual, passionate, trusting, hopeful, accepting, adventuresome, and creative. And although she shone through when it really mattered, there were more times than not when her inherited characteristics took over. She conformed to being insensitive, judgmental, submissive, compliant, defensive, deceptive, and perfectionistic. For over forty years, I feared being perceived as bad because I had abandoned my instincts to preserve the goodness of my soul under the safety of the memory of a weeping willow tree.

Instead, I fell hard into the trap of acting the way I thought others wanted me to be—like them—all for the sake of a perception of love that turned out to be not what I wanted. I was in my mid-forties when I realized that the uncomfortable fight to be right would always be a frustrating unfulfilled prophecy of love, tempting me day in and day out. Being true to who I am became something highly integral for me to achieve and the very definition of love. I was awakened to the fact that simply being me without having any need or desire to explain how I show up was the moral and ethical thing for me to step into. But that's easier said than done.

I walked a very long journey to realize that I didn't have to blame anyone, including myself, for my fucked-up-ness anymore—I was the only person responsible for making sense of the constant, chaotic screaming in my head. I could make it stop if I started by not sabotaging my authenticity. I read extensive research that indicates that the perception of someone's motivation or behaviour determines whether it negatively or positively affects your own or another's well-being. For example, I worked really hard to live and breathe what I thought my parents' expectations were, but that made me feel crazy. And yet, experiencing decades of the ill effects of trying to please them confirmed my sanity because my interpretations of their intentions became blatantly clear to me—my perception of their absurdity was real.

From the day I was able to emotionally and intellectually decipher situations and interactions with others, I blocked those very emotions and thoughts for fear of someone trying to convince me otherwise. I faltered by not having the confidence to articulate what I knew to be accurate, so ill feelings of anger, resentment, and blame manifested within me to a harmful degree for me and everyone involved. But over time, I only had so much capacity to carry the weight of trying to make something so very wrong, right. That burden took far too much energy.

I find love incredibly complicated because it isn't a tangible, black or white, all or nothing kind of thing that is predictable or constant, but rather, an ever-changing emotion that shifts with my personal evolution. On top of that, it requires adapting to transformational fluctuations experienced by the person giving their love or receiving my love. It has been a crapshoot when at a crossroads of self-discovery because my ego urges me to move in the direction of that incessant right or wrong mentality: *This is my love mould, and I need you to fit into it.*

After five decades of living in an emotional, over-thinking shit-show, I finally

Around The Table

determined that acceptance defines true love. Unfortunately, in my parents' case, the child in me only focused on my lack of belonging. Simply put, I didn't think I fit into their model of love to the degree I needed to in order to receive it fully and unconditionally. This was the glitch that I could never seem to overcome because I couldn't genuinely adapt to their way, which always seemed to hurt me.

I finally discovered that it isn't selfish to want to feel worthy of love—as long as I feel authentic, genuine love. I recognized that it's also okay to disagree with withholding love through prerequisites that others believe define said worthiness—the same method of approaching love that motivates exclusion. I now know that I don't need to accept what is painful or uncomfortable within anyone's act of love towards me. In other words, I can love someone but not accept the way they love me. I can still love them as a human being but not allow their way of loving to negatively affect me: intimidate, scare, shame, control, or manipulate me. No one has permission to make me think I am going insane. Logically, this makes sense, but it can become emotionally ambiguous when the person you think loves you disagrees. That's where my confusion set in; I was the only one who thought my way of loving and being loved made sense. Thus, I experienced a life-long struggle to co-exist with those who say they love me yet don't show up within my interpretation of how love should be experienced. They believed I should love the way they do, and they all seemed to love the same way, so I was the odd one out. In their rule book, I must have been doing something wrong.

Inevitably, every now and then, inherited familial characteristics escape from within me and present themselves to the world. They just pop out when I least expect them to, and some serve me well while others do not. Those that affect me and everyone around me positively don't need to be analyzed because, well, they encompass *gezelegheid*, so I freely let them out. However, the ones that trigger the almighty self-righteousness I grew up with need to be carefully evaluated because, well, they cause harm to everyone around me through acts of betrayal and require immediate attention. On the one hand, I can be obsessed with wondering why someone is this way or that, and sometimes, the exact way I am. While on the other, I understand our past dictates our behaviour, and I become disappointed with my lack of compassion for everyone involved, including me. Ironically, I do not doubt their love for me or my love for them. Unfortunately, I have to include myself in this equation, even though our conditional behaviour is contrary to what love means to me. By default, I adapted to their love model, having grown up surrounded by it while desperately fighting its adverse consequences.

When I was a child, my perception of their love included control, fear, and shame, and it carried much more impact than the empowering love that Hank inspired in me. I never resonated with the tactics my parents and their parents before them used to ensure that the people they loved were loyal to them no matter what. And yet, I often ignored the signs telling me to shift in another direction—far away from betrayal.

Escaping the Cycle of Betrayal

Just like all those who came before me by virtue of genealogy, I was a child being sculpted into a replica of my parents without knowing what was happening. Until I suddenly did. Somehow, by the grace of the Universe, I became aware that something wasn't right. I seemed to know better from a very early age. And without even knowing what I was fighting, I began my battle to find and maintain my authenticity. Oh yes, I faltered for years at a time, even decades. There were moments when I didn't think I would ever find my way because I was held captive in the belief that my parents were doing the best they could. And yet, there was a tiny, thin thread in the background that kept tugging at me, knowing that they couldn't do any better because this was all they were willing to give. There was no solace in that, and I was told time and time again that forgiveness would set me free. I tried to commit to this wonderfully fantastical theory for periods of time. Still, it just did not resonate with me, given that the people I was supposed to forgive continued to turn their backs on me, Hank, and my children. There was no admission of guilt and no request for absolution. As a result, this story doesn't likely end the way most do, gloriously happy with everyone accepting and forgiving each other and going merrily on their way. Sadly, it's the exact opposite.

Hank and I moved many more times—17 in all. And we often contemplate why. Maybe, we kept searching for a better place than the one we were in before. There is a tale sharing a young woman's quest to seek the ultimate destination of happiness. She travels from city to city and province to province, looking for the perfect climate, terrain, and scenery, but she disregards the people who surround her. When she arrives at each location and takes in its newness, she sighs in relief, believing she has landed at her last. However, after a brief time, she tells herself that something is missing because she lacks an inner sense of joy and connection—*gezelegheid*. Every time, she packs her belongings and begins searching again until one day when she reaches Tofino, British Columbia, an old-growth rain forest village at the most western terminus of Highway 4. She cannot go any further because this is where the land ends and where the ocean begins. She is devastated and seeks solace in the people living in her community and begins experiencing the connection that her neighbours willingly bestow upon her. She finally realizes that it is not the destination that provides ultimate joy, but instead, those who surround her who create the connection she has been ignoring her whole life. Happiness was everywhere she went; she just needed to embrace the people who surrounded her. She unpacks her bags one last time and never leaves.

I think that Hank and I always had the black cloud of my parents' interference hanging over us. Instead of coming right out and letting them know, we betrayed them by subconsciously seeking relief by moving to new houses and different areas to find ultimate happiness. Had we taken the time to address their obtrusiveness earlier, we might not have felt the need to find something better by creating distance from them every couple of years. However, I believe what stopped us from staying was that we knew they would not listen. So, we kept running but never far enough to provide enough of a distraction from the unrest they caused.

In 2010, we took a trip to visit our best friends in Vancouver, British Columbia, and we took a weekend out of our stay to drive to Kelowna to look at houses for sale. We bought one on the spot and decided to rent it out for five years until Hank retired with the plan to move out there. But over the next year, Hank began experiencing extreme exhaustion, and he could barely walk up the stairs from the garage at the end of each day. He went to the doctor, but they could not determine what was wrong. He finally decided to retire in December of 2011 because he just could not go on. A few weeks later, he stood at his retirement dinner, giving his farewell speech, and he could not control his hand from trembling. He joked, saying he must be nervous.

Then one night, while watching TV, I noticed that he had a similar tremor in his right foot, and I asked him what was going on. He replied that he didn't know, but it had started the day before. He went to the doctor the following week and was diagnosed with Parkinson's Disease. My heart broke for him as he navigated a disease that instantly controlled his life. I knew what this felt like because I had been managing rheumatoid arthritis for several years at that point. However, his Parkinson's was a whole other ballgame when it came to how it impacted his day-to-day living. We decided to leave our family home after living there for ten years because we couldn't keep it up any longer. Simon was busy following his dream of becoming a pro golfer, and Olivia would be off to university in a few years, so we bought a smaller house in another neighbourhood.

Hank suffered for another year because the neurologist could not come up with an effective medication regime, and we found ourselves catapulted into a level of betrayal I never thought my mother was capable of inflicting upon us. Once again, my naivety of expectation created the shock of my mother's overt display of arrogance, and I was jolted into realizing how far she would go to get what she wanted. At this point, I had not yet uncovered her deception around my sister's death, so what occurred next far exceeded anything else I knew she had done to date. My response was reactive yet very confidently decisive. I wanted to rip her heart out and alienate her forever.

Hank spent that previous year going back and forth to a specialist in a city two hours away as part of a Parkinson's research study, and he was worse than ever—it was clear that he got the placebo. He could barely get through a day, so we discussed Christmas, and he indicated there was no way he could sit in a packed room at either of our parents' apartments. His Parkinson's had triggered a high level of anxiety, and I told him not to worry; our families would understand. So, I emailed every member on both sides of our family to get the word out as efficiently as possible. For some reason, I was confident they would rally together to support my husband:

Escaping the Cycle of Betrayal

October 13, 2012

Hello everyone,

Hank and I were having coffee the other day, and we were talking about how quickly fall has passed, and before we know it, Christmas will be here. We have made a lot of changes in how we are managing our lives over the last year due to several transitions we have had to face, and we have decided that we need to make another change in regard to how we move through the Christmas season so that it serves us and our children well.

We would like to spend the main part of the season, Christmas Eve and Christmas Day, in our own home and Boxing Day as a day to enjoy relaxing and going shopping. We are past the days of rushing around and would instead like some peace and ease around the holidays. We also feel that mom and dad are past the point of hosting Christmas as it is a very big job having us all in their home. As a result, we are wondering if you would agree to us all celebrating together before or after the holidays by going out for dinner to a nice restaurant; we could all pay for our own meal, and that could be the gift to us all....being together. We are really not interested in monetary gifts and feel that all of our money would be better spent by spending time together.

We would love to have Mom and Dad stop by our house for a drink and visit on Christmas Eve or Day, and perhaps each of you would like to do the same; that would, of course, be entirely up to you.

If you agree with this, we would like to propose that we have our family dinner out on one of the following dates Friday, Dec 21st, Saturday, Dec 22nd, Sunday, Dec 23rd, Friday, Jan 4th, Saturday, Jan 5th, or Sunday, Jan 6th. We know that this is a big change from what we have normally done, and we by no means want to dictate how Christmas will be celebrated this year; it is simply a suggestion, so please let us know what you honestly think about it.

Much, much love,
Diana and Hank xoxo

This was an invitation to my family to discuss with us how Hank could experience Christmas without added stress. I was asking my family for help. It seems embarrassing now to think that I expected this would have been responded to with anything but compassion. I have always had the shortcoming of not taking past history with my mother into consideration when navigating seeking support from her. Back then, I was still chasing that ominous path of hope, still ignoring those whispers from my soul.

Around The Table

As much as Hank and his sister had their issues, she was the first to reply the next day, letting us know that she understood and also welcomed a less-rushed Christmas. I called Hank's mother because she didn't have email, and she said she would do whatever worked for Hank. Then I waited to hear from my family, which would typically be within a day or two at the most. But not one of them called or replied to my email that day, or the next, or the next, or the next—not my mother, my father, my sister, or my brother-in-law. I waited for seven days until October 20th, when I decided to call my mother. When she didn't answer, I left a message on her answering machine asking her to call me back to discuss my email. It was so obvious that my mother was home because she replied to my initial email to everyone within moments indicating that she needed time to think about it and decided to keep her traditional Christmas on Boxing Day in my parents' apartment. She hoped we could all come.

About two hours later, once having received my mother's reply, my brother-in-law and his wife responded to everyone, saying, *We will be there.* And 47 minutes later, my sister replied to everyone as well, *We would love to celebrate at your house on Boxing Day.* The matriarch had spoken. I felt like I was on the show, Survivor, being eliminated from the competition after a long battle of fighting for the sole survivor spot. None of them bothered to email or pick up the phone to discuss our situation with me after I emailed them. It was evident to Hank and me that my mother called each of them to tell them she would not be flexible while leaving us out of the conversation—she likely told them not to reply to me, given none of them did. My mother went behind our backs and convinced the rest of the family that they should do Christmas the way she had always done it instead of considering how they could support my husband.

There are no words for the long-term damage her decision created that day or how the cowardice of each of my family members set a precedent for how we would respond to them in the future. The pain I experienced while channelling Hank's disappointment far exceeded the intimidation my father created at the dinner table when I was five or the control my Opa inflicted on me at the age of twelve when he whacked my shin with his cane. Their response to my cry for help was more harmful than the jealousy I witnessed between my aunts and the rejection I experienced when my father intentionally swam away from me. It wasn't the same as the shame that God inflicted upon me for not wanting to share my sins with Him, or the manipulation my mother used on my wedding day. However, all of those traumas bubbled up with each reply I read, backing up my mother's decision to betray my husband. And then I was angry.

I experienced a massive revelation when I became very clear about what had just happened, and my loyalty to my husband moved me to do something that I will never regret. My mother had not just hopped over the line into insanity, but she had taken her whole family with her to form an alliance, backing up her decision to exclude my husband and me. I could not get my head around how to forgive her.

Escaping the Cycle of Betrayal

I could not. I just could not. Suddenly, co-existing without trust did not seem feasible anymore because I realized that the child she gave birth to 52 years ago and the man she chose for that child 24 years later were only ever worthy of her love if we did exactly what she wanted. She had reminded us of that time and time again. And, yet, I had ignored those reminders until this happened, and I processed her hints of passive-aggressiveness after avoiding fully confronting them. This time, I made no excuses for her actions and took what she did for what it was: a very evil intention mixed with the façade of goodness. This time, I witnessed and sensed the bad more than I ever had, and it overrode the good by a longshot; she was about to discover that her loyalty to my father was nothing compared to the loyalty I had for my husband.

I commend her for being an excellent match-maker because Hank and I complement each other in so many ways. However, the success of our relationship was not conducive to the reasons she initially set us up—that was sheer luck. I believe she was worried I wouldn't be able to take care of myself. After all, I was just a young woman, so her goal was to find someone for me with a reputable career who could support me financially—that's what she thought would make me happy. In her mind, Hank was a good fit because he was a teacher, and this fell in line with her value of being well-respected in the community and making a decent income. The bonus was that Hank's family was Dutch, so he would fit easily into our culture. But she didn't bank on him not adapting to her codependency and addiction to controlling every facet of our lives. She constantly determined what we did wrong and then came up with a solution to fix it; she believed we should conform to her way—all the time. Hank tolerated her suggestions for a while, but she wasn't happy when he disagreed and got tired of her interference.

Over the years, her failure to assess his true personality transitioned into her disappointment in him. Hank is an independent thinker who does not need to agree with or please others, regardless of their status in a familial or societal hierarchy. This became evident long before our children came into the picture when we moved out of our first house and bought a three-story townhouse mid-town. We had just gone through a disastrous partial house-build with a contractor who installed kitchen cabinetry and a furnace that were sub-par from what we had ordered. The builder was struggling financially and cut many corners, so we ended our contract and searched for another place to live. The townhouse was perfect because it allowed us to live closer to the downtown area, where we enjoyed shopping and meeting friends for breakfast and dinner. We moved further away from our families and looked forward to a bit of distance from them. However, when Hank simultaneously decided to leave teaching high school after twelve years to follow his dream of being an entrepreneur, my parents questioned why in the world he would do that. My mother realized Hank no longer fit into the perfect mould she originally put him in, and the worst part was that I fell into my parents' reactive-judgement syndrome. Sadly, I responded to my husband in a way that he interpreted as unsupportive, and rightfully so.

Around The Table

From my heart, I understood when he told me he didn't think he could continue teaching. I experienced a wave of empathy when he told me he was suffering emotionally. And I believed he needed to take time off to determine what was next for him. But instead of outwardly encouraging him to process all that, I reacted as if I didn't understand, empathize, or believe in him. I showed up the way my mother and father did, asking him to think about whether or not he really wanted to throw away a secure job with good pay and benefits. I made him think he had to defend himself and justify his emotions. He was so angry and disappointed in me that I didn't think we would ever get through that time. But we did because Hank knew that wasn't me, and I was feeding into how I was brought up instead of who I truly was.

Hank has been through a lot with my parents, and he saw the best and the worst of my mother, but even he was shocked at her response to my Christmas request. More than that, he was hurt. He doesn't often get involved in the dynamics of my family until they have crossed that crazy-making line, and he made sure everyone knew how he felt by replying to all:

October 20, 2012
7:47 p.m.

Hi folks,

I'm really sorry to be writing this email, but I'm saddened and hurt by the way this has gone...not so much with the decision to continue celebrating Christmas on Boxing Day but rather the way it was decided! Diana wrote you an email to explain how we felt with all that has gone on in each of our families this past year and for concern for you, Oma and Opa, and to suggest what we felt would benefit all of us. It was a suggestion open for discussion, compromise if necessary and hopefully a solution that would benefit all of us. No one bothered to contact her to discuss or to express an opinion until Oma and Opa made the decision to ignore our concerns and suggestion, and then the other two families immediately agreed....it was almost as if you had all discussed this behind our backs!?! This is not the way families support each other! We were not dictating how we should celebrate Christmas, only suggesting and asking for your input.

Sorry, but we will be celebrating Christmas as Diana outlined in her email.

Hank.

My sister replied immediately to everyone, saying that they would do what our parents wanted because they enjoy celebrating at their home. They were sorry we were choosing not to come. My mother replied, saying that it was not her idea to celebrate Christmas in a restaurant and that she finds it difficult to communicate by email. She hoped we would still come over.

My mother didn't get it. She was still adamant about making me understand that she was not willing to change Christmas because she liked it the way it was and did not even mention the intention of supporting Hank. Her self-centredness poured off the computer screen. Interestingly, she shared the difficulty she had communicating by email—her way of telling me I shouldn't have reached out that way in the first place. And yet, she still chose to email instead of picking up the phone. And then, because I didn't reply to her email right away, she finally phoned the next day, leaving a voicemail, indicating she wanted to talk. Unfortunately, both Hank and I were well beyond having an in-person conversation with her, still licking our wounds of exclusion. I decided to stop the madness and responded to her with yet another email:

October 22, 2012
7:04 p.m.

Hello Mom,

We received your voicemail this morning. We are not interested in getting together with you at this time because we are very upset. As Hank indicated to you in his email, we are hurt by your lack of support. Even after Hank explained to you that we were asking for your help in giving us some ease over the holidays, you still made this about what you wanted; we received your message loud and clear—your main concern is about what you want only. There is nothing to discuss at this point because you told us what you want and that you have decided that you want Christmas at your house on Boxing Day, and that is what you are going to do. You made this decision without including us in the discussion and thus without compromise. You indicated that you don't like emails, and yet you chose not to phone me after our original email or after I left you a voicemail a week later asking you to call me to discuss this. You, yourself, indicated that you didn't have the courtesy to discuss it with the rest of the family either. It is interesting that you feel that you are the only one involved in making these types of decisions and that your opinion is the only one that matters. By not asking others' opinions, you actually believe that you are the only one who is important in these matters. The reality is that you wanted Christmas at your place on Boxing Day, and that was that. You didn't call me because you didn't like my suggestion, and you ignored what I was saying in my email, which was that I needed help. You were not opened to talking about it, and you wanted to find a way to shut down the chance that Christmas might be something other than what you wanted, and that is exactly what you ended up doing. You got your way.

I know that this is probably not what you want to hear, but this is the trade-off when you put yourself ahead of your family's needs. I rarely ask for help, but I went out on a limb

Around The Table

to ask for it this time because Hank and I are exhausted and in total emotional survival mode. My worst fear came true when you ignored me and did not return my phone call. Deep down, I knew what your reaction would be, but I was hopeful that I would be wrong this time and that you might move from a place of compassion and love.

We will respect what you want, and we ask that you respect our decision as we are now also not willing to discuss or compromise on our end. You got what you wanted, Mom, so accept it and enjoy it; we are fine with it. Our initial offer to have you visit over Christmas is now off as we feel that this would be very uncomfortable for all of us, and our goal is to have as little stress in our lives as possible; we will not deviate from this as our immediate family is dedicated to supporting this goal. This is a value that we have always held strong. I would like to ask that you not share this email with others as this issue is between you and me. If you do choose to share it, you will certainly be betraying my trust.

I need time to process this, so please do not call me, email me, or drop by because I will not respond at this time; I will contact you when I am ready. I ask you to also not try to contact Hank about this as he has enough on his plate and does not need anything more added to his stress.

Diana

    For once in my life, I created a clear-cut boundary. Although I am deeply opposed to excluding anyone, I needed to create space between my mother and me to make her understand what I was not willing to accept within our relationship. My mother believes she has the freedom to push and hurt people as long as they don't push back—it's her right to inflict pain, and if her victims don't acknowledge it, it doesn't exist. However, once her selfish deeds are ousted, her guilt throws her into deep anguish over her misgivings. She becomes triggered into dramatic displays of remorse to redeem herself because she experiences the same hurt and exclusion she creates for others.
    Not surprisingly, she did not respect my request to leave me alone, and on November 6, 2012, she phoned me. I let it go to voicemail as per my therapist's suggestion to give me time to process her message and prepare my genuine response rather than my make-my-mother-happy one. So, I waited and naively hoped she would be calling was to make amends. She didn't like me not being in her life—that was not an ingredient in the perfect family. And true to form, when I called her back, I was immediately drawn into her act of humility and regret. She begged Hank and me to meet with her and my father. I foolishly agreed because she was very convincing, and I actually believed she wanted to apologize for what she had done. So, we set a date, and my mother assumed we would go to them, but

Escaping the Cycle of Betrayal

I asked them to come to our place for coffee—I needed the confidence of being in the comfort of my home rather than sitting around their intimidating table.

I intended to try to forgive and move forward, and my perception was that's what they wanted as well, or maybe that's just what I wanted to hear. I did not want any drama, so I made a vow that I would not throw what they did to us in their faces. Instead, I would be gracious and grateful that they were willing to apologize and start over. To this day, I have no idea where my heart and mind went when it came to giving them the benefit of the doubt.

They arrived at 10 o'clock in the morning, and unfortunately, Hank was having one of his worst days yet. He still had on his pyjamas, and he had a horrible migraine accompanied by out-of-control tremors in his right hand and leg. I had the coffee ready just like when I invited my parents to our first home. When the doorbell rang, I pushed the coffee machine button and went to let them in. We were all cordial, but I didn't anticipate the frigid air that gushed in with them. Hank took their coats, and I invited them to sit in the living room—the House of Brougham pine coffee table had long since been replaced with a more modern set of large ottomans. I wondered if a comment would be made about them.

I shared that I had brought out the small Dutch coffee cups and saucers that I had served coffee in so many years ago because I knew my mother preferred them, and she scoffed defensively at me, asking why I said that. I told her I meant no harm—it was a gesture, letting her know I was thinking of her. At that moment, I knew that my parents were not there to say they were sorry but rather to make sure I knew they were right. So, I served the coffee and sat down on the sofa adjacent to my father. My mother chose the easy chair across from me, and Hank sat at a distance in a desk chair at the other side of the room trying to manage his migraine and my parents' visit; he was suspicious of their intentions the moment I told him they were coming. As soon as I took my seat, I turned to my mother on my right and noticed her pursed lips. Oh shit, I thought, and my stomach began to curdle. I braced myself, and sure enough, she let me have it, *Well, what have you got to say?*

Although I was semi-prepared, having felt the kick in my ass coming for approximately ten minutes, it was not enough time to recalibrate from thinking they were there to apologize to realizing they were there to shame me with their we-were-right-and-you-were-wrong mentality. It all happened so fast, and I was still adjusting to realizing that they had played me. This was not the same woman who swooned me with her sweetness on the phone; no, this was the same mother who scammed me my whole life.

I inhaled and exhaled, *What do you mean?* Then I immediately noted that I had just invited her to blast me with all the reasons I was a horrible person and ruined her Christmas. And that's exactly what she did. I said one thing at the end of her speech, *Mom, I was just trying to find a way to support Hank through Christmas; I wasn't trying to ruin yours or anyone else's.* This prompted my father to take aim from the left. His shoulders twitched uncontrollably as he accused me of something he should never have. I knew his insecurities were elevated, and he defaulted to the verbal abuse he was so adept at, *You know what you are? A narcissist! That's what you are!! Do you know what that is?!* Hmmm, this was interesting—I was a narcissist because I wanted to help my husband get through Christmas, and my father was not because he refused to...

Before I could even reply, I saw my husband out of the corner of my eye, coming from behind me. He stepped past me with his confident, calm energy, walked in front of the new ottomans, and leaned over my attacker. Then, trembling uncontrollably and without saying anything, he took my father's elbow, lifted him out of his seat, and walked him to the front entrance. Still holding onto him, he opened the door, put him out on the step and said, *Stay out of my house.* He then closed the door and locked it. My father began relentlessly ringing the doorbell while repeatedly screaming, *Give me my coat.* We all ignored him, including my mother, and Hank sat down in the open-concept office beside the entryway without saying a word. I got up and sat closer to him on the stairs leading up to the second floor, and my mother followed me.

She stood in front of Hank and got brave, pursed her lips, and went into a sudden accusatory frenzy, *How can you do that to your father-in-law?* But when Hank just glared at her and did not answer because he did not want to say anything he would regret later, she segued into her classic panicked from-warrior-to-victim mode within seconds. I knew she had crossed the infamous line from being as sane as she could to being desperately insane, and it saddened me to see her drop to her knees in front of me, pleading, *You know you are my favourite, don't you? Just like Olivia is for you.* Wow, we were back to that game. Everything suddenly went quiet. Coincidentally, even my father stopped trying to get our attention, turned around, and walked down the front steps to his car.

Looking down at my mother, I was overwhelmed with so many emotions; seeing her in such a submissive state made me pity her, but I could no longer endure her manipulation. I thought my head would explode, listening to her crying in desperation while seeing my husband trying to manage his pain within another one of my family's deranged episodes. I was overpowered by the anger towards my father for calling me a narcissist, the disappointment in my mother for resorting back to comparing me to my sisters, and the disdain towards both of them for coming to my house with the intention to prove themselves right. Within a few seconds, a massive wave of shame encompassed me, knowing I could not bring myself to forgive them for what had just transpired. And yet, I still struggled with tearing myself away from their emotional abuse. What was wrong with me?!

I wanted it all to end, but instead, I turned to my mother with one final attempt at saving her, *Mom, how can you say that? I do not have favourites!! What would Emily think if she knew you said I was your favourite? How would it make Fran feel if she knew you were saying that to me right now?* At that moment, a flip instantly switched in my mother's brain—she promptly stopped crying, squinted her eyes at me,

Escaping the Cycle of Betrayal

and slowly and methodically replied, *They will never know.* And then alternately pointing at me and then her, she reiterated, *That's our secret.* She was like an adopted child on a quest to belong; if I was her favourite, she could fulfill her mission of being loved. I understood, but I could not be a part of her antics.

And I would certainly not engage with my father, who had accused me of being the one thing I knew I was not. I got his coat, told her that we needed another break, and asked her to leave. I'm sure my mother went home and projected all the blame onto my father for what he said to me because later that day, I received an email from him that I knew he would never have initiated on his own. He said he apologized, that people say things they don't mean, and *please forget about it.* Oy, that last line!! My heart sank with its resurfaced message that only ever dismissed me. My father had never picked up the phone to call me in my entire life. He never emailed me to see how I was doing—ever. In all the houses we lived, no matter how close or far away, he never once came to visit me on his own. He never inquired about any of my work projects or my career.

My father appeared as disinterested in me as he would any stranger on the street. And yet, I received this email from him claiming to apologize after looking straight at me, accusing me of being a narcissist. When he apologized, I was slightly moved because it was so out of character to admit that he was wrong. And then, my hopes were squashed when he erased his regret with the excuse that *people say things they don't mean.* He signed the email, *Love, Dad.* This was a man who never told me he loved me, but I'm sure because of my mother's insistence he signed it using that word. He didn't even know my email address and sent it to Hank's. Their loyalty to each other is remarkable, yet I saw right through how destructive it was to those associated with them.

My sister contacted me one day, telling me that she wanted to get together to discuss what had happened. I expected a repeat of my parents' fiasco but agreed, being prepared this time. We met for coffee at Starbucks. While sitting at a table for two, she told me that she didn't mean for things to go the way they did. She said it was a miscommunication, and we needed to move forward from it. I appreciated that she initiated our visit, and she wanted to get past the uncomfortableness that loomed over us. Then, as quickly as I agreed, she began acting as uneasy as my father does when he is about to blurt something inappropriate out, *But, you know, you were dictating how Christmas should be in that email you sent.* I almost spit my coffee out, having been misled again, *Are you kidding me?* I told her that I showed my email to half a dozen people and asked them to honestly tell me if I was out of line with my request, and every one of them said to me that I was not. She told me she was sorry, but she disagreed, and I told her that tricking me into our meeting was way out of line. She had become my mother.

I didn't speak to my mother for another three months, and Olivia convinced her dad that a puppy would be good for us after putting down our Britany Spaniel, Jake, just months before. When Hank and I went to the breeder to pick her out,

Around The Table

Lucy the cockapoo sat sweetly in his hand. Her demeanour was subdued, and she didn't let out one peep. However, from the day Simon and I picked her up, Lucy was a handful. She howled the entire car drive home, and we wondered what we got ourselves into. In the meantime, Hank abandoned the Parkinson's study and was referred to a specialist in Toronto, who prescribed a shocking number of prescriptions to manage his symptoms. But they worked!! His friends talked him into going on their annual golf trip with them, and he left before Lucy arrived in November. He really didn't want to go because he knew he probably couldn't keep up with the others, and that was the case. He spent a lot of time in the cart and told the others to play on without him. The three-day car ride there and back was very taxing on him, and that golf trip ended up being his last. I know how disappointed he was as the reality of his Parkinson's was becoming crystal clear.

While he was away, Lucy and I spent every day together, and she became very attached to me—so attached that when Hank returned, she became very possessive of me and the pack leader of us all. She was aggressive and challenging to manage, and by the time Christmas rolled around, no one wanted to deal with her. The frustration level in our house rose because I was trying my best to create a memorable holiday for my children, given the fallout we experienced with my family. At the same time, I was training a puppy who decided to take over our household and everyone in it. Overall, it was stressful, and I didn't realize how much of what happened with my parents had adversely manifested in both Hank and me. However, we enjoyed our intimate Christmas with just the kids, and we all agreed that it did us all good to be separated from my side of the family for the holidays.

I didn't speak to any of my family until February 2013, when my mother phoned me and asked if we could get together. I knew she would be having a hard time not having any contact with me and that she likely couldn't sustain the separation. So, I agreed to meet with her at the Starbucks down the street from me. At that point, I was not prepared to have her come into my home, and I had no interest in meeting with my father—he and I had definitely lost any chance at creating a connection. Hank was not ready to see either one of them—indefinitely. Once again, she seemed very grateful to meet with me, but my guard was up because I didn't trust her anymore. I questioned why I always let her back into my life. What was it about her that drew me back in every time? Deep down, I loved her and could not let her go.

We shared a lot of things that day. She made no excuses for what happened at Christmas this time and owned what she had done. She told me she should have reached out to me when I emailed the family for help and asked me to forgive her. I told her I did, but I really didn't. She asked me if Hank would forgive her, and I told her I didn't know; that was between the two of them. She never spoke to him about it again—as if it never happened. I know that in her mind, he should have contacted her.

Escaping the Cycle of Betrayal

I believe my mother admitted her guilt to me for the same reason she said she was sorry to her sisters when they landed in the demise of turmoil. I believe my mother thought she was going to lose me, and she knew what she had to do and say to keep that from happening. I understood. I had reached out to her in the past for the same reason, fearing that if I didn't, all the energy we put into our relationship would have been for not. As insane as it sounds, I care about my mother. Even after what she put me through all those years, I don't think she ever meant to cause me the heartache she did. It's easy for people to tell me that forgiveness is the answer, but it isn't always easy to achieve. To release her of her guilt, I had to understand how her mind works and what takes her to the devious decisions she makes. Being hurt repeatedly, losing her trust, and never feeling like I belonged were massive barriers to overcome, and I can only be fully transparent, saying that I don't think I ever will. However, my passion for supporting others to achieve inclusion was developed over decades of experiencing familial and societal exclusion. That compelled me never to walk away from her completely. I refused to continue inflicting her with the same pain of rejection she manifested in me because I knew that isn't who she genuinely is—from her soul.

I agreed to meet with her once a month for coffee from then on. My mother liked the scheduled date and wanted to hold me to it, but I was sharper this time and told her she had to be flexible. I had a job, children, and a husband who needed me, and there might be times when I had to cancel or meet on another day of the week. She agreed, and things went well for a while. However, one of my downfalls is being sucked into the illusion that I can trust her. I think it's because I crave the bond that comes alongside my fantasy-based mother-daughter relationship. I obviously also yearned for some sort of connection with my father because, during one of our coffee visits, I suddenly found myself having a vulnerable conversation about him with her. I shared something I had only ever told Hank—that I didn't remember my father ever telling me that he loved me. It just popped out of my mouth, and I knew I should never have shared it with her as soon as it did.

Then one day, she asked me to meet her at a different coffee shop across the street from her apartment, *For a change*. I felt bad that I hadn't thought of that because she had to drive to Starbucks. When the day arrived, I drove to the café, and she walked across the street to meet me. We were sitting there when suddenly, my father walked in. I was pretty surprised because I had not seen him since he called me a narcissist, and he had never before joined us in all the years that I met with my mother outside of our houses. He sat down, and my mother told me that my father had come because he wanted to tell me something. I looked at her and then him, and she broke the silence by saying, *Tell her!!* With his usual smirk and jerky shoulders, he turned to me and said what my mother told him to, *You know I love you, don't you?*

Although incredibly awkward, he said the words that I wanted to hear from my father but never had. However, his discomfort in doing so immediately moved

Around The Table

me towards compassion for him because he was pressured to express a sentiment that did not come naturally to him. Saying those words were not within his level of comfort. And at that moment, I wondered if perhaps his father had never shared those words with him. I couldn't come up with anything else to say but, *Of course, Dad.* But I didn't mean it.

I understand my mother's need to provide what her child needs—that her daughter feels loved. However, my perception at the time was that she was trying to create something that felt right for her but didn't for my dad. Both she and I wanted my father to express his love for me in a way that didn't resonate with him, and it meant nothing to me. I sincerely wished that my mother had kept our conversation confidential, but once again, she overrode my trust in her and moved into her mode of making things right instead of accepting what was—something I had learned to do as well. I just wanted her to listen and understand me, but she chose to try to fix my dad and our relationship. I was beyond angry with my mother for breaching my trust in her. Still, I was also taken aback by the fact that she put herself way out on a limb to convince my father that he needed to verbally express his love for me—I'm still in awe that she was able to pull that off; she stood up for me, and I will never forget that.

The next time I had coffee with my mother, I let her know that it was not okay to put my father and me in that position. But she didn't like being told that she had misbehaved, and before I knew it, she changed the subject, accusing me of not spending enough time with her. As I sipped my latte and watched her lips transition to that far too familiar pose while waiting for my reply, I let her sit in her shit in silence. Then, not being able to wait any longer, she pulled out her day timer to prove the meagre eight times I had visited her at her house the year before. I looked at her and asked her if taking her out for Mother's Day lunch and to the spa counted. I asked her if I got points for making chocolate-covered strawberries for her birthday. I asked her if taking her to the conservation area for a walk was included in her score-keeping or if our monthly coffee dates gave me a different rating on her scale of what a good daughter does. She was quick with her reply, saying, *No, I'm talking about the number of times you came to my house.* I told her that I couldn't keep up with her rule book, and we would not be having coffee anymore.

Seven months later, Hank and I didn't hesitate when we decided to pack up and move across Canada to live in Kelowna. I experienced no guilt for leaving my parents because my mother had made it very clear that it would never be enough no matter what I did—I would always be reminded of what I didn't do. I also recognized that the critical component of her disappointment was that, even though I did things for her, I didn't do them her way, and that wasn't good enough. I tried so hard to express my love to her, but I didn't meet her criteria. Her expectations of me were far too high to sustain, so I chose to run away again. I hoped that the extra distance between us would allow us to maintain a connection without the added pressure that comes with living close together.

XII

Escaping the Cycle of Self-Righteousness

I was diagnosed with rheumatoid arthritis in 2006 after working for two years as a house manager for a billionaire who owned a 26,000 square-foot home. He was an arrogant European authoritarian, and yet, I accepted the position, working under him as if I was a servant to a king. I despised everything he represented. And yet, strangely, I was extremely comfortable with how he treated me because I knew every misogynistic move before he made it. I also knew what he would say before he said it—I was very accustomed to the I-am-right-and-you-are-wrong script.

This man decided to fire me for inconveniencing him because I had to take time off for doctor's appointments. I'm not sure if he actually believed he could get away with that in Canada, but I let him know that he couldn't legally use my ill-health as a reason to let me go. He agreed to lay me off with a severance package. I didn't fight to stay because I finally realized that constantly trying to gain his acceptance was not worth the pay, car, and benefits—all the things I was still using to validate my existence. Although my father never told me, I knew he thought I should be proud of this job.

After six years of trial-and-error medication menus, I took the maximum dose of Celebrex prescribed for RA and injected monthly doses of a biologique to support the management of rheumatoid flares for seven additional years. Unfortunately, the internal ramifications of decades of manifested emotional trauma had not yet dawned on me. My physical and mental health were incredibly compromised, but I did not link the two, thinking I was just unlucky, having been diagnosed with a crippling disease.

After I left there, I went back to school and received my esthetics diploma in 2008. I opened a spa in our home, but that only lasted a few years because my body could not take the physical stress. My inner voice told me what a failure I was, and I ended up spending months sitting in a local Starbucks, drinking lattes in an easy chair by the fireplace. Without any purpose outside of my immediate family, I reflected on my life and accomplishments but mostly my perceived failures and lack of worth. After many conversations with strangers who frequented the cafe, I realized how many experienced the same kind of emotional trauma I had. Their well-being was as affected as mine was, if not more in some cases. I was astonished at how vulnerable and willing they were to share their stories. I wondered how I could move forward purposefully to support myself and others with the repercussions of emotional trauma.

Around The Table

Then, one day, the friend who recruited me to sell RESPs years ago walked in and sat beside me. I told her about my very premature plan of creating space for others to share their stories in a relaxed, conversational way. She told me that her sister-in-law in Vancouver did just that. Synchronistic? I'm still not sure about that, but I heard somewhere that the Universe eventually corrects all wrongs. I believed I was long overdue, or maybe there was a God, and He finally recognized I deserved a break. I already had a trip booked to Vancouver the following week, so I called my friend's sister-in-law, and she invited me for tea.

That cup of tea changed me and my life in exponential ways. I became certified with her leadership company and began running programs, supporting individuals' emotional well-being. I finally landed in a place where I could navigate in a way conducive to who I genuinely am. I clarified the expectations that were in line with my values and which ones were developed from what I believed others wanted me to be, particularly my parents. I discovered how to self-manage extreme arcs of dysfunctional energy when triggered by my past and current emotional trauma. And I learned that I didn't have to be a victim anymore; I could respond to others in a way that honoured my intuitive belief system without trying to prove I was right or they were wrong. There was even a possibility that I didn't have to exclude people from my life who I believed had harmed me. However, that was still under negotiation.

And then all hell broke loose that Christmas in 2013, and I had the rude awakening that I had a long way to go—literally all the way to British Columbia—to get my shit together. As much as I experienced relief alongside our decision to move out west, it was created by my need to run away from my family, so I was curious to understand what about being that far away would make a difference. There is no doubt that I deserted the city where I took my first breath to finally escape the cycle of insanity that followed that initial exhale. Yes, I was running away from them, but I discovered that it was definitely to make space to breathe and heal from my trauma with ease. I also didn't feel inclined to defend the reason why I left to anyone.

Ontario did not feel like home anymore because the one thing that kept me connected to it had completely dissipated—that familial *gezelligheid* I clung to as a life raft to achieve sanity all my life had sunk along with my mother's latest betrayal. I was left with a deep void of disconnection, and before I continued trying to focus on loving and connecting with others, I had to start loving myself and reaching out to that scared little girl who sat at the table with a spilled glass of milk. Strangely, as much as I was committed to getting to know her, there was something in her that resisted losing her parents—the very people she believed put her in this mental mess.

We sold our house in June of 2014, put our belongings in storage, and stayed at a cottage we rented long before we decided to move to Kelowna. After four weeks, we got a month-by-month apartment rental in our hometown until it was time

Escaping the Cycle of Self-Righteousness

for the movers to drive across the country with our things. When late September arrived, I flew out with Lucy, and Hank drove for five days to get our car there. That was difficult for him, physically and mentally, but he could still endure the ten-hour days while recuperating in hotels at night.

I arrived a few days before him and cried the whole way on the plane, grieving the death of my girlfriend and regretting our decision not to postpone our trip. This was a big move, and besides my guilt over missing my friend's funeral and not being there for her sister, I was leaving behind my son, daughter, and many dear friends. Most of the time, being 54 and starting over seemed like an adventure, but now and then, trepidation set in, and I became unconvinced I should leave my loved ones—my inner critic told me that I was a lousy parent to leave my children, and they might eventually drift away from me. I worried that my friendships would fade away over time.

Besides needing space from my family and needing a fresh start to heal, I often questioned my motive for leaving the city where I had deep-rooted ties. After a lot of reflection, I realized I didn't need one, and I didn't have to defend myself because I was doing what was right for me; it was okay to do something without trying to please others. Releasing that lifelong obligation provided me with the definition of being sane. It had nothing to do with comparing my level of sanity to others, but rather, confidently stepping into what I considered being sane was. That was being my unique self, and I no longer desired fighting for that right because, although acceptance had defined love throughout my life, I knew it did not validate my worth anymore. I discovered that the validity of my story existed simply because I did, and I wondered if this epiphany was the forgiveness my inner-child sought. And could I extend that same forgiveness to others—wasn't their story as valid as mine, even if it hurt me?

There was no doubt I wanted the freedom that enveloped me to be the result of forgiving those who brought me dis-ease, but sadly, that was not the case. I still struggled with giving them a pass because, even when I tried to forgive them, they continued thinking they were right and betrayed my trust, time and time again. Ironically, I also attempted to forgive myself for my sins but continued to condemn myself. Thus, the constant running away because I had to get away from who I was when I was around them. But I could not create distance between my adult self and my child, so I focussed on blaming them and controlling their need for my reverence and my need to provide them with it. I was hopeful that was the key to the door of everlasting peace, but I was soon reminded that nothing is that simple.

My friend in Kelowna met Lucy and me at the airport, and Hank arrived three days later. She and her husband welcomed us into their home until our moving truck arrived. They supported us to celebrate our new beginning in the beauty of the Okanagan. And once we settled into our new house, we truly embraced everything it had to offer: the mountains, the wineries, the warmth of the summer and moderate winters, and best of all, the new friendships we made. I started a hiking club to meet new people, and Hank golfed the first year we were there, although he had to use a cart more than he would have liked.

My health also continued to decline, but I fought tooth and nail. The year before we moved out west, I opted for a uterine ablation because I could not manage the anemic exhaustion I experienced caused by my period's excessive blood loss. I was told that the ablation would stop the monthly bleeding, but I would still experience cramping. During an ultrasound, the doctor also found a cyst on one of my ovaries and told me they would keep an eye on it to see if it grew. Hank took me to the hospital on the day of the procedure, and after recovering for several hours, the doctor sent me home because I was showing no signs of distress. I fell asleep in the back seat of the car during the drive home, and when Hank stopped for gas, I woke up burning up from the inside out. Hank told me that my face was swollen up like Fiona's on Shrek, and I tried to rip my leggings off, desperate to cool myself down. We were close to our house, so he drove like a madman to get there and pumped Benadryl into me. It didn't take long for it to take effect, but what happened next reminded me of the level of inner stress I was managing.

Every night for a week, I woke up at three in the morning sweating so profusely that I soaked through my pyjamas and bedsheets. I thought I was still experiencing an allergic reaction to the sedation for my procedure, so I continued taking the antihistamine. I never had another hot flash after that. A few years later, while living in Kelowna, my gynecologist discovered the ovarian cyst detected a few years prior; it was growing rapidly and had to be removed. He was trying to assess whether or not I was menopausal because if I was done, he could remove both ovaries to lessen the risk of future cysts, and I wouldn't need to take hormone replacement supplements. I told him that I only had hot flashes for a week and thought I was done. He kind of chuckled, but when he received my hormone test, he confirmed I had already gone through menopause, which made sense because I had no period symptoms since the last brutal hot flash years before. He determined that I had gone through stress-induced menopause right after my ablation. I did menopause in a week!! Whenever I went through a medical crisis, my awareness heightened about how much my emotional trauma affected my inner well-being, causing inflammation and ill-health.

I was advised to have a complete hysterectomy, and a week before I went to the hospital, I received a call from Simon, asking me how to manage my mother's guilt tactics. I asked him why, and he shared that since we moved away, she called him frequently with reminders of how little he called or visited her. He didn't want to hurt her feelings, but he also didn't want to be harassed by her pressuring him into seeing her more than he could. He was busy working on his career and did not have the time she expected from him. This was all too familiar to me, and I became very protective of my son. So, I called her and calmly told her that I wanted to support her because pressuring her grandson would not motivate him to visit or phone her more often. I told her that it would push him away as it did me, and she was better

Escaping the Cycle of Self-Righteousness

off letting him come when he wanted rather than when she expected him to. She instantly reacted, telling me I had nothing to say about her grandson because I gave up my right to give advice about him when I moved away, leaving him stranded.

Once again, I hung up on my mother as I absorbed her spiteful words. Deep down, I realized that she couldn't help herself and that it really wasn't about me abandoning my son but likely about her feeling abandoned by me. I don't even think my mother understands how her mind operates within those two-point-five seconds between standing on the ledge of sanity and jumping off of it. But at that time, I knew that I had to share what she said to me with Simon because I wanted to spare him the decades of insanity I had coped with. I wanted him to understand what he was dealing with when it came to my mother and the way her mind works and reacts when she doesn't get her way and loses control of the people she loves. He needed to learn how to manage her manipulation if he wanted her in his life. I also assured him that I would never come between him and his grandparents.

After my hysterectomy, I went home to recuperate, and Hank and my friends took excellent care of me. A few days into my recovery, a bouquet of flowers was delivered to my house. They were from my mother just four days after she implied that I was a neglectful mother. I got caught up in our familial game of not wanting to be the one to phone her first because I was so angry—she had definitely crossed a line by using my son as ammunition. But her rule about being thanked within 24 hours was tattooed on my brain, and I was torn between being right and letting her misbehaving go. I could hear my father say, *Just forget about it*, but my mind spiralled out of control within her classic game of hurt me, ghost me, then send a gift that requires thanks. *Fuck!!!*

Of course, I called her. And yes, I thanked her. But I was cold, and she knew I was still upset. So, I kept the conversation light and short and didn't talk to her for months afterwards. I learned long ago that there were times in our relationship when I had to take sentimentality out of the equation to make emotional room to cope with my pain. Through the years, many conflicts and disagreements with my mother arose over telephone calls; it became apparent that moving away was not the perfect solution.

Then one day, after a particularly heated argument with her on the phone, I found myself teetering on the same line my mother struggled with; my soul begged me to decide which way to go. I wanted to scream and have a tantrum but instead went out to the living room and performed my usual rant to Hank. As his usual calm self, he said, *You just have to let it go*. That's not what I wanted to hear because was that not the same as *Just forget about it?* I wanted him to tell me I was right, and she was wrong, but I had reached a breaking point because I turned around and left the house with his words echoing behind me. Nothing he said or what my mother and I had argued about mattered anymore; I just got in my car and drove and began chanting aloud, *Let it go*. Instinctively, I drove to the yoga studio I had been frequenting since we moved. Once I arrived on my mat, I continued to repeat the phrase as if I was in a trance of sorts, and a surge of calm came over me. I began my practice and couldn't stop repeating the words because they seemed to provide me with a level of comfort I had never experienced. Ten minutes into the hour-long practice, I moved into a subconscious state and didn't remember anything after that. My next conscious recollection was finding myself sitting in the yoga studio lobby conversing with a group of fellow yogis and the instructor.

I was baffled about how I got from the studio to this bench, so I asked the instructor what happened after the first sequence of poses. She was surprised that I didn't remember and explained that I moved through my practice with incredible intention, including going deep into the pigeon pose. She also shared that I sobbed uncontrollably each time I pushed through it. I did not remember any of this and found it somewhat frightening. I wondered how I could have done all that without any memory of what happened.

The pigeon pose had always been the most difficult one for me to endure; it was painful and unsustainable for any length of time. It focuses on the hips, where one stores the emotions related to relationship trauma—anxiety, fear, sadness, shame. Normally, it caused me significant physical discomfort due to the stiffness in my hip joints because I would not allow those uncomfortable emotions to the surface to release—I was mentally stoic like my mother and emotionally detached like my father. However, I allowed that release that day, refusing to succumb to the insanity of self-righteousness…if only for a while. This endeavour includes a lifelong process, a battle that, although I would like to say I have fully conquered, I have accepted I may never win.

Hank and I were thrilled when Olivia joined us in Kelowna in January 2015, just months after moving. She met the love of her life there, and within two years, they moved to Vancouver Island. Soon after, we went for a visit, and they asked if we would consider moving there because they wanted us to be closer to them. We were excited about the prospect of living on the island and experiencing it with them, but I was terrified, given the problems we had with my parents living so close to us. Hank was also leery, not wanting to cause issues with our daughter and future son-in-law. So, we compromised and moved to Qualicum Beach, about 45 minutes from where they lived in Port Alberni—the same distance my sister had when she moved after getting married. The kids eventually bought a place in Tofino, the village in the infamous fable where ultimate happiness is said to be found. This provided even more physical distance with less frequent visits, and Hank and I were more comfortable, knowing that more time between visits would create more welcomed ones. We did not want to damage our relationship with them.

On Father's Day, June 17, 2017, our daughter and her fiancé were married in Ucluelet, a small village just east of Tofino. I remember being so excited that my sister, her husband, my mother, and Hank's mother all decided to come. We had a beautiful time filled with the *gezelligheid* I continued to create. My mother praised me for being the ultimate host as I cooked daily meals and took my family out to

Escaping the Cycle of Self-Righteousness

local shops and attractions. Hank and I took everyone out for supper several times, and his mother even paid for both sides of the family once. My sister and her husband had to leave before our mothers did, and they were staying in an Airbnb, so we invited them over for breakfast before they left for the airport. I was so happy she came to celebrate my daughter's wedding, and I will never forget that special time we had together.

However, there were some tense moments because our mothers had a strained relationship created by several condescending things my father had done and said to my mother-in-law in the past. For example, she had confided in Hank that at a community coffee group in their apartment building, my father had finished his first cup and called out to my mother-in-law, *Hey*, while tapping his mug on the table—that was his way of telling her to refill his cup. This was just one of many ways he belittled her. She told Hank not to tell me because she didn't want to upset me, but he convinced her that it was okay to let me know. I was furious and sat down with her one day to tell her that she didn't need to take my father's emotional abuse just because we were related; she didn't have to socialize with my parents to make me happy if she was uncomfortable. She graciously accepted the freedom from any expectation she thought she had and agreed to share a room with my mother since my father could not attend the wedding.

I moved through one of my most reflective transitions about a year later. Although I didn't want to admit it, my most extraordinary insight throughout this time was that my daughter and I began walking down the same path my mother and I did. I perceived her as pulling away from me, and I responded by hanging onto her. This déjà vu moment prompted me to take a step back to digest the perilous waters in which I was dipping my toes. I struggled with the fear of losing her but knew that this could not be about me—I didn't want to repeat history by possibly destroying the deeply-rooted relationship I had developed with my daughter. I did not want to create a divide between us for the sake of feeding my ego.

I now understand what my mother went through because I experienced the same thing with my daughter—the fear of losing someone I loved so dearly. When she pulled away, I reacted by holding on for dear life. But every time this happened, I caught myself and slowed down to recalibrate. She was venturing into the world of adulthood, making her own decisions, and committing to values developed with her husband. She discovered an expanded side of herself—her authentic self—outside of me and anyone else who might have influenced her until then. She understood and found clarity about what was right for her. I knew it was time for me to release and honour her to transition into this new way of being that included an accumulation of her past and present self-awareness. She deserved to be confident about processing her thoughts and emotions and stepping into her authenticity. I realized that it is possible to give someone the freedom to embrace their uniqueness while simultaneously loving them to the moon and back.

If I learned anything about the dysfunctional relationship I had with my parents, it is that my way is not necessarily my children's. I'm also aware that how I perceive them, whether I think they are right or wrong, cannot determine how I choose to respond to them. My job is very straightforward—to respect them as human beings and support their choices. My hierarchal positioning in our family does not give me the right to manipulate them, their partners, or their children into believing that I know better than any of them. If anything, I have discovered a lot about myself, having had the honour of experiencing part of my life with them. They have become my greatest influencers, and I savour the wisdom they continue to share with me.

Hierarchy is everything I do not connect with. And yet, I lived with and managed it all my life—I still struggle with the repercussions it created from a very early age. That little girl never had a chance to develop the degree of strength her mother tried to instill in her to fight the misogynistic warfare society threw at her. But my matriarch tried—really fucking hard. And as much as I always believed she could have done better, my self-righteousness got in the way of not giving her credit for doing the best she could within the scope of insanity we were both dealt.

I had a total knee replacement in November 2017 before our second Christmas there. Years upon years of inflammation chose to attack and deteriorate another body part. As always, I was a good patient and passed my recovery with flying colours. I noticed that Hank worked hard at supporting me, but he was struggling physically and emotionally. We got through those hard months; however, the endless dark, rainy winters did not support his mental health. So, we decided to move in September 2018 and returned to Kelowna.

Before we left and within two months of living on the island, I met the two most beautiful souls ever to exist. And, organically, they and I created something so significant that it altered everything about me and my life—and I think theirs too. From the day I met them in November 2016 to the day I left, we developed and expanded a movement that continues to inspire people to connect through the art of storytelling. I didn't have a business plan, but our initial conversations and subsequent storytelling events naturally transpired into a book publishing business that supports others to discover their stories and share them with the world in the written word. It was a sombre day when I said goodbye to them after loading the moving truck to return to Kelowna. Incredibly, after all this time apart, I still connect with them multiple times every week on the phone. They are deeply embedded in my heart.

My vision was that Hank would begin thriving upon returning to the Okanagan, but that was me falling back on my go-to of running away to try and fix something that couldn't be. And even though that pattern still crept in from time to time, I was much more grounded and in tune with myself than I ever thought possible. So, when Hank's mother's birthday approached, we managed to squeeze in a visit to Ontario in April 2019 because she was turning 90, and my father was turning 92. I had a book launch coming up, so I scheduled an in-person

Escaping the Cycle of Self-Righteousness

book signing at Indigo in the mall by my parents' apartment from two to four in the afternoon on a Saturday. I told my mother about it long before we arrived, and then she decided to schedule my father's birthday dinner the same day—ironically, he got the exact kind of celebration I indicated I preferred years before. I wasn't worried so much about them being on the same day because anyone who came would have enough time to do both, and I would have plenty of time to pack up from the signing and meet everyone at the restaurant.

The two hours went by quickly as I greeted and chatted with many people I knew and many I had never met before. It was a huge success, and I appreciated that my sister flew in at one point, but it was apparent she was in a rush when she told me she couldn't stay long because she and her husband were heading downtown. About midway through the event, I briefly wondered if this would be the day I would remember when the rest of my family popped in to support my career success, but they did not. My mother had already told me that she couldn't come because it was raining—she lived around the corner, and I wondered why my sister didn't offer to bring her along when she arrived. And even though he regularly walked to the mall back then, I knew my father wouldn't attend because he never expressed any interest in my book signing at all. As for my brother-in-law, sister-in-law, and nephews, I just figured they couldn't fit one more thing into their day because they were travelling from the perspective cities where they lived.

When Hank and I arrived at the dinner, we walked in on a conversation between everyone but my parents about how much fun they had at a local bar downtown that afternoon. I found myself in one of those moments where the clarity of truth struck me like my opa's cane on my shin. This was not an ambiguous perception but rather an actual fact that they were sharing amongst themselves as if it would have no negative impact on me. They all chose to go drinking in a bar instead of coming to my book signing. The sense of separation from them was intense as I found myself going to that state of being perceived as a bad little girl who needed attention; I was being punished for my past wrong-doing. I quickly assessed what had happened, realizing that I had given everyone the benefit of the doubt, thinking they were busy, travelling, or at the very least, disinterested. But no, they had the time and were at a bar during my book signing; they intentionally did not come. Within moments, I recalibrated, said hello to everyone, and sat down. I ordered from the menu as if nothing ever happened. My mind raced with the awareness that the curse of jealousy had strategically woven itself through our lineage right down to the youngest generation. All the slanted tales of ridicule my mother had told them behind my back had created a family divided, with me on one side and them on the other. Their actions spoke volumes—I was wrong, and they were right.

We carried on through the week, and at one point, my mother told me that she would love to have everyone over for pizza but didn't think she could manage so many people in her apartment. I reflected on every Christmas she was adamant and continued to host, including the one of betrayal back in 2012. Shaking off the memory and attempting to make my mother happy, I suggested she ask my sister to have us over since she had a house with more space. She called her, and my sister told her that she didn't have the energy because she worked full time. Once again, my mind spun around, envisioning me in my kitchen back on the island cooking and cleaning for her and her husband when they came for my daughter's wedding. I worked full time as well and was thrilled to do that for them. But standing there listening to my mother tell me that my sister was too tired to order pizza for me took me to a place of unworthiness for something I will never comprehend. I looked at my mother and told her we could easily do it at her apartment, and I would help her. My sister took the time out of her busy day to come and have a slice. Hank and I were relieved to get on a plane a few days later, heading back to Kelowna.

My rheumatoid went into complete remission after having thumb joint surgery on my other hand in November 2019. Twenty-five years after having my left thumb operated on, I had the right one done. Years of trauma continued to remind me to stop the madness. I was placed on a waiting list at the beginning of September but didn't know when they would call me, so I immediately stopped taking all my immunosuppressant medication because they could schedule me from one day to the next. This was a risk because the longer I was off of my meds, the greater chance I could have a flare, and research dictated, it would be a doozie. I was called in for the surgery at the end of November and wasn't allowed to go back on my meds for two more months to give my thumb time to heal without any immune suppression. I was worried I would have a flare by the end of December because two months was generally how long that took without the support of medication. However, by the time the end of January 2020 rolled around, I was scheduled to resume my monthly biologique injection, but I was still flare-free. It had been five months after my last dose, and the inflammation in my body had not returned—I was in natural remission. I wondered if the distance from my family had finally provided the space that I needed to heal enough emotionally to support my physical well-being.

And then President Trump declared a state of emergency on March 17th that year when COVID invaded the western world, and Hank and I found ourselves putting a for sale sign on our front yard again. This time, we headed to the very place we had fled from six years before. I never thought we would ever move back to Ontario, but I yearned to go home to be close to our son and his soon-to-be wife. This time, I heard a different, gentle whisper that told me to go home to be near them. They were thinking about having a baby, and Hank and I couldn't imagine being so far away from our grand baby, so we called and asked them how they felt about that. They were thrilled.

I also craved being surrounded by my friends and the familiarity of the city where I was born and grew up. I wondered if my mother experienced this when

Escaping the Cycle of Self-Righteousness

she left Canada to be with her family back in Holland over 40 years ago. It also occurred to me that I was trepidatious about living near my family again and the expectations that were already filling my mind. I reflected on the irreparable damage that resulted over 55 years of our combined, layered self-righteousness. The difference was that I was not fearful this time. I believed that I was ready to be me and could allow them to be them. Perhaps we could co-exist.

Olivia and her husband drove from the island to help us pack; we could never have done it without them. When it was time for them to go home, we cried buckets because we didn't know when we would see them again. Along with this emotional toll, this was a particularly challenging move because my husband's Parkinson's had significantly progressed. We ran into some obstacles due to the side effects of the pandemic, with several air flights booked and cancelled within a week. We also struggled with finding a way to get our car across the country because the train and truck services were all booked, and very few wanted to travel due to the fear of contracting COVID. We were stuck, having decided that we couldn't risk another flight cancellation because we had Lucy as well as Rodger, a five-year-old Havanese we adopted along the way. There was no guarantee there would be room for them in cargo on a newly-booked flight. After the third cancellation, we sat in our living room with boxes piled up around us, and Hank asked me, *How are we going to get to Ontario?* I looked at him and hesitated for a moment, knowing that what I was about to say would push him into a worried state. But I had no option because we only had one way to get home, *We are going old school and driving across Canada; we will alternate driving and take our time, sleeping in a hotel every night.* Our motivation was to get back to our son who was anticipating our arrival back home.

We drove five days, ten to twelve hours a day, and Hank was stubborn doing all the driving for the first three. By the fourth day, his shoulders seized up, and he could barely hold his arms up—pride can be self-defeating with the best of intentions. The adventuresome picture I painted on social media was very different from what we experienced because we did not savour every moment but rather raced through each to get our trip over with as quickly as possible.

There was an element of safety, sitting in our car protected by the ambivalence of what was happening outside of it. Interestingly, being confined in a small space without a mask beside the security of my husband provided some courage to possibly fight the unknown at that point. However, when we stepped outside of our vehicle for lunch or a pee break, I was filled with the fear of potential danger. The only person who ever provided me with courage and calm was the one I needed to protect now; Hank would not do well with COVID.

We arrived in Ontario at the end of a sunny day in July of 2021, a few days after my mother's birthday. I made sure to phone her en route, knowing she would be waiting for the call. The kids waited for us at the condo we rented until our house was built in the same subdivision where we lived before leaving six years ago.

Around The Table

They became our bubble, and we did our due diligence, going into quarantine and choosing not to see our extended family or friends for the required two weeks. My mother seemed excited about us moving back, but our isolation allowed me to segue into the closer proximity of our relationship with caution—my intuition told me she might be apprehensive as well. And when it came time to visit my parents, even though he was struggling greatly with his Parkinson's and the stress of our transition, Hank volunteered to accompany me to their apartment.

Although we had flown to visit them several times over the years, it was difficult seeing my parents in their more elderly state. My mother turned 90 the following July, and my father was now 93. They were both quite spry but needed walkers, and my father could barely hear and didn't adapt well to his hearing aid. Nevertheless, we were all very amicable, keeping our conversation focused on the weather and the state of the pandemic. I noticed my father's shoulder tick now and again, and I took a breath each time, preparing myself for any comments that might trigger my defence default. I was grateful that he squashed any urges he may have had to debate something during our visit. I was also conscious of behaving myself. After about an hour, we left to visit Hank's mother, who lived in the same building, and while there, I noticed how much more relaxed my husband was in her presence as opposed to with my mother and father.

I saw my parents and my sister a few more times and spent August catching up with friends I had not seen in a long time. My 60th birthday was approaching, and distant memories of my 45th and 50th birthdays hit me. In my crazy mind, I thought maybe my sister would take me out for a coffee or lunch, but that never happened. I went to that dark place of unworthiness until three of my friends invited me to the most beautiful celebration in one of their homes. She had decorated every room with 60-themed birthday streamers and balloons. Initially, I was uncomfortable because I had been shamed into believing that I didn't deserve such special attention. But as the evening progressed, I was honoured because I noticed they had gifted me with precisely what I resonated with—sitting around the table, connecting over conversation and good food. We had been celebrating each other's birthdays for over 20 years, and as I sat in the gezelegheid of what they had created, I realized how much I had missed their unconditional love. Another friend took me out for lunch the next day, and we laughed and chatted about so many things; I never feel uncomfortable being who I am with her.

I continued to deviate from having my family at my house on my celebratory day, using the implications of the virus on my husband. My children had planned a dinner at their house, so my mother asked me to go to her apartment on the following Tuesday—it wasn't the day of my birthday, but it was my sister's day off, so it worked for her. She brought a lovely cake, and I appreciated them taking the time to do something. When my sister came in, she handed me a bouquet of flowers, and as awkwardly as my father would, she said, *I would have gotten you a*

Escaping the Cycle of Self-Righteousness

present, but it's COVID. I smiled, thanked her for the flowers, and replied, *Oh, no worries, I understand*.

But I really didn't. It's not that I needed anything more than the flowers, but I wondered why she was drawing attention to the fact that she didn't get me more. Did she feel the need to justify not getting me something more because I had gotten her something special for her 60th?—that's not who I am. I began questioning myself again. Maybe I was nuts! I wondered if I created an expectation that she thought she had to fill—that's my mother. What did she actually mean by *but it's COVID*—was is it some sort of passive-aggressive comment that I triggered because Hank and I were being careful? I was right back in the thick of my chaotic mind.

I remember ten years before, after my 50th birthday, asking my mother why she didn't do anything special for my milestone birthdays over the years, and she said, *Your sister told me you don't like birthday parties*. Hmmm. It was true that I said that in passing, but I couldn't help thinking that my mother used that as an excuse to not provide me with any kind of special celebration as a punishment for not doing them her way. She was like an elephant who never forgets and then blames one of us for her bad behaviour. But I never forgot either; we all carried that self-righteousness tool in our belt. I was definitely back in crazy-making land.

We finally moved into our new home at the end of October, and Hank and I chose to follow all restriction guidelines because his health was at risk should he contract this strange, and for some, deadly virus. As a result, we did not socialize with anyone other than our kids until the following spring. My publishing company and coaching business was a good distraction because I could facilitate it online, and Daring to Share Global™ was thriving. We hibernated for the winter, feeling safe and at ease in the comfort of our home; we were so grateful. My mother often called me and told me that she missed me, and as much as I wanted to believe she was being genuine, what I heard was, *You never come to see me*. I used to scold myself when I initially thought poorly of my mother, but in this case, it wasn't long after when someone shared that my mother told them that I never visit her. Instead of sharing my intention of sparing Hank the contraction of COVID, she implied that I didn't care about her. And although she has told me that she understands that I place Hank ahead of her, there is always an undertone of jealousy. I am enough when I give her what she needs, but when my husband comes before her, she feels slighted.

As restrictions lifted in the spring of 2021, I began visiting my parents now and again. I know it wasn't as often as they, and my mother, in particular, would have liked, but I did the best I could, given my workload and the time I wanted to be home with Hank. My sister had been my parents' primary caregiver since I left in 2014, and she was recovering from a surgery. She told me that her husband was helping her with my mother's errands, so I felt an obligation to reduce their workload and offered to do my mother's weekly groceries. I asked her to give me her grocery list by Sunday because I would do hers along with mine on Mondays and drop them off right after. I told her it was a workday for me, so she offered to meet me down in the lobby of her apartment building, and I brought a grocery box to put on her walker to get them upstairs. I was happy she agreed to this because I was well aware of how she could talk me into a visit with her when I needed to work. I think she knew that I was firm on not being able to visit because she was very accommodating and thanked me profusely while giving me the cash to pay her bill.

She followed with making a point of saying she loved me, and I suddenly found myself being that little girl, equating doing something right with being loved. It wasn't fair assuming that's what she was doing, but that's what bubbled up after years of not being enough. Ever since the day she coerced my father into telling me he loved me, she has told me the same hundreds of times more than she normally would. And every time, it sounds as though she is meeting an expectation I have set, but that's her not me. I want to push away the desperation of her intention while, simultaneously, accept what I wish her intention is. I answered, *I love you* and turned around to go home.

I thought I had done my duty to God and the Queen until my phone rang the next day, and my mother told me that she needed a few more things from the grocery store. I was surprised and asked her why she didn't have them on her list the day before; she said she didn't think of it. I know she's elderly, and when I share this with anyone, I initially get the give-her-a-break talk until I explain to them that, no, this is what I have managed my whole life—the I've-given-you-an-inch-and-now-I-want-a-mile game. It's a tactical move that manipulates me to see her more often—something I understand she values, but I don't appreciate being tricked into. And yet I did that time and went out to get the additional items she wanted. When I dropped them off, she asked if I wanted to come up to visit with her and my dad. I told her the truth, explaining that I couldn't because I had an upcoming appointment and had to get back to my office. She looked disappointed, and I do not doubt her lips were pursed under her mask.

The following day, I received yet another call from her, asking me to get her a BBQ lighter to light her candles. Really? I told her I would get it the next Monday when I went for groceries. I quickly realized I was getting sucked back into the vortex of the making-my-mother-happy mindset that included the doing-equals-loved pattern, and I had to stop the madness. So, I told her that this wouldn't work for me because the only time I could spend on her groceries was when I went on Mondays because of my work commitments and caregiving role with Hank. I added that if there was an emergency, she could call me. Her reply, *I thought you wanted to do something for me like your sister does.* Her automatic default was still inflicting guilt. I told her that getting her groceries wasn't working for me and requested she give me grace by asking my sister and her husband to get them for her again. She agreed because my mother had my sister at her beck and call, and I refused to do that.

On Tuesday, June 29, 2021, I texted to my sister. It was her day off, and I

Escaping the Cycle of Self-Righteousness

asked her if we could discuss my mother's birthday. We had a month to organize her milestone of turning 90 on July 26th, and it was a tricky time because a strict pandemic lockdown was still in place. Because Ontario was doing well, we were told that as of June 30th, we would enter step two of lifting restrictions and could have 5 people at an indoor social gathering and 25 outdoors. There was a possibility that we could move into step three with even fewer restrictions within 21 days, but we couldn't count on that. I was going to suggest going to a conservation park on the water in the east end of town for a birthday picnic. But my sister replied that she hadn't thought of it with COVID, and she was off to do groceries. I didn't hear back again, so I figured she was busy and thought I would leave it for a few days.

By the following Tuesday, July 7th, I wondered why she hadn't contacted me, and flashbacks of our Christmas episode so many years ago popped up in my head. My inner voice told me that something strange was going on, and sure enough, I received a phone call from my mother a few hours later. She was agitated and told me that she had arranged her birthday, and it would be at her apartment. I asked her why she was organizing her 90th birthday. *Well, it's a few weeks away, and no one has done anything yet!* I indicated that I had texted my sister a week ago and was waiting to hear back from her, and we still had plenty of time. My mother told me that she had confirmed having it at her place with both my sister and sister-in-law the previous Sunday and told them to let the kids know. I thought, *What about me?*

I'd like to say that I was surprised, but I was not. I wasn't even hurt. I told my mother how disappointed I was in her, but that wasn't the case at all—I was definitely disappointed in myself. How in the world was I back here, back in the same self-destructive place I always put myself in? I seemed to continuously set myself up for failure by trying to make my mother happy, knowing I could never meet her standards.

I calmly told her that she would be breaking protocol if she had the whole family there and that I had an idea I was going to share to do something outside. She said, *Everyone is vaccinated, so we don't have to worry.* I told her that wasn't the case and wondered if she had even thought about the risk to Hank. My mother began to backtrack, realizing that her brain had taken her to that self-righteous mindset. And then I asked her, *Mom, why did you exclude me from the conversation again?* The only answer she had was that she was planning on telling me what she had decided—telling me but not including me in the discussion.

She then asked me what my outdoor idea was, and I told her about the beach area, but I also told her that I didn't want anything to do with it anymore, and I would not be at her apartment for her birthday because I could not risk compromising Hank. Once again, this was something she didn't think about. I didn't want to talk to her anymore because I knew I would explode, so I hung up the phone and texted my sister to let her know how disappointed I was that she and my mother excluded me from yet another decision. I shared my outdoor party idea but told her it was all good; I was out.

Around The Table

Since I arrived home from out west, my sister had been nothing but gracious and kind, checking in on me through texts and phone calls. I really believe she was happy that I came back home, so when she reached out to me later on July 7th and told me that she should have gotten back to me sooner, and it was her fault, I was empathetic and realized that she too got swept into old familial patterns of accommodating our mother. She probably would not say this, but her mother-pleasing skills are so fine-tuned that I don't think she realizes how programmed she is.

Four days later, she reached out again and asked if I would be opened to having the party in her backyard. I was still processing and hanging on to being right, so I curtly answered, *If that is what you want to do*. Thankfully, she stepped up and phoned me, and we had the conversation we should have had in the first place. She told me that she was overwhelmed and felt pressured that Sunday when my mother started asking about her party. My sister had been working full time through the pandemic as a front-line worker while supporting my parents to stay in their apartment. I recognize that was a lot of work. I have thanked her many times for all she does, and she remains humble, genuinely saying it's no problem. In my eyes, she is a superstar; she is a loyal and loving daughter in my mother's, who celebrated her birthday in my sister's garden.

A year passed since Hank and I had travelled across Canada to come home, and for many months and numerous times before my mother's birthday, I asked my mother and father to get together to discuss their will with my sister and me. Along with my sister, I am one of the executors and powers of attorney, and I wanted to ensure that everything was in order. However, every time I brought it up, my parents told me it could wait. My mother looked me in the eye and leaned forward, *We're not going to die tomorrow!* I remember looking back at her and saying, *Mom, no offence, but you and Dad are in your 90s, and you could die anytime!!* I knew it sounded awful, but I also knew how horrible dealing with an unmanaged will would be if one of them passed away. Next, I asked my father why he was adamant about not showing me his will. As if it made total sense, he explained that it didn't matter because he would be dead, and it wouldn't affect him if something were amiss. At this point, nothing surprised me, but I told him that if the will wasn't in order, it would negatively affect his daughters. Again, he said he would be dead, so it wouldn't matter.

I have sat with my father so many times and tried to connect with him on a deeper level—any level really—using conversation, intellect, music, world events, and even sharing my emotions. There were times when we laughed over a joke, but he has never given me the grace of honouring my opinion, passions, purpose, or extended a morsel of tenderness. I used to approach him for a kiss on the cheek when I arrived at my parents' house or when I left to say goodbye, and he would turn his head away to avoid contact. When my son was younger, he would go to his opa with his arms extended to hug him, and my father would step back and reach his arm out to shake Simon's hand. My mother complained that my children never ran and jumped into his arms as they did with their other grandfather. She wanted to know why they were so comfortable with him and not with my father. I dreaded those questions back then because I didn't have the guts to tell her that her husband was emotionally-detached and never got out of his chair to greet my kids. I wanted to tell her that a child senses when an adult shows up within self-righteousness void of emotion, and it is not just uninviting but also ignites a fear of not being loved. I knew this because I grew up with him and experienced the consequences of his indifference.

Mid-September 2021, my sister asked me out for coffee to celebrate my 61st birthday—I wondered why this one was more special than my 60th While we chatted, I gently explained the importance of reviewing my parents' will, and she agreed. I told her that it would be better for her to ask them for a meeting because they didn't seem to welcome the topic with me. She agreed. As I drove away, I was overwhelmed that I had to share my unworthiness with her in order to do the right thing for my parents. It was like I was begging for the same respect she had to make sure their affairs were in place. I believed my parents didn't trust me, and I wondered why I continued to fight for the same honour my sister had earned.

The four of us met, and we discovered that some details needed attending to. They were more than happy to have me take care of the issues because, *You're good at that*. So, I took care of them, and a few months later, my father's health began to decline at the beginning of December. I had since been laid up due to major foot reconstruction surgery at the end of October—even though I was in remission, thirteen years of RA left me with crippling toes. I was just beginning to use a knee scooter to get around when he was sent to the hospital by ambulance for the first time on December 3rd because he did not have the strength to get himself out of his chair. He told the doctors it was his arthritic knee that was bothering him because he didn't want to stay in the hospital. So, they didn't check him any further and sent him home, instructing him to take Tylenol. My mother called an ambulance the next day when she couldn't get him up again. I wondered if he was having mini-strokes.

We were not allowed into the hospital due to the pandemic restrictions, so early on the morning of the fifth, I called my mother to see if she had received an update. She was irate, saying someone called her in the middle of the night to ask what my father's wishes were should his heart stop. She said that they should not have woken her up. This news was a red flag for me, recognizing that calling in the middle of the night likely meant he had declined to the degree that needed immediate attention. She said they wanted to know what to do if his heart failed. I understood she was anxious, given her age and the situation and asked if she would like me to call the hospital to find out what was going on and if she would like me to field the calls from then on. She agreed. So, I called, and the nurse on his case told me that his breathing became laboured in the middle of the night, and they discovered he had a lung infection. He was still in the emergency department because the ICU was full, and I asked if he could have any visitors, knowing my mother would want to be with him. She apologized, telling me that no visitors were allowed due to COVID. So, I asked her if the doctor could call me when she became available.

I phoned my mother and sister to update them. My sister was working but was getting off early to go to our mother, so I asked her if she was willing to pick me up on her way and bring me home after the visit because I couldn't drive with my foot yet. She agreed, and we went to my parents' apartment to spend time with my mother. From this visit on, my sister and I worked as a team. I was so grateful to her for supporting me and my mother, getting us in and out of cars and buildings and repeatedly hoisting my scooter and my mother's walker into the trunk and out again. I became aware of my sister's caregiving expression of love that I hadn't experienced before.

At nine in the morning on Monday, December 6th, I got a call from the ER doctor, who told me that my father was on 60 percent oxygen because he had trouble breathing. She told me she would call if anything changed. Two hours later, she contacted me again and said one of us should come because he was not likely going to make it. Because his condition worsened, they were allowing one person in, but I calmly told her that there were just the three of us, my mother, my sister, and me, and asked if it was at all possible for us all to come. Even though I wasn't close to my father, I wanted him to be surrounded by his loved ones. Just like any human being leaving this realm, he needed his family with him during his final hours, and his family needed to say goodbye to him—like my sister who passed many years before, he deserved not to be frightened and alone in his final hours.

The doctor said she would ask and called me back ten minutes later, saying she would meet us at the door. Under no circumstances could we leave once we came in because they would not allow us to return. I told her that we would do whatever was required. I phoned my sister right away and told her that she needed to leave work and pick up my mother and then me. When we arrived at the hospital, my father was on 80 percent oxygen, and the doctor told us that the next step was life support. I knew that was not what my father wanted because we had just discussed this when we reviewed his will three months prior. My mother held and stroked his hand and searched his eyes with tears in hers. My sister was on the other side, crying and watching him as he anxiously scanned the room. I stood behind her and witnessed his suffering as he gasped for tiny breaths. We all tried to reassure him by talking to him, but his breathing was so laboured that we could not decipher what he tried to say in response. I told my mother to tell him anything she wanted, and she told him she loved him. He smiled. My sister told him she loved him too. He smiled. Finally, it was my turn, and it felt awkward. And at that moment, it dawned on me that I had never told my father that I loved him—not that I could remember.

The doctor came back and nodded her head to me. I turned to my mother and told her that it was time, and as much as she didn't want to, she agreed to say goodbye. So, I turned to my father and took his hand and asked, *Dad, are you tired of this?* He looked at me, squeezed my hand, and smiled. I asked again, *Are you ready to let all of this go?* He smiled and squeezed my hand again. I turned to the doctor and told her that he was ready. And then I held my father's hand up in my two hands, and as he looked into my eyes, I said, *I love you.* A shiver migrated from the top of my spine to the bottom, and when he smiled at me one last time, it occurred to me that perhaps I had finally done something right. I thanked God.

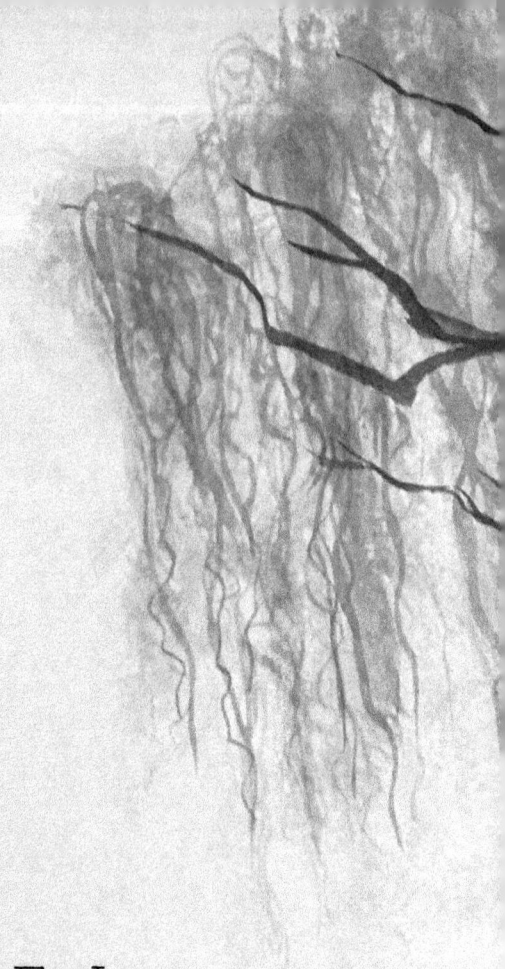

The End

Diana Reyers

About the Author

Diana has this wondrous way of transforming fear of vulnerability into heartfelt connection between author and writer, and speaker and audience, and even strangers who bravely say hello after turning the pages in one of her books. Despite the personal hardships, and emotional trauma Diana has faced, she continues to rise above all adversity by shining light on darkness and exposing truth with courageous love. These are just some of the gifts Diana brings along with her each time she dares to share, while inspiring countless others to do the same. Grateful to know her and love her, Diana has become a cherished confidante and lifelong friend.

Michelle Elleana Nadeau,
Co-Author, Daring to Share Deception to Truth

www.ingramcontent.com/pod-product-compliance
Lightning Source LLC
Chambersburg PA
CBHW072151100526
44589CB00015B/2175